Contents

Illustrations

Figures

Tables

Acknowledgments

I am indebted to a number of people for their support, advice and encouragement at various stages during the preparation of this book.

My greatest debt is to the 52 'offending' girls and young women in the study, for allowing me to interview them and for giving so generously of their time and expertise. They shared with me stories – which were often difficult and distressing to tell – about their lives and loves, their pasts and their hopes for the future. I was continually impressed by their spirit, interest and enthusiasm, not to mention their knowledge of local fast food restaurants! I am most grateful to them for imparting many words of wisdom about youth culture, crime and justice, and I hope that this book will have a positive impact on their lives or on those of their younger sisters.

The managers of 'Midshire' and 'Castleshire' Youth Offending Teams and the deputy director of the 'Secure Training Centre' provided considerable encouragement and practical assistance, without which the research would not have been possible. I am also very grateful to the youth justice practitioners in the three sites, and to those I interviewed in the YOTs' partner agencies, for sharing their views and considerable knowledge and experience with me and for facilitating access to the girls and young women under their supervision.

The Economic and Social Research Council funded the doctoral research from which this book grew and Loraine Gelsthorpe was a wise and kind supervisor during my time at the Institute of Criminology in Cambridge.

Gwen Robinson, Jo Phoenix, Loraine Gelsthorpe and Layla Skinns provided generous and very useful comments on various draft chapters of the book. I am particularly grateful to Gwen for being such a good friend and colleague in the School of Law at Sheffield over the past three years. Tim Bateman kindly drew my attention to ASBO and sanction detection data, which proved invaluable in making sense of recent trends in young women's offending and criminalisation. Chris Strevens at the Youth Justice Board supplied information on black and minority ethnic young women in custody. Julia Willan has been as patient and kind a publisher as I could have hoped for.

Closest to home, special thanks are owed to Mark for his love, friendship, patience and cooking during the very long time it has taken this project to come to fruition. I was eight and a half months pregnant when I finished writing the book and, unlike me, Mark always believed I would get it finished before the baby arrived.

Abbreviations

ABC	Acceptable Behaviour Contract
ABH	Assault Occasioning Actual Bodily Harm
ADHD	Attention Deficit Hyperactivity Disorder
AQA	Assessment and Qualifications Alliance
ASBO	Anti-Social Behaviour Order
Asset	Assessment Tool Used with Young Offenders
BME	Black and Minority Ethnic
CLAIT	Computer Literacy and Information Technology
DfES	Department for Education and Skills
DTO	Detention and Training Order
GBH	Assault Occasioning Grievous Bodily Harm
GCSE	General Certificate of Secondary Education (national school examination taken by pupils usually aged 15 or 16)
HMIP	Her Majesty's Inspectorate of Prisons
ISSP	Intensive Supervision and Surveillance Programme
IT	Intermediate Treatment
LSD	Lysergic Acid Diethylamide (a psychedelic drug)
NCRS	National Crime Recording Standard
NEET	Not in Education, Employment or Training
NOMS	National Offender Management Service
NVivo7	A Qualitative Data Analysis Software Package
NVQ	National Vocational Qualification
OBTJ	Offences Brought To Justice
Ofsted	Office for Standards in Education, Children's Services and Schools (the body that inspects child care, education and training services in England)
PRU	Pupil Referral Unit
PSR	Pre-Sentence Report
STC	Secure Training Centre
TWOC	(Vehicle) Taken Without Owner's Consent

YCC	Youth Conditional Caution
YISP	Youth Inclusion and Support Panel
YJB	Youth Justice Board
YOT	Youth Offending Team
YRO	Youth Rehabilitation Order

1 New offending girls?[1]

At the dawn of the twenty-first century, panic about girls' offending in Britain seemed to have reached fever pitch. No longer sugar and spice, a 'new breed' of girl, the 'ladette',[2] was reported to have emerged – a hedonistic, violent, binge-drinking young woman whose crude and very public uncouth behaviour differed little from that of her male underclass counterparts. Published crime statistics lent considerable, albeit superficial, support to these claims. For example, official figures indicated that recorded offences committed by girls in England and Wales had increased by 38 per cent between 2002/03 and 2007/08 (Youth Justice Board, 2004a, 2009), and that violent crimes attributable to young women had risen even more starkly. Popular commentators were quick to attribute this 'shocking trend' to the 'dark side' of girlpower. As reflected in the newspaper headlines below, girls were believed to be enacting the gains of feminism in problematic ways, and 'ladette culture' was widely purported to be the cause of the apparent dramatic increase in female youth crime:

> Britain is in the grip of an unprecedented crime wave among teenage girls.
> (Patrick Hennessy, *The Telegraph*, 10 May 2008)

> British girls among most violent in world, WHO survey shows. Link to binge-drinking 'ladette' culture feared.
> (Mark Honigsbaum, *The Guardian*, 24 January 2006)

> The female of the species is now just as deadly as the male.
> (Jan Moir, *Daily Mail*, 2 August 2008)

> Scourge of the ladette thugs: rising tide of violent crime committed by young women.
> (James Slack, *Daily Mail*, 30 January 2009)

> Violent attacks by teenage girls treble in seven years.
> (Richard Edwards, *The Telegraph*, 1 March 2009)

Politicians, senior criminal justice professionals and even some academics lent credence to these popular stereotypes by uncritically accepting the 'evidence' on which such stories were based. A typical newspaper article about 'violent ladettes' published in *The Times* cited a professor of child forensic psychology, who asserted that 'there was evidence to suggest that girls were becoming more violent and aggressive' and even that '[t]here is beginning to be evidence that girls are capable of being perpetrators of sexual crimes in their own right' (Ford, 2009). Judge Alan Berg, who sentenced a 20-year-old female student to eight weeks' imprisonment after she attacked a paramedic (she was later released on appeal), was reported in *The Telegraph* to have claimed that 'booze-fuelled yobs were behind the sharp spike in "mindless" violence that had left many people fearing for their safety'. Judge Berg went on to claim that '[t]here is this ladette culture which creates these problems. There is a culture among a certain sector of female society of drinking until they are senseless' (Hough, 2010).

Not all girls have prompted such anxieties, however. Images of high-achieving, successful and glamorous 'self-made' young women are perhaps as ubiquitous as those of 'ladettes' and girl gang members. Indeed, the 'girlpowered' (Aapola *et al.*, 2005[3]) young woman is commonly 'championed as a metaphor for social change' (McRobbie, 2004: 6). The ideal modern subject, she is celebrated for enjoying unprecedented achievements in education and employment (and has delayed motherhood so as not to hinder her career prospects), considerable freedom in her sexual relationships and success and glamour in the field of consumption (Harris, 2004). She is cast as a deserving beneficiary of the gains of feminism. Such images throw the offending girl into particularly stark relief: she is unable (or refuses) to keep within the narrow boundaries of respectable and ladylike behaviour; she makes poor consumption choices (drinking heavily, using drugs and behaving violently); and she has dropped out of school and has no interest in educational advancement. She is also far less likely than her girlpowered counterpart to be white and middle class. Together with her alter ego, the economically unproductive lone teenage mother who is dependent on the state for financial support, the offending girl is the subject of widespread public and political anxiety. It is these young women, this 'certain sector of female society', to use Judge Berg's terminology, who are the subject of this book.

'Old', 'new' and 'new-old' anxieties about girlhood deviance and criminality

Contemporary anxieties about 'bad girls' are by no means unprecedented, although the purported emergence of a 'new breed' of girl criminal is often presented as a new phenomenon. A steady growth in the female share of youth crime in England and Wales during the second half of the last century attracted widespread commentary: the sex ratio fell from approximately 11:1 in the late 1950s to around 6:1 in the early 1970s, and to 3.6:1 in 1995 (Rutter *et al.*, 1998), subsequent rates remaining fairly stable. In fact, as I show in Chapter Two, concerns about offending (or, at different historical junctures, 'wayward' or 'delinquent') young women can be traced back more than 100 years, during which time 'successive generations of girls in England and Wales have been cast as posing an ever-new threat to social order requiring ever-new restraints' (Cox, 2003: 3). However, changes in the classification of girlhood delinquency and lawbreaking over time mean that a young woman's 'offending' behaviour today may bear little resemblance to that of her 'delinquent' counterpart half a century ago, which casts doubt on the validity of long-term historical comparisons of female crime rates.

From 'liberated' to 'ladettes'

During the twentieth century, girls' 'emancipation' was continually identified as a primary source of their moral deterioration, and unsupervised young girls without domestic responsibilities to curb their morals or their finances were perceived to threaten state stability as well as the future of the family (Cox, 2003). As long ago as the 1800s, as Sprott and Doob (2009: 11) document, it was claimed that 'every step made by a woman towards her independence is a step towards that precipice at the bottom of which lies prison' (Pike, 1876: 527).

The belief that rising female crime rates are attributable to a growing number of women adopting 'male roles' (entering paid employment in greater numbers), and to women's increasing expectations and opportunities – a theoretical perspective that came to be known as the 'liberation hypothesis' – dominated popular accounts of female lawbreaking in the 1970s. It was widely claimed that women's roles had changed in ways that were threatening to the social order, and that this had resulted in more women being brought within the control of the criminal justice system (Morris and Gelsthorpe, 1981). This popular belief was supported by two American academic studies by Freda Adler and Rita Simon, both published in 1975. In contrast with earlier theories emphasising biological and psychological sex differences, and considerably more liberal in their view of women's emancipation, Adler and Simon claimed that 'social position and social-role expectations are more important than sex in determining behavior' (Adler, 1975: 47). The rising female crime rate during the 1970s was purported to represent the 'dark side' of women's liberation, a position Simon outlined as follows:

> The women's movement … claims that women are no more moral, or conforming, or law-abiding than are men; and that women should neither bask in their superiority over men nor feel they are trapped into wearing a mask of morality and goodness … If one of the consequences of sexual equality should turn out to be higher crime rates among women, the women's movement would not feel that it has all been in vain.
>
> (1975: 106)

Despite the considerable moral panic created by Adler's book, in particular,[4] the available empirical evidence lent little support to the liberation hypothesis. In fact, the women's movement had the greatest impact on white, middle-class women, while it was (and still is) working-class and black women who are most likely to come into contact with the criminal justice system. Darrell Steffensmeier, in a review of statistical evidence on female crime rates in the United States in the 1970s, concluded that '[t]he new female criminal is more a social invention than an empirical reality and [...] the proposed relationship between the women's movement and crime is, indeed, tenuous and even vacuous. Women are still typically non-violent, petty property offenders' (1978: 580).

Box and Hale were of much the same opinion in their analysis of British female violent crime rates: they found that the sex composition of the police force (the proportion of female police officers was steadily growing), but not the 'masculinisation' of women's roles, was significantly related to female conviction rates for violent offending. Their conclusion, consistent with a 'labelling' hypothesis, was that media exaggeration of female violence had 'sensitized both public and police to the alleged relationship between violence and female emancipation [which in turn had apparently led to] a harsher stance towards females suspected of violence' (1983: 43).[5] The liberation hypothesis has been enjoying a sustained renaissance in Britain in recent years, primarily in the guise of moral panics about girls and violence. Fears about the 'liberated' female criminal abound in contemporary media representations of 'ladettes', female violence and 'girl gangs', and newspaper headlines, such as those reproduced above, have once again stirred up respectable fears that girlhood criminality is increasing rapidly.

From sexuality to violence

Throughout the majority of the last century, definitions of girls' delinquent and troublesome behaviour were closely tied to ideas about 'respectable' femininity, which precluded sexual experimentation outside wedlock. Indications that the usual familial controls were proving unsuccessful in constraining girlhood enterprise and adventure were reflected in legal definitions which included being 'beyond parental control' or 'in moral danger', and girls admitted to carceral institutions – many of whom had not actually broken the law – were routinely tested for pregnancy and venereal infections. Indeed, the moral policing of girls' sexuality, which appears to have been a central objective of the juvenile justice system for the major part of the twentieth century (Gelsthorpe and Worrall, 2009), not only created the impression that girls' delinquency was, for the most part, sexual in nature, but also kept much of their 'ordinary' lawbreaking out of the criminal courts (Cox, 2003; Sharpe, 2008).

In the late twentieth century, a *new* threat to the gender order – girls' violence – was identified, and the preoccupation with girls' sexuality that had long been evident in both popular and criminological discourse was eclipsed to a large extent by panic about violent young women. But what brought about this shift in focus? Expectations about what it means to grow up female have undergone considerable change over the course of recent decades and young women today are invoked to put the 'old' markers of feminine success – marriage and motherhood – on hold until they reach at least their mid-20s. Moreover, chastity is no longer expected or considered desirable (in many Western cultures, at least), and youthful female (hetero)sexuality – as long as it does not result in pregnancy – is no longer widely condemned as 'unfeminine'.[6] Anita Harris has argued that three domains – professional ambition, consumption and motherhood – are most significant for identity work for contemporary young women, and that success and failure are manufactured in these contexts (2004: 183–5). However, success in *reproduction* has, for teenage girls and young women, been overtaken by success in the spheres of *consumption* and *production* – as evidenced by a new focus on (and celebration of) young women's educational achievements and their enactment of successful employment and glamorous 'lifestyle' choices.[7] Today's young women feature as much, if not more, in governmental discourse for their productive as for their reproductive capacities (McRobbie, 2009).

It is perhaps also culturally untenable that overtly sexual young women today might be considered to be in 'moral danger'. According to sociologist Ros Gill, young women have been transformed – in the media and, subsequently, by themselves – from sexual objects to sexual subjects, and there has been a broad cultural shift in recent years which she refers to as 'the knowing and deliberate *re-sexualisation* and *re-commodification* of women's bodies' (2003: 101). Gill argues that new femininities are being constructed, 'organised around sexual confidence and autonomy', wherein young women are represented not 'as passive objects but as knowing, active, and desiring sexual subjects' (p. 103).[8] This 're-commodification' has arguably been further encouraged by the mainstreaming of the pornography industry and the proliferation of sexual entertainment/ encounter venues in the city centre night time economy, as well by the influence of such developments on the content of 'lads' magazines, women's and 'celebrity' weeklies and the popular press. The contemporary 'hyper-culture of commercial sexuality' (McRobbie, 2009: 18) makes the governance of young women from a 'moral danger' perspective extremely difficult to uphold.[9]

Despite the shift of attention from young women's sexuality to their violence, certain historical continuities are in evidence. The public display of sexuality and promiscuity by young women is now tolerated, indeed celebrated, at least within certain parameters.[10] No longer considered evidence of female pathology, the coming forward of young women as sexual subjects, as opposed to objects, is seen as a sign of 'empowerment'. Young women in the twenty-first century are free to make individual sexual and reproductive choices relatively unfettered by moral censure. A significant exception here is when girls' reproductive choices end in teenage pregnancy. In fact, old anxieties about promiscuity have not entirely disappeared, but they have become more narrowly focused on teenage pregnancy and motherhood; indeed, the financially unproductive young woman who is dependent on the state has been constructed as a new, near-criminal major social problem requiring urgent government intervention (Duncan *et al.*, 2010; see Chapter Five). And while the condemnatory gaze may have shifted from girls' sexuality to their violence, what is believed to constitute girlhood deviance continues to be embodied and the working-class female body continues to be scrutinised and found wanting. Today, as before, it is young women's assumed lack of physical and self-control and restraint that is a central source of moral censure. Fascination about girls, coupled with anxiety about them, is greater now than ever, and there are many more avenues – with girls and women themselves the chief consumers – through which such concerns can find expression: magazines, 'chick lit', media commentary, online fora, TV chat shows, and so on. The claim that 'girls, including their bodies, their labour power and their social behaviour are now the subject of governmentality to an unprecedented degree' (McRobbie, 2001, cited in Harris, 2004: 14) is perhaps no exaggeration.

A number of authors have argued that feminism, in the twenty-first century, has been denounced as no longer relevant (Griffin, 2004; McRobbie, 2009, *inter alia*). This repudiation arguably allows for girls' problems and failures, as well as their achievements and successes, to be individualised, thus situating blame – or credit, as the case may be – at an individual, rather than a social, level, thereby rejecting the notion that opportunity remains structured by social class, gender and ethnicity (Aapola *et al.*, 2005; Furlong and Cartmel, 2007; Walkerdine *et al.*, 2001). Anita Harris has suggested that the structural barriers and exclusionary policies that working-class girls are confronted with have been largely erased from understandings of their behaviour, and that their 'failures' are thus easily constructed as 'bad' personal choices for which they have only themselves to blame (2004: 29–30). This has arguably enabled new and more pernicious forms of vilification and stigmatisation of the offending girl to emerge.

Anxieties about unruly young women from the early twentieth century and subsequently have been closely and consistently linked to the belief that gender differences are being eroded (Jackson and Tinkler, 2007). However, an intensified focus on the behaviour, and also on the physical appearance, of 'underclass' young women (aided significantly by colour photography and the proliferation of online media) can be discerned in the twenty-first century, and questions are frequently raised about the 'trashiness' and also the sexual orientation of the contemporary female offender (Chesney-Lind and Eliason, 2006), perhaps denoting a new desire to re-instate gender boundaries and heterosexual norms. In May 2008, for example, the *Daily Mail* newspaper ran a story about the 'terrifying rise of violent girl gangs' (Bracchi, 2008). The unnamed protagonist of the article, a 14-year-old girl from North Yorkshire, is described as having 'emerged from her house with a mobile phone glued to her ear and a cigarette hanging out of her mouth', to be permanently dressed in 'a chav T-shirt and tracksuit bottoms', and to play football. Readers are further informed that she 'weighs in at around 13 stone'. The undertones of class denigration and homophobia are obvious.[11] Paul Bracchi, author of the article, goes on to claim that

there has been a dramatic coarsening in the behaviour of an entire underclass of young women – driven partly by the destruction of the nuclear family and the lack of a strong father figure, but also by a celebrity culture in which female so-called 'stars' – famous only for appearing on Big Brother or its equivalents – are photographed blind drunk and fighting in the gutter with other women outside nightclubs.

Leaving aside the fact of the frequent appearance of such 'stars' in the pages of the same newspaper,[12] the message that we are left with is that '[s]ometimes beneath a cap or a "hoodie" it is hard to tell one sex from another any more' and that girls, too, now regularly commit 'the kind of nihilistic, violent crimes ... that we used to associate with men not women, boys not girls. The truth is there is little difference any more – which is perhaps the most shocking indictment of all' (Bracchi, 2008).

'New' offending girls?

I have argued so far that a shift in popular concern about unruly girls has taken place in recent decades. However, we know little about what exactly *is* new about the 'new' offending girl, nor to what extent the life circumstances and behaviours of girls and young women caught up in the contemporary youth justice system fit with popular stereotypes that a 'new breed' of criminal young woman has emerged. The purpose of this book is twofold. My first aim is to examine who is the twenty-first century young female offender and what, if anything, is 'new' about her behaviour. How, and in what ways, does she differ from her twentieth-century forebear? What continuities and changes are in evidence? To what extent do popular stereotypes problematising female youthful behaviour and purporting that today's girls are acting like boys resonate with the accounts of criminalised young women themselves, or with those of youth justice professionals?

My second object of analysis is young women and youth justice. While the criminalising and net-widening tendencies of the 'new' youth justice system in England and Wales have been subjected to substantial critique in recent years (Goldson and Muncie, 2006; Morgan, 2009; Muncie and Goldson, 2006; Smith, 2007, *inter alia*), this body of critique has remained at a distance from the 'messiness' of everyday practice. And although the popular spotlight on girls' law-breaking and their behaviour in public space has been intense, the rapid influx of girls into the youth justice system in the early twenty-first century has received relatively little critical attention (Sharpe, 2011; Sharpe and Gelsthorpe, 2009; Worrall, 2004). Moreover, the few organisational analyses that have addressed youth justice have ignored young women.[13] In this book, I explore contemporary responses to female youthful lawbreaking through the lens of an empirical study of the 'new' youth justice system in England and Wales. My analysis reveals that many 'old' stereotypes about girls' behaviour and its causes, as well as ideas about how best to respond to them, are still in evidence. In addition, new stereotypes and new socio-cultural pressures affecting offending girls can be discerned.

This is not another book about girls' violence. It is somewhat regrettable that the majority of recent criminological texts about young women have 'violence' or 'fighting' in their titles, when girls' violence is in fact relatively rare and the bulk of young women's offending is non-violent. While the best examples of contemporary criminological and sociological research[14] challenge stereotypical representations of 'violent' girls, a near-exclusive focus on violence in the academic literature since the mid-1990s has perhaps fuelled popular stereotypes that girls are becoming more violent and that fighting has become an 'equal opportunity' pursuit. As I argue in Chapter Three, such stereotypes are unsubstantiated.

Layout of the book

My analysis of the 'new' young woman in the twenty-first century youth justice system begins some time ago, in 1908. In Chapter Two, I examine how the 'delinquent' behaviour of the modern-day offending girl's female predecessor was theorised, assessed and responded to in England and Wales in the course of the twentieth century and how definitions of young women's offending have changed in recent times. A central question of this book is whether the *contemporary* panic about an 'unprecedented crime wave' among girls is supported by robust evidence. I argue in Chapter Three – which examines recent trends in girls' lawbreaking and criminalisation – that it is not. In fact, the growing number of criminal(ised) young women in Britain in recent years has been the outcome not of girls 'getting worse', but of changes in youth justice processing enacted from within a crime prevention paradigm. Interventionism within the framework of the formal youth justice system in the name of preventing (further) offending has had a profound effect here. In addition, the criminalisation of welfare matters appears to have had a particularly net-widening impact on girls. After outlining the background to the study in Chapter Four, Chapter Five examines the lives of 52 offending girls in the contemporary youth justice system. In light of enormous social and cultural change since previous British research in this area, as well as shifts in expectations of what it means to grow up girl, I pay particular attention to historical continuities and changes both in the backgrounds and life histories of criminalised young women, and in their explanations of their lawbreaking. I argue that social-structural problems continue to be a central determinant of young women's pathways into crime and into the criminal justice system.

Historically, girlhood has tended to be located within the analytical frameworks of private and domestic worlds. More recently, although narratives of girlhood have become more publicly visible (Harris, 2004), girls' own more complicated stories have been subjugated or silenced. Young women's voices have been notably absent from recent debates about female crime. In Chapter Six, I present the accounts of 52 offending girls of the motivations underlying their lawbreaking. In contrast to popular representations of lawbreaking girls as hedonistic and acting like boys, the circumstances that structured the young women's life chances were gendered, but also classed and generational. What was particularly striking was the contrast between the adversities that they had to attempt – sometimes through criminal means – to negotiate, resist or simply endure, and the absence of adult social-structural support to do so. Chapter Six further examines the role of consumption in young women's lives and in their offending.

The focus of Chapter Seven is youth justice professionals' accounts of girls' pathways into and out of crime, as well as their perspectives on interpersonal work with young women. This chapter also examines the extent to which popular claims that 'girls are getting worse' have entered contemporary youth justice discourse. Chapter Eight examines – through the contrasting perspectives of young women and youth justice practitioners – the extent to which the 'new' youth justice system is delivering justice for girls and young women. Finally, in Chapter Nine, I conclude with a discussion of the implications of the study for theory, policy and practice with offending girls in the twenty-first century.

2 Historical perspectives on offending girls

As long as there are conventional gender orders to disturb, bad girls will have the power to disrupt.

(Cox, 2003: 172)

In this chapter, I chart definitions of delinquency, offending and 'troublesomeness' as they have been applied to girls in theory, policy and practice during the course of the past century. My primary focus is youth (formerly juvenile) justice interventions. However, the regulation of young women through the education and child welfare spheres is also important, since legislative and policy changes have periodically altered the sites within which young women are governed, and their delinquency or lawbreaking diagnosed, treated and punished. In education policy and provision, in particular, there are clear parallels with youth justice with regard to the socialisation of girls: schooling plays a crucial role in both inculcating and reflecting social mores, and in shaping children's perceptions of themselves, their capacities and the options open to them (Hunt, 1991). Moreover, the social regulation of women and children has historically been effected largely through the informal policing of private and domestic behaviour. Indeed, the effectiveness of informal means of social control has frequently been put forward as the primary explanation of females' lesser participation in crime (Heidensohn, 1968, 2000).

The year 1908 signalled the formal beginning of a separate youth justice 'system' in England and Wales, and thus serves as the starting point for my historical analysis. I review how girls' challenging behaviour has been understood at different stages since then, highlighting ways in which legal and professional constructions of (certain types of) female youthful behaviour as problematic exemplify broader social and political concerns about gender and youth. The ways in which 'offending' girls' and young women's deeds and needs are defined and represented in empirical research are historically contingent and influenced by trends in criminological theorising and by broader sociopolitical concerns. As changes in theory, legislation, policy and practice occur, so does the profile of girls and young women in the youth justice system (see Chapter Three).

1908–32: child-saving and moral rescue

A distinct category of juvenile offender emerged at the beginning of the nineteenth century, prompted by a number of official enquiries into the 'epidemic' of youth crime. The Youthful Offenders Act of 1854 subsequently gave official recognition to reformatory schools in England and Wales, marking a hiatus between the earlier ideology of punishment and retributive justice for children and the newer aims of reform or child-saving (Giller, 1982). The modern youth justice system in England and Wales dates back to 1908, when the first Children Act created the juvenile court, which established the principle of dealing with young offenders under 16 separately from adults and ended the imprisonment of children under 14. Predating the Children Act by just one year, the Probation of Offenders Act 1907 had already introduced probation and recognisances for offenders under certain circumstances: where offences were of a trivial nature; if there were extenuating circumstances; and/or if, having considered the character, previous record, age and mental condition of the offender, nothing more than a nominal punishment was warranted. Despite the Children Act's abolition of child imprisonment, a separate network of secure institutions was established by the Prevention of Crime Act, also of 1908, thereby creating a parallel system of child institutionalisation, albeit under the more benign guise of reform and training (Gelsthorpe and Morris, 1994).[1] Aylesbury borstal in Buckinghamshire was the only such institution for young women until the 1940s.

While the incarceration of children might seem draconian, locking up children has for many years been couched in utilitarian terms as being for the greater good, a humanitarian gesture which benefits individual deviant children while simultaneously protecting society from their troublesome behaviour. And incarceration for 'welfare' reasons, rather than in response to lawbreaking activity, has a long history for young women (Cox, 2003). Efforts to rescue girls deemed in danger of 'falling' were reflected in the high proportion of 'wayward' girls, or girls who might be at risk of 'moral contamination', among the (nonetheless small) female industrial school population. Victorian conceptions of proper womanly behaviour centred on middle-class values of respectability and domesticity: a woman's place was in the home and not in the public arena. Consequently, correctional institutions for girls focused on educating and socialising delinquent females into what was perceived to be gender-appropriate behaviour. For example, the main task of reformatories and borstals was domestic training to prepare girls for their future as a wife and mother, servant or both (Gelsthorpe, 2005a).

The assessment and treatment of delinquent girls during the period were clearly influenced by prevailing ideas and stereotypes about the aetiology of female crime. Cesare Lombroso, an Italian psychiatrist writing in the late nineteenth century and now infamous proponent of biologically determinist explanations of female offending, believed that women in general commit less crime because they are less atavistic than men, criminality being a sign of atavism or biological underdevelopment, and offending being antithetical to 'normal' femininity. Lombroso, together with his son-in-law Ferrero, maintained in his 1895 work, *La Donna Delinquente*, that *all* women are inferior to men; furthermore, the female criminal, they believed, was more masculine than the law-abiding woman (the authors' 'evidence' for this was female prisoners' apparent physical abnormalities); she was 'doubly exceptional' – statistically deviant both as a woman and as a criminal, and hence a 'true monster'. Lombroso and Ferrero further argued that prostitution was the 'natural' female form of deviance. Rafter and Gibson, in their recent analysis of Lombroso's apparently contradictory assertions about women's inferiority and their normally law-abiding behaviour, point out that 'Lombroso assigned himself the very difficult task of arguing that women were less criminal than men because of their inferiority to men' (2004: 9). Moreover, in the early editions of their work, at least, Lombroso and Ferrero largely neglected the social and economic contexts in which offending by women occurred, leaving unquestioned the contemporary social and legal preoccupation with regulating female sexuality.[2]

William Isaac Thomas focused more explicitly on the assumed relationship between female crime and sexuality. In his early work, Thomas (1907) described females as 'anabolic' (passive), compared with males who are 'katabolic' (active), thus assuming essential physiological sex differences. Later, in *The Unadjusted Girl*, published in 1923, Thomas defined girls according to their domestic and sexual roles – dominated by biological imperatives – and as emotional and irrational. More benevolent than Lombroso, Thomas viewed crime primarily as a social pathology rather than a biological abnormality, and thus believed that wayward girls could be 'saved' through early intervention in the form of individual treatment which would help delinquent, 'undersocialised', girls to 'readjust'.

It is important to note the contemporaneity of the emergence of psychological theories of female crime with the rise of medical and psychiatric models of deviance during the second half of the nineteenth century (Gelsthorpe, 2004). Questions of diagnosis and treatment were central concerns in criminal justice practice as well as in theory. In mid-Victorian England, prostitution, or 'vice', had come to be seen as the greatest social evil of the day, leading to state attempts to control sexuality and curb the spread of venereal disease through a series of Contagious Diseases Acts (Heidensohn, 2000). There was also widespread concern about the declining birth rate, youth unemployment and the health of the nation in the aftermath of the Boer War (Gelsthorpe and Morris, 1994). Consequently, young women's sexual choices – the primary rationale for their moral policing – had very public ramifications. This ensured that for girls, delinquency and youthful sexuality were closely associated with one another (Shore, 2002). Pamela Cox's (2003) historical study of 'bad girls' in Britain during the first half of the twentieth century has demonstrated that while the proportion of female defendants appearing in the juvenile court was very low, rescue homes and other private or charity-run reform and child-saving institutions accounted for the hidden policing of a significant additional population of girls. The police either ignored female criminal misbehaviour or at least processed it differently (Godfrey, 2004) and women and girls were more frequently classified as 'feeble-minded', 'irresponsible' or certified lunatics, than criminals (Zedner, 1991). It also appears that the majority of girls resident in industrial schools in the early part of the twentieth century had been admitted on a 'voluntary' basis, rather than committed by the courts, which explains their near-invisibility among the officially sentenced population.

1933–68: identifying and reforming wayward girls

During the 1930s, British institutions for 'delinquent' children were seen as places of treatment, rather than punishment. The Children Act of 1933 was the first piece of legislation that required the court to have regard to the welfare of the child, and girls who had previously been described as having 'knowledge of evil' or 'immoral antecedents', were now defined as 'being beyond control', 'lacking proper parental control' or 'in need of care and protection' (Cox, 2003). The 1933 Act amalgamated reformatories and industrial schools into schools approved by the state, or 'approved schools', which remained in place until the Children and Young Persons Act 1969, when they were again renamed, becoming 'community homes with education'. It was not until 1948, when local authority children's departments were created by the Children Act, that the state took on the role of regulating work with juvenile delinquents. Alongside concerns about the welfare of troublesome children, the 1940s heralded a reaffirmation of punishment, and in 1948, the same year in which remand homes were introduced, a Labour Home Secretary accepted the idea of youth detention centres (Gelsthorpe and Morris, 1994).

Girls admitted to correctional institutions during the mid-twentieth century continued to be routinely tested for pregnancy and venereal infections, indicating that it was still their sexual behaviour that was under strict surveillance. Such moral scrutiny was not confined to Britain. Sheldon and Eleanor Glueck, in their North American study, *Five Hundred Delinquent Women*, published in 1934, advocated sterilisation and lengthy sentences in reformatories for delinquent young women: four-fifths of their sample were under 21, most had been incarcerated for sexual (mis)behaviour, and the majority had venereal infections. The Gluecks believed that 'a major problem involved in the delinquency and criminality of our girls is their lack of control of the sex impulse' (1934: 96). The following excerpt from their work illustrates both popular and professional contemporary fears surrounding the social threat that 'fallen' women represented:

[F]ar more is involved in the careers of most of our women than an occasional lapse from moral conventions. We are dealing not only with a complicated network of biological and socio-economic deficiencies, but with such socially dangerous consequences as the spread of venereal infection, the unrestricted birth of illegitimate, underprivileged children, and like tangible ill effects of unrestrained sexual indulgence.

(Ibid: 322)

In spite of the continuing sexualisation of female juvenile crime, working-class girls in Britain during the first half of the twentieth century were rarely brought to public attention as a result of sexual delinquency – that is, potential or actual sexual activity outside marriage – alone. Rather, a girl's sexual activity had to be accompanied by some other factor or behaviour indicating dubious morals, such as the commission of an offence, adults in the family having been subject to moral scrutiny in the past, or if the girl's sexual activity was assumed to be dangerous, unsuitable, unconsenting or had resulted in pregnancy or infection. The assessment of what kind of family a girl came from was thus of great importance, since 'questions of poverty and propriety, of class and conduct, were closely linked' (Cox, 2003: 4). Parents, as well as the courts, had a vested interested in upholding double standards for their sons and daughters in terms of sexual behaviour, since 'the power of the family rested on its female children's marriageability, and daughters who were "better preserved" than those of other families made more desirable marriage partners' (Donzelot, 1979: 174). Young women who had only committed offences apparently often escaped the purview of the juvenile justice system altogether: 'respectable' girls were often competent thieves during this period, though relatively unlikely to be prosecuted if apprehended (Cox, 2003). And in the case of girls who *were* prosecuted for theft, it was not uncommon for the aetiology of their acquisitive crimes to be understood as psychological, rather than financial. Prominent juvenile psychiatrist T.C.N. Gibbens, for example, declared that girls' acquisitive offending, which he believed was superseded by sexual delinquency in mid-adolescence, resulted from unhappiness and a lack of love and that stealing 'represented a substitute for affection' (1959: 86).

Several authors, Gibbens included, went as far as to contend that there was little need for any conceptual distinction between girls appearing before the courts on the grounds of waywardness or sexual delinquency and those charged with indictable offences. Despite the fact that three quarters of the girls in Cowie and colleagues' approved school sample[3] had been institutionalised as a result of 'misbehaviour, mainly sexual, of a kind not subject to legal sanctions after the age of 17', while just one quarter had committed indictable offences, the authors confidently asserted that 'authorities are agreed that not too much should be made of this difference' (1968: 67). Helen Richardson, also studying girls in an approved school in the 1950s, observed that although girls were often known to have stolen as well as being deemed beyond parental control or in need of care and protection, they were frequently, 'out of thought for [their] future record [...] committed only on one of the latter charges' (1969: 83–4). The clear underlying assumption was that it was more acceptable and less stigmatising for young women to be labelled immoral than criminal.

The institutionalisation of young women on non-criminal grounds – for reasons of 'moral danger' or 'protection' – continued relatively unabated into the 1960s (Smart, 1976) in spite of the Advisory Council on the Penal System's recommendation in 1968 that the only existing detention centre for girls (on the grounds of Moor Court open prison in Staffordshire) be closed without replacement, since it was 'not appropriate for girls' (Home Office, 1968: 1).[4] According to the Ingleby Committee Report of 1960,[5] although 95 per cent of boys were sent to approved schools because they had committed a criminal offence, this was true of only 36 per cent of girls.

The majority of British empirical studies of offending girls undertaken between the 1950s and the 1980s were based on institutional samples, including remand homes, approved schools and borstals. Their authors continued to focus on an assumed relationship between psychology and delinquency, pointing to high levels of emotional instability, poor self-image, psychological disturbance and even physical unattractiveness in delinquent girls (Cowie *et al.*, 1968; Hoghughi, 1978; Richardson, 1969).[6] A key theme in these academic depictions was 'that unhappiness, sexual promiscuity and familial rejection [were] all seen as features of the girls' problematic behaviour' (Gelsthorpe, 1989: 6). Representations of delinquent girls as lonely and socially isolated individuals, acting out their psychological disturbances, were also commonplace. Konopka (1966) linked what she perceived to be adolescent girls' emotional disturbance, 'frightening' sexuality brought about by puberty, and loneliness, to their participation in (usually sexual) offending and to their chances of future 'success' in life. Arriving at such conclusions from observations of an institutional sample of 14- to 19-year-old young women, Konopka characteristically failed to recognise the wider social context of the behaviour of the 181 girls she studied, namely that many of them had been institutionalised precisely because of their (often only suspected) sexual behaviour which, had they been adults or indeed boys, would most probably have been ignored. Others attributed delinquency among girls to a kind of psychological 'acting out' because of family dysfunction (Blos, 1969), or to sexual dysfunction (being either undersexualised or oversexualised). Given the courts' practices of institutionalising girls due to precocious and unmarried sexual behaviour or on other moral welfare or 'protection' grounds, such studies have been criticised for being unrepresentative of actual (criminal) lawbreakers, as well as for their uncritical acceptance of the sexual double standard that led to girls' institutionalisation (Smart, 1976).

It is likely that the foregrounding of girls' sexuality as both cause and expression of their offending in much psychological theorising reinforced, and was in turn reinforced by, legal definitions in which girls' delinquent behaviour was understood as sexual – particularly though the category of 'moral danger' – in ways which that of boys was not. A significant precept of the majority of traditional psychological, as well as biological, theories of female offending was the assumption that girls' and boys' delinquency have distinct causes, which are based on essential sex differences, rather than on gender-differentiated social-structural influences. The influence of Freudian psychoanalysis was also in evidence until at least the 1960s (see Gelsthorpe, 2004): female criminality, Freud contended, stemmed from a 'masculinity complex' originating in penis envy (Belknap, 2007: 35). Psychological theories have frequently situated the origins of girls' offending within deficient families; furthermore, they have variously implicated women's 'natural' inferiority (or, contradictorily, their natural superiority), passivity and mothering instincts in the aetiology of their offending. Freud himself 'believed criminal women to be neurotic, maladjusted, sexual misfits who were not content with their roles of wife and mother' (Morris, 1987: 13).

1969–98: from welfare to justice

The Children and Young Persons Act of 1969 sought to blur the boundaries between deprived and delinquent children, decriminalising the latter to an extent, and aiming to provide a common service for troubled and troublesome children by bringing children's welfare within the remit of the juvenile court (Giller, 1982). The Act thus effectively transformed the juvenile court into a body allocating services on welfare grounds. Children under 14 years of age were not to be referred to the courts solely on the basis of offending behaviour; it had also to be demonstrated that they were not receiving the care, protection and guidance that a good parent was expected to give, thereby extending the discretion of social workers and increasing their power (Gelsthorpe and Morris, 1994).

Confusion between the care and control aims of the youth justice system persisted for almost 30 years with particular consequences for girls, whose criminal deeds continued to be (and still are) much less frequent and serious than those of boys. Shacklady Smith (1978), for example, found that girls deemed to be in need of care or protection and control *and* known to have had sexual intercourse underage were seven times more likely to be sent to an approved school than girls convicted of criminal offences, independent of social class,[7] and in 1977, while similar numbers of males and females received care orders, seven times as many girls as boys did so as a result of being 'in moral danger' (Campbell, 1981: 9). The coexistence of welfare needs and lawbreaking was particularly significant in the punishment of young women. Kerry Carrington (1993) examined the case records of a random sample of girls and boys appearing before the courts in Australia for both welfare and criminal matters in the 1970s and early 1980s, and found that 19 per cent of girls appearing in court on welfare grounds were committed to correctional institutions, compared with just 6 per cent of girls charged with criminal offences. However, Carrington's findings complicated the 'sexualisation thesis' that prevailed in feminist academic work of the period (e.g. Chesney-Lind, 1974) – that is, the idea that the courts punish sexual behaviour in girls that they would ignore – or at least deal with relatively leniently – in boys. Rather, she discovered that girls were not in fact over-represented in the courts for welfare matters, but that when the same girl appeared in court multiple times for welfare *and* criminal matters, it was for the welfare matters that she was dealt with more severely. This led Carrington to the conclusion that the central issue in determining punitiveness was not the sex of the child, but the nexus between welfare and punishment.

Intermediate Treatment (IT) was introduced in England and Wales in the late 1960s, its primary objective being to reduce the level of juvenile offending by addressing the needs of (potential) young offenders.[8] Girls were much more likely than boys to be involved in IT schemes on a 'voluntary' basis and for reasons other than the commission of offences; indeed, only a quarter of girls in mixed sex units, compared with two-thirds of boys, were offenders (Bottoms and Pratt, 1989; Bottoms *et al.*, 1990).

Youth justice in the 1970s was marked by a 'bifurcation' (Bottoms, 1974): a rise in punitive disposals, particularly custody, was accompanied by an increase in the use of diversion through cautioning. This was a largely unintended effect of the 1969 Act: despite its ideological emphasis on welfare and on a needs-based approach, in practice, some have argued, 'the full machinery of courtroom adjudication was retained for those who saw juvenile offenders as responsible and who believed in the symbolic and deterrent value of such appearances' (Gelsthorpe and Morris, 1994: 965). Thus the relevant professionals as well as the courts needed to know which type of offender they were dealing with – a transient lawbreaker, or one whose family background and circumstances were more problematic or pathological (ibid.). Moreover, while overt punishment has not always been the official legislative aim in youth justice, it has often underscored decision-making by the police and by magistrates in relation to the imposition of more restrictive disposals on young people. It is also possible (and this applies today as much as ever – see Chapter Eight) that some sentencers, as well as policy-makers, considered incarceration to be an effective way of meeting young offenders' welfare needs.

The White Paper, *Young Offenders*, published in 1980, and the ensuing Criminal Justice Act of 1982, attacked the root of the social welfare perspective underlying the 1969 Act and represented 'a move away from treatment and lack of personal responsibility to notions of punishment and individual and parental responsibility' (Gelsthorpe and Morris, 1994: 972).[9] The Children Act 1989, implemented in October 1991, further separated justice and welfare approaches to children by abolishing the use of the care order as a disposal available to the courts in criminal proceedings, as well as removing the offence condition in proceedings justifying state intervention into family life. During the 1980s, welfarism had been increasingly criticised by academics, albeit on different grounds: the role of the court was confused; the court had the power to impose sentences which were disproportionate both to the seriousness of the young person's offending and to the risk they posed to the public; girls' behaviour was effectively being policed on 'moral danger' grounds and the net of the youth justice system was widening, drawing in children who had welfare needs but no history of lawbreaking (B. Hudson, 1989).[10] A return to just deserts thus seemed to be a positive move for girls. The justice model of the 1980s meant that girls who had previously been committed to institutions 'for their own good' were now to be judged on the basis of their behaviour alone, but with the emphasis now on the *offence* rather than the individual characteristics of the *offender* came the risk of eroding the distinction between young people and adults. Girls who had broken the law were now to be judged not according to criteria of youthful silliness or experimentation, but as inadequately socialised (female) adults. As Hudson argued, the justice model 'tend[ed] to encourage even further this judgement of girls' delinquency against standards of adult femininity rather than juvenile immaturity' (ibid.: 110).

In youth justice policy and practice, gender-differentiated assessments of and responses to youthful lawbreaking – based on assumptions that the needs and deeds of boys and girls are essentially different – were overtaken from the 1990s onwards with gender-neutral, or gender-blind, policies and practices, wherein girls are assessed and treated identically to boys (Worrall, 2000, 2002). While this may seem, in some ways, to be an improvement on earlier discourses that pathologised girls delinquency, criminalised their welfare needs and established female sexuality as the principal rationale for youth justice control, this gender-blindness fails to recognise the distinct needs of young women and the fact that their criminal careers are shorter and less serious than those of young men.[11] Anne Worrall has argued that feminist critiques of welfarism in the 1980s inadvertently led to concerns about the sexual waywardness of 'delinquent' young women being overtaken by individual psychological explanations of girls' offending, which either emphasised girls' 'empowerment' and personal responsibility, or refuted the role of gender in their offending altogether. Either way, according to Worrall, this retreat from welfarism ultimately resulted in greater numbers of girls being criminalised and imprisoned (see Chapter Three):

> As the 'welfarisation' and 'soft policing' of young women's behaviour, by both formal and informal social control mechanisms, has now given way to the straightforward 'criminalisation' of that same behaviour, we are seeing increasing numbers of young women being incarcerated, not on spuriously benevolent welfare grounds, but on spuriously equitable 'justice' grounds.
>
> (2004: 43)

Meanwhile, empirical research from the late 1980s was beginning to reveal the importance of victimisation in the aetiology of young women's offending. Feminist scholars have emphasised the significance of 'blurred boundaries' between victimisation and lawbreaking and, particularly in the Untied States, of 'the central role played by the juvenile justice system in the sexualization of girls' delinquency and the criminalization of girls' survival strategies' (Chesney-Lind, 1989: 11; see Chapter Three),[12] most obviously via status offences, such as running away from home and 'incorrigibility'. British empirical work, too, has highlighted how involvement in the 'looked after' residential care system over-determines young women's routes into penal custody (Carlen, 1987; Taylor, 2006).

Girls have long been shown to be 'more sinned against than sinning' (Hartless et al., 1995), experiencing frequent harassment and sexual victimisation by adults. Anderson and colleagues (1994) surveyed 1,150 young people aged 11–15 in Edinburgh about their victimisation experiences, and interviewed 120 young people face-to-face. Over half of the girls and one-third of the boys reported having been harassed by an adult. Furthermore, 26 per cent of girls and 9 per cent of boys had been sexually harassed by an adult male at least once,[13] and for girls, contrary to boys, likelihood of victimisation increased with age. Studies of young women in the youth justice system have consistently revealed remarkably high rates of child-hood victimisation.[14] Chesney-Lind and Shelden's (2004) North American review indicates that reported rates of sexual abuse among delinquent girls vary from 40 per cent to 73 per cent, while a raft of studies of incarcerated girls and young women in the United Kingdom (Batchelor, 2007a; Douglas and Plugge, 2006; Howard League, 1997; Wilkinson and Morris, 2002) and across the Atlantic (Acoca, 1998; Belknap and Holsinger, 1998, *inter alia*) have demonstrated that girls in penal custody have significantly higher levels of mental, physical and sexual health needs than both their adolescent male and adult female counterparts. Goodkind, Ng and Sarri found that girls who have experienced sexual abuse are much more likely to be 'placed' in closed residential settings, leading them to surmise that 'a history of abuse continues to work against young women in risk assessment […] and detainment decisions' (2006: 22).

There is now a large body of evidence linking childhood abuse and victimisation with adolescent delinquency and adult lawbreaking. David Smith, analysing data from the Edinburgh Study of Delinquent Development, found 'evidence for a genu-ine causal link between victimisation and offending, running in both directions' (2004: 3). Repeat victimisation and being a victim of assault with a weapon – in particular, robbery – were strongly associated with teenage delinquency, although Smith did not disaggregate his findings by gender. In the United States, Smith and Thornberry (1995) found a significant relationship between child maltreatment and both self-reported and official delinquency for both sexes, with children who had been abused starting to offend earlier and offending more than their non-abused counterparts. Cathy Spatz Widom's extensive prospective research into the relation-ship between child abuse and neglect and offending has revealed that a history of childhood abuse significantly increases the likelihood, for both sexes, of gaining a criminal record as an adult. Widom found evidence of a larger effect size among females in terms of adult convictions: 15.9 per cent of abused females (cf. 9.0 per cent of non-abused ones) were arrested as adults, compared with 42.0 per cent of abused males (and 33.2 per cent of male controls). Abused girls were significantly more likely to be arrested as adults for property, drugs and 'order' offences, although not for acts of violence (Widom, 1989; see also Kaufman and Widom, 1999). Cernkovich *et al.* (2008) similarly found that childhood physical abuse dra-matically increased females' likelihood of adult criminality by between 579 and 605 per cent, while sexual abuse victimisation resulted in a comparable increase of between 264 and 334 per cent, indicating a significant long-term but 'lagged' effect of victimisation on future lawbreaking.[15]

Despite this growing body of research linking girlhood abuse with offending, the intervening processes and mechanisms between childhood victimisation and later criminality are poorly understood and under-theorised (Daly, 1998; Hollin and Palmer, 2006a, 2006b). The fact that the majority of maltreated girls do *not* become delinquent, at least not by official measures, suggests that resilience or protective factors, such as attachment to education and success at school, are also important.[16] Limitations to our understanding of exactly how victimisation increases the probability of subsequent offending among abused girls and young women notwithstanding, the available evidence strongly supports the claim that a 'comprehensive explanation of adolescent females' involvement in deviant behavior *must* take account of past and present victimization' (Lanctôt and LeBlanc, 2002: 175, my emphasis).

Offending girls in the third millennium: a new risky population?

A major change of direction took place in youth justice in England and Wales at the dawn of the twenty-first century. The Crime and Disorder Act 1998, whose reforms were implemented nationally in June 2000, ushered in a 'new' youth justice system which was 'significantly more interventionist and correctionalist than the approaches that immediately preceded it' (Bottoms and Dignan, 2004: 25). Underpinned by four key principles – the primacy of offending prevention, reparation, efficiency and 'responsibilisation' (ibid.) – the casework supervision of young offenders in England and Wales within this reformed system is the responsibility of multi-agency Youth Offending Teams (YOTs), overseen by the Youth Justice Board (YJB), an executive non-departmental public body.[17] The Act introduced a raft of new court orders for young offenders. The most significant of these, symbolically, was the detention and training order (DTO), a custodial sentence which includes a period of incarceration (the first half of the order), followed by supervision in the community. One consequence of the DTO was a sharp rise in the number of young women sent to prison.[18]

The new central concern of preventing offending[19] must be seen in the context of a broader shift towards a 'risk society' (Beck, 1992) in the late twentieth century. Sociologists including Beck, as well as Giddens (1990, 1991), have identified processes of 'individualisation' and risk which characterise life in late modernity. Briefly put, the risk society thesis emphasises that relatively predictable 'modern' social structures and pathways – including jobs for life and stable communities and families – have weakened in influence such that individuals can no longer rely on what were previously more-or-less pre-written biographies determined largely by social class. In addition to creating a breakdown in 'ontological security' (Giddens, 1991), these new uncertainties have meant that risk has become individualised, as opposed to being defined with reference to social groups or collectivities. In late modern society, individuals are required to make reflexive choices regarding education, employment, marriage and so on, and there is an expectation that, in the process of creating their own, personalised, biographies, individuals will self-monitor or plan and thus make the 'right' choices. One consequence of 'reflexive modernisation' (Beck *et al.*, 1994) is that 'failures' or crises are increasingly regarded as individual shortcomings, rather than outcomes beyond people's personal control (Furlong and Cartmel, 2007), and 'new lines and demarcations are drawn between those subjects who are judged responsive to the regime of personal responsibility, and those who fail miserably' (McRobbie, 2009: 19).

The late modern preoccupation with risk has been particularly significant in the penal sphere, as evidenced in a shift away from social work with offenders – where offenders are seen as individuals in need of treatment – towards 'offender management' (as it is now called in the adult arena[20]), wherein offenders are seen as populations requiring control (Feeley and Simon, 1992; Garland, 2001). The risks that offenders present must now be assessed and managed, if not eliminated (Hudson, 2003). In penal policy and practice, parallel changes have been identified, from normalising strategies (which promote *inclusion*) to management strategies (which are underpinned by *exclusion*, either actual or threatened), together with a shift in diagnosis and assessment techniques from clinical to actuarial judgements of risk and need (ibid.; Kemshall, 2008).

The new youth justice focus on preventing offending first and foremost has been accompanied by an unprecedented emphasis on actuarial risk assessment derived from risk factors research – an approach commonly referred to as the Risk Factor Prevention Paradigm, or RFPP (O'Mahony, 2009; Paylor, 2010).[21] Risk categories in generic assessment tools, such as Asset, the youth justice assessment tool in England and Wales,[22] are based on results derived from samples of male offenders, but women's and girls' 'criminogenic' needs may be rather different from those of boys and men (Hedderman, 2004; Shaw and Hannah-Moffat, 2000).[23] Moreover, while apparently a morally neutral 'scientific' activity, risk assessment is imbued with professional subjectivity and value judgements; indeed, it has been argued that '[d]iscretion is not done away with, but it is boxed into categories and systematized and thereby presumed to be more neutral' (Maurutto and Hannah-Moffat, 2007: 480). Elsewhere, Hannah-Moffat has contended that need in contemporary criminal justice is narrowly defined and fused with risk, with the result that the welfare needs of offenders have either been reframed as 'criminogenic needs', or else ignored altogether where they are not amenable to change through criminal justice intervention:

> Correctional interventions are prioritized according to what is pragmatic, rather than what may be meaningful to the offender but 'unachievable', because interventions hinge on broader social and structural inequalities, or gaps in services. [As a result, i]ndividuals are positioned as potential recipients of predefined services, rather than as active agents involved in processes of self-identifying needs.
>
> (2005: 43)

For young women in particular, there is some evidence of a 'hybridisation' of risk and need. Girls who were, in decades past, defined as being 'in moral danger', 'vulnerable', 'needy' or 'at risk' – *objects* of risk – have to some extent been reconstructed as risky or dangerous *subjects* requiring criminal justice intervention that targets their 'dynamic risk factors' or 'criminogenic needs' (Hannah-Moffat, 2005; Maurutto and Hannah-Moffat, 2006, 2007). In effect, this means that young women whose needs might previously have been met via welfare mechanisms are now being reclassified as being at risk of offending and thus drawn into the youth justice system in order to manage and reduce their assessed criminogenic risk factors (Sharpe, 2009). Worrall has argued that a major implication of actuarialism for offending girls is that 'a group which hitherto has been assessed as too small and too low-risk to warrant attention is now being re-assessed and re-categorised' as violent, drug abusing and so on, and consequently 'subjected to the same forms of management as young men' (2001: 86).

The evidence presented so far refutes Worrall's claim that girls' offending was *previously* considered insignificant and unworthy of attention; rather, as we have seen, girls' offending and delinquency has been defined differently to that of boys and thus responded to in distinct, though no less punitive, ways, despite being dealt with primarily via 'welfare' mechanisms. Nonetheless, her contention that girls today are now treated like (or *as*) boys – because the gendered contexts of their deeds and their needs as *female* children are ignored – is an important one.

A further recent and significant development in youth justice in England and Wales is the introduction of a 'Scaled Approach', which 'aims to ensure that interventions are tailored to the individual, based on an assessment of their risks and needs'.[24] Based on the RFPP, the Scaled Approach has substantially intensified the risk focus in youth justice practice and promises to facilitate the 'effective' targeting of resources, namely by matching the intensity of intervention with each individual young person's assessed risk of reoffending and causing serious harm to others. The implications for girls – in terms of risk amplification or, alternatively, their risk being assessed as too low to warrant any intervention (or help) – should be obvious from the foregoing discussion.

Despite claims that the RFPP is now the dominant discourse in youth justice policy (O'Mahony, 2009) and that the system is now 'consumed by "risk" and determined around risk factors' (Paylor, 2010: 31), the extent to which the risk paradigm has infiltrated youth justice practice has, so far, received limited empirical attention (although see Sutherland, 2009). Studies of individual YOTs pre-dating the introduction of the Scaled Approach have revealed that while the traditional social work ethic has survived (Burnett and Appleton, 2004; Field, 2007), welfare concerns have to some extent been reconstituted as risk factors. In other words, individuals' welfare needs are understood in instrumental terms, as an appropriate focus for intervention only insofar as addressing welfare problems is a means to the end of reducing (risk of) reoffending (Field, 2007; Phoenix, 2009; Sharpe, 2009).[25] The gendering of risk is particularly important in light of the fact that the youth justice system has also expanded significantly to incorporate a range of 'pre-crime' interventions targeting young people 'at risk' of offending, as well as convicted offenders. Given the long-standing tendencies to confuse vulnerability and dangerousness, 'at-riskness' and risk to others, discussed earlier in this chapter, there is considerable potential within an increasingly risk-focused youth justice system for net-widening and for the criminalisation of girls who have not in fact broken the law.

Conclusion

This chapter has highlighted continuities and changes in representations of offending girls in the course of the past century. While girls have continually been defined as a risk or danger to society and as being worse than boys for displaying the same behaviours, popular concerns have shifted in recent years from girls' sexuality to their violence as the central site of moral opprobrium. As I argue in Chapter Three, robust evidence in support of the claim that we are witnessing a 'new' girlhood violent crime wave in the twenty-first century is as absent as evidence that girls in the twentieth century were any more involved in sexual delinquency than their male counterparts.

In policy, as well as in popular discourse, a further shift has occurred: an earlier gender-specific focus on girls' sexual delinquency and the assumed-to-be essentially different needs of delinquent girls and boys has been largely displaced by assumptions that girls' offending behaviour is almost indistinguishable from that of boys. Neither the Crime and Disorder Act nor the White Paper, *No More Excuses*, which preceded it (Home Office, 1997) makes any reference to the gender of offenders, and policy documentation relating to the Scaled Approach, too, has been silent on issues of gender, as well as ethnicity, within the new risk-oriented framework. Girls and young women are therefore all but invisible in contemporary youth justice policy. However, as the following chapter shows, recent policies have had a significantly criminalising impact on young women and the youth crime prevention agenda, in particular, has had gendered consequences.

3 The construction of a girlhood crime wave

Recent trends in young women's lawbreaking and criminalisation

In Chapter One, I analysed claims that a new female crime wave had emerged in late twentieth-century Britain and that a new species of disorderly and menacing young woman, who mimicks the anti-social exploits long enjoyed by her male counterparts, was behind this new trend. In Britain in the third millennium, statistical 'evidence' appeared, at first glance, to support such claims. However, appearances can be deceptive, and on closer inspection, robust evidence in support of a new female youthful crime wave is non-existent. While the contention that there is a 'new' breed of girl criminal appears to be built on sand, the following analysis indicates that there is a new and expanded population of *criminalised* young women. This has implications both for practitioners' perceptions of girls who offend and for criminalised young women's evaluations of the youth justice system, issues to which I shall return in Chapters Seven and Eight, respectively.

In this chapter, I review recent trends in the nature and scale of young women's lawbreaking. After subjecting to detailed critical scrutiny the official criminal statistics that have fuelled popular claims that girls are 'bad in ways they never used to be' (Chesney-Lind and Irwin, 2008), I contend that the interventionist and net-widening tendencies of youth and criminal justice policy and practice in England and Wales since the mid-1990s have had a disproportionately criminalising impact on girls and, of particular note, that such policies and practices have artefactually inflated the population of young women labelled 'violent'. My main contention is that the increased statistical visibility of young female offenders is largely the result of political strategies to 'get tough on crime' and the introduction of targets to increase sanction detections which consider neither the gender or age of the offender nor the context of their lawbreaking. While changes in policing have had the greatest impact on the volume of girls entering the youth justice system at the 'front end', principles of progressive interventionism in the name of crime prevention and risk management have propelled a substantial number of young women deeper into the system, including into custody.

The extent of female youth crime

Recurrent panics about apparent increases in girls' offending deflect attention from the actual nature and context of their lawbreaking. One of the few 'facts' about crime is that girls and women offend substantially less than boys and men. Young women who do break the law commit less serious offences, less frequently, than their male counterparts (Gelsthorpe and Sharpe, 2006). Girls are responsible for just one-fifth (22 per cent) of recorded youth crime in England and Wales (Ministry of Justice, 2011) and are similarly under-represented in crime statistics internationally. In the USA, for example, girls constituted 30 per cent of youth arrestees in 2008 (Federal Bureau of Investigation, 2009), and just one-quarter of Canadian young people charged with property and violent offences are female (Sprott and Doob, 2009). In Scotland, young women are responsible for an estimated 13 per cent of crime committed by under 21-year-olds (DTZ Pieda Consulting, 2005), although Scottish youth crime data are not disaggregated by age and gender, making accurate calculations difficult.

The gender differential narrows when self-reported offending is considered. Data from the Offending Crime and Justice Survey (OCJS), the most recent study of self-reported offending in England and Wales, indicate that 26 per cent of males and 17 per cent of females aged 10–25 years admitted having committed at least one offence during the previous year. However, a rather larger proportion of males than females reported serious or frequent offending or both (Roe and Ashe, 2008).[1] A Scottish study of youth offending has similarly found that while gender differences in 'broad' delinquency are small, the gap widens significantly when 'serious' delinquency is considered (Smith and McAra, 2004).[2]

Female offending is a particularly youthful phenomenon. This is largely due to the fact that young women 'grow out of crime' (Rutherford, 1986) earlier than young men: over a quarter of female arrestees, compared with one-fifth of males, are under 18 (Ministry of Justice, 2010a). Estimates of the peak age of offending have for some time been lower – at 14 or 15 years – for females than males, and one in four girls in this age group reports some involvement in offending in the past year (Roe and Ashe, 2008).[3] Self-report studies indicate that the gender gap in offending is smallest (although still very much in evidence) among younger teenagers, after which male offenders outnumber females significantly, the gender differential increasing with age (Graham and Bowling, 1995; Flood-Page *et al.*, 2000). Persistent youth offending is also gendered: reconviction data indicate that four in ten young male offenders, compared with just one-quarter of comparable females, are apprehended for re-offending within 12 months of sentence; moreover, male juvenile recidivists re-offend at almost twice the rate of females (Ministry of Justice, 2010b).

The nature of girls' offending

Recorded crime statistics, while representing only a minority of offences committed, confirm the predominance of minor property crime among young women (see Table 3.1). Theft and handling has topped the female criminal statistics for over 100 years (Cox, 2003) and continues to account for the lion's share of detected female youth crime, followed (but not at all closely) by violence. The

Table 3.1 Young offenders found guilty or cautioned by offence type, sex and age, 2008 (indictable offences only)

%	10–11 years		12–14 years		15–17 years	
	Females	*Males*	*Females*	*Males*	*Females*	*Males*
Theft and handling	83	48	74	44	63	33
Violence against the person	8	19	14	18	15	16
Criminal damage	3	15	3	9	4	5
Burglary	3	11	2	12	3	10
Drug offences	0	1	2	6	6	22
Robbery	1	2	2	5	2	4
Fraud and forgery	0	1	1	1	3	2
Sexual offences	–	2	0	2	0	1
Other (excluding motoring)	2	2	2	4	4	6
Motoring	–	–	0	0	0	1

Source: Ministry of Justice (2010c).

scale of girls' offending is eclipsed by that of boys in both categories, however. In 2008/09, only around one-quarter of youth arrests for both theft and handling (28 per cent) and violence (26 per cent) involved girls, and overall young men were arrested at four times the rate of young women (Povey *et al.*, 2010).

A slightly different picture is painted by self-report data, which indicate that assault, followed by 'other thefts', are the offences most frequently committed by young people (see Figure 3.1), both peaking in prevalence at the age of 14–15 years for males and females. Among young women who do report offending, their crimes are almost exclusively restricted to assaults and property crimes, which together account for 93 per cent of their lawbreaking (Roe and Ashe, 2008).

Assaults constitute a higher proportion of crime among young females than among males – according to both officially recorded and self-report measures – on account of the fact that young women rarely commit other, more serious, types of offence, notably burglary. Young women's theft and handling and violent offences accounted for 37 per cent and 26 per cent, respectively, of their total offences resulting in a disposal in 2009/10, the comparable figures for young men being 17 per cent and 18 per cent (Ministry of Justice, 2011).[4] However, girls are substantially less likely than boys to report violent offending and serious violence perpetrated by young women is particularly unusual: among 10- to 15-year-olds, one-quarter of assaults perpetrated by males, compared with just one-tenth of those committed by females, result in injury (Budd *et al.*, 2005).

Minority ethnic young women and crime

Already a minority within the youth justice system, young women who offend have tended to be treated as a homogeneous group. This situation is reinforced by the fact that British criminal statistics do not report ethnic differences in either

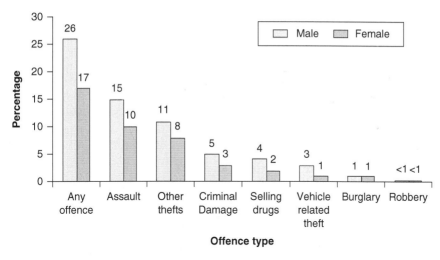

Figure 3.1 Percentage of 10- to 25-year-olds reporting offending during the last 12 months by sex, 2006.

Source: Roe and Ashe (2008: 13).

crime or criminalisation trends by gender for any age group, despite evidence of racial discrimination in the treatment of women and girls within the criminal justice system (Feilzer and Hood, 2004; Gelsthorpe, 2005b). Indeed, it might well be claimed that minority ethnic young women's experience, like that of their older sisters, 'remains subsumed in the experience of black men and homogenised with the experience of white women' (Chigwada-Bailey, 2004: 183).

Self-report data from the OCJS do, however, reveal some interesting ethnic differences in patterns of youth offending by gender. Among males aged 10–25 years, those of white and 'mixed' ethnic origin report similar levels of lifetime involvement in offending, while black and Asian respondents are significantly less likely to say they have committed an offence. Such ethnic differences are less apparent among young women, whose lifetime participation in offending is almost identical across all ethnic groups, with the exception of Asian females: one-quarter of Asian young women aged 10–25 years, compared with over two-fifths of girls in the other three ethnic groups, report ever having offended. The proportion of females aged 10–25 years of 'mixed' ethnic origin reporting lifetime serious and/or violent offending is rather higher than that of both their white and black counterparts and several times the rate of Asian young women. However, the percentage of females in this age group classified as having offended frequently or seriously during the past 12 months does not differ between white, 'mixed' and black groups: 4 per cent of young women in each group are classified as frequent offenders and 7 per cent report any serious offending, twice the level of their Asian counterparts (Sharp and Budd, 2005).

Racial disproportionality in sentencing is particularly under-researched in relation to female defendants. One study that did consider gender, 'race' and sentencing found that African-Caribbean girls, in particular those aged 14 and 15 years and identified as 'black other', are up to six times more likely to be prosecuted than similarly placed white females (Feilzer and Hood, 2004). The authors also found that black and mixed race young people of both sexes were significantly more likely to be prosecuted than was justified by their case characteristics, and that black and mixed race offenders sentenced to custody received longer sentences than their white counterparts, with Asian youths more likely than average to be incarcerated. A recent examination of differential treatment at various stages of the youth justice system also found evidence of disproportionality towards mixed race boys and girls who, compared with white young people, were more likely to be prosecuted than given a pre-court disposal, and were more likely to receive a community sentence as opposed to a first-tier penalty. The converse was true for Asian girls, however, who were least likely to be prosecuted (May *et al.*, 2010).

A recent study of magistrates' considerations in youth court sentencing (National Audit Office/Audit Commission, 2003) found that, according to their self-reports, the presence or absence of parental and family support and information about family background were most likely to affect magistrates' sentencing decisions. Just 11 per cent of magistrates stated that gender influenced their sentencing decisions, and only 7 per cent highlighted ethnicity as a relevant consideration. However, perceptions of what constitutes adequate parenting or family support are likely to be both gendered and raced (Gillborn, 1998). Four-fifths of magistrates in the same survey reported that a young person's attitude and demeanour in court 'influences their sentencing decision to some or a great extent' (National Audit Office/Audit Commission, 2003: 30). White middle-class expectations of gender-appropriate behaviour and demeanour both within and beyond the courtroom have no doubt contributed to the over-representation of black and working-class females in the criminal justice system.

Interventionism and criminalisation

As I outlined in Chapter Two, the contemporary youth justice system in England and Wales is premised on preventing offending, and is characterised to a large extent by interventionism and correctionalism. These imperatives have had a significant impact on the policing and sentencing of young lawbreakers in recent years. In addition, 'disorderly' and 'anti-social' youthful behaviour has become increasingly regulated through the imposition of civil sanctions, thereby blurring the boundaries between youth crime and nuisance behaviour. In the following section, I analyse the impact of changes in pre-court intervention and youth sentencing, as well as the rise of the anti-social behaviour (ASB) agenda, on the criminalisation of girls and young women.

Diversion and pre-court intervention

Girls who commit offences are significantly more likely than boys to be diverted from court, the gender difference being largely accounted for by the lesser seriousness of girls' offending. Pre-court disposals account for 57 per cent of all disposals given to girls, compared with 36 per cent of disposals received by boys (Ministry of Justice, 2011).[5] However, young female lawbreakers in the twenty-first century have been rather less likely to be diverted from prosecution than their counterparts a generation ago. From the early 1990s, following a significant expansion in the use of cautions for over two decades on the grounds that they reduced the likelihood of further offending while avoiding the 'labelling' effect of a court appearance, the practice of repeat cautioning (albeit in reality relatively rare, particularly where girls were concerned) was subjected to increasing criticism. According to the 1996 Audit Commission report, *Misspent Youth*, 'the deterrent impact of the law was being eroded...the factors associated with offending were typically not being addressed and re-offending was happening with impunity' (Morgan, 2009: 57). The ensuing White Paper, appropriately titled *No More Excuses* (Home Office, 1997), and the Crime and Disorder Act 1998, the flagship legislation which followed, heralded a paradigm shift from diversion away from the youth justice system to prevention through criminal justice intervention. The principal aim of prevention within the 'new' youth justice system in England and Wales represented a significant move away from earlier principles of limited retributivism. The current system is predicated on the belief that youth crime prevention is best effected by way of intervening through the youth justice system, as opposed to via welfare mechanisms or, alternatively, by eschewing formal intervention altogether. Accordingly, the 1998 Act replaced youth cautions – which, in theory at least, could be imposed an indefinite number of times – with a more restrictive 'two strikes and you're out' pre-court system of reprimands and final warnings, leaving cautions in place for adult offenders. Both reprimands and final warnings may, unless there is a significant lapse of time, only be used once (and in that order), after which any further offence, no matter how minor, will result in prosecution.[6]

   This shift from diversion from the youth justice system altogether to pre-court intervention in the name of preventing crime has in turn been criticised; for example, on the grounds that concerns about crime control now take precedence over proportionality and due process considerations (Evans and Puech, 2001) as well as the fact that the police, ironically, now have less discretion to divert children from the courts than they do with adults (Morgan and Newburn, 2007). Few critics have addressed the gendered impact of the reforms, however. Among 15- to 17-year-olds – the group most likely to come into formal contact with the police – cautioning rates among young women charged with indictable offences fell from 81 per cent of those found guilty or cautioned in 1992 to 62 per cent in 2002 (Home Office, 2003: 34), propelling many more girls into court, in spite of a sizeable drop in recorded female juvenile crime during the period.

Sentencing

A brief review of recent sentencing patterns provides further evidence of the crimi-nalising consequences for young women of the interventionist turn of youth justice policy in England and Wales. Two changes in particular have had a substantial impact on girls. First, the Crime and Disorder Act 1998 severely restricted the use of the conditional discharge, formerly the most common sentence handed down to girls.[7] Second, the Youth Justice and Criminal Evidence Act of the following year introduced a new rung into the sentencing ladder in the form of the referral order, a 'first tier' penalty which has substantially displaced both the conditional discharge and the fine.[8] All young offenders being sentenced for the first time and pleading guilty must now be given a referral order unless the offence is considered so seri-ous as to justify the imposition of a custodial sentence.[9] Between 1998 and 2008, the use of discharges and fines for young female offenders declined steadily (see Table 3.2), while referral orders constituted four-tenths of court disposals by 2005, just three years after their introduction.

While the *proportion* of young women (and indeed of young men) sentenced to each disposal has remained relatively stable since the early 2000s (a shift away from fines and discharges towards referral orders notwithstanding), the *number* of young women receiving every sentence type increased until 2008/09, when all disposals fell, as illustrated in Table 3.3.[10] Most notable here is the expansion of community sentences, which rose more steeply among girls than boys.[11] The figures in Tables 3.2 and 3.3 do not include the growing number of penalties imposed on young people under the substantial expansion of out-of-court summary justice which, as discussed later, has had significant net-widening consequences with large numbers of young women being criminalised for beha-viour which would previously have been ignored or dealt with informally.

Table 3.2 Proportionate (%) use of sentences for girls aged 10–17 years, England and Wales, 1998–2008

Sentence	1998	1999	2000	2001	2002	2003	2004	2005	2006	2007	2008
Discharge	42	43	34	24	16	15	14	13	13	13	13
Fine	22	17	16	15	9	8	7	7	5	6	6
Referral order	–	–	–	–	28	37	39	41	42	41	42
Community sentence[a]	31	33	42	50	38	33	33	33	34	34	34
Custody	3	4	4	4	5	4	3	4	3	3	3
Other	2	4	4	6	4	4	4	3	3	3	2

Source: Ministry of Justice (2010c).

Note

a Includes reparation orders, action plan orders, attendance centre orders, supervision orders, community rehabilitation orders, community punishment orders, drug treatment and testing orders and curfew orders. All of these community orders were replaced in November 2009 by the generic youth rehabilitation order (YRO), to which any of a 'menu' of 18 requirements may be attached.

Table 3.3 Youth justice disposals by sex, 2002/03–2009/10

	Girls								Boys							
	Pre-court		First tier[a]		Community sentence		Custody		Pre-court		First tier		Community sentence		Custody	
	n	%	n	%	n	%	n	%	n	%	n	%	n	%	n	%
2002/03	18,949	60	8,442	27	3,490	11	498	1.6	54,793	40	49,938	37	24,352	18	6,463	4.8
2003/04	21,076	58	10,331	29	4,349	12	476	1.3	57,439	39	57,787	39	27,158	18	6,468	4.3
2004/05	24,528	60	11,218	27	4,872	12	554	1.3	60,842	39	58,286	38	28,875	19	6,308	4.1
2005/06	27,606	60	12,220	27	5,495	12	623	1.4	66,929	40	61,613	37	31,283	19	6,473	3.9
2006/07	28,116	59	12,422	26	6,164	13	621	1.3	68,072	40	60,582	36	33,558	20	6,476	3.8
2007/08	26,579	58	12,692	27	6,328	14	612	1.3	62,695	38	60,329	37	34,914	21	6,241	3.8
2008/09	22,877	56	11,091	27	5,976	15	621	1.5	52,251	36	53,378	37	32,557	23	6,099	4.2
2009/10	19,894	57	10,013	29	4,564	13	416	1.2	43,241	36	47,333	39	25,654	21	4,714	3.9

Source: Youth Justice Annual Workload Data, 2002/03–2009/10.

Note

a Includes discharges, bindovers, compensation orders, fines, reparation orders, deferred sentences and referral orders. As noted earlier, data are collated slightly differently in the Ministry of Justice *Sentencing Statistics* and the *Youth Justice Annual Workload Data* and are thus not directly comparable.

Anti-social behaviour

Also relevant here is the ascendancy of the ASB agenda during the past decade and the associated growth of civil sanctions which has blurred traditional boundaries between crime and disorder and, many have argued, circumvented the due process protections of the criminal law (Ashworth *et al.*, 1998).

The anti-social behaviour order (ASBO[12]), the most controversial of the ASB provisions, was also introduced by the Crime and Disorder Act and can be imposed on anyone aged 10 years or above who has acted 'in a manner that caused or was likely cause harassment, alarm or distress to one or more persons not of the same household as himself'.[13] The ASBO is a 'two-step prohibition' (Simester and von Hirsch, 2006), breach of which constitutes a criminal offence (the second step) carrying a maximum sentence of five years' imprisonment for adults and two years for youths. ASBOs last a minimum of two years and can be indefinite in length, even when imposed on a child. Criticised by the Council of Europe Commissioner for Human Rights for constituting a 'personalised penal code' which was 'drawn up in such a way as to make its breach almost inevitable' (Gil-Robles, 2005: 36, para. 116), the ASBO comprises prohibitions such as refraining from entering particular areas or associating with named individuals, and restrictions on certain behaviours. In addition to civil liberties concerns, the ASB agenda has attracted criticism in respect of 'regulatory creep' and its preoccupation with the governance of youth (Crawford, 2009a). Concerns about the ASBO specifically have focused on the minimum length of the order and the frequently excessive number of prohibitions imposed, both of which make breach more likely (Morgan and Newburn, 2007).

National data relating to breach of ASBOs are only publicly available up to the end of 2007. Data from 1 June 2000 to 31 December 2007 indicate that 540 girls and 5,488 boys aged 10–17 years received an ASBO, a female-to-male ratio of one to ten.[14] During the same period, almost two-thirds of ASBOs given to under 18-year-olds were breached (compared with around half of those imposed on adults) and one-third (33 per cent) of young women sentenced for breach of an ASBO received a custodial sentence.[15] This compares very unfavourably with an overall custody rate of 3 per cent of all sentences imposed on girls (Sharpe, 2011).[16]

Are girls getting worse ... ?

In the opening chapter of this book, I reproduced a selection of media headlines which reported that crimes committed by young women under 18 in England and Wales had increased dramatically in the early twenty-first century. The apparent rise was widely attributed to 'ladette culture' and binge drinking. Journalists relied heavily on Youth Justice Board figures, which did indeed indicate that recorded offences committed by girls and young women had increased substantially during the mid-2000s. The scale of the increase was biggest in respect of violent crime, official data denoting a 78 per cent rise in girls' violent offences in just three years between 2002/03 and 2005/06 (Youth Justice Board, 2004a, 2007).[17] Similar statistical trends have been documented internationally.[18]

In attempting to interpret percentage rises in relation to a small population such as young women who offend, it is important to note that such increases are susceptible to two 'small numbers' problems. First, a small numerical increase from a low baseline may translate into a very large rise in percentage terms. Second, small numbers are inherently unstable, hence increases (and indeed decreases) calculated over short periods may be particularly deceptive (Sprott and Doob, 2009: 14). The need for interpretative caution notwithstanding, the sheer scale of the apparent growth in female youth violence over such a short period calls into question whether such a rise can be accounted for by behavioural change alone. It is perhaps instructive to consider the situation a decade or so earlier. Between 1992 and 2002, the number of recorded indictable offences committed by girls fell by almost a third (Bateman, 2008b), attracting no press interest whatsoever. If the subsequent 'rise' in female youth crime is, as so many journalists have claimed, a consequence of the 'dark side' of feminism, why did this only affect female youth offending rates from 2002 onwards?

Young women themselves reported no more involvement in lawbreaking in 2006 than they did in 2003. Self-report data from the annual OCJS over the same three-year period reveal no evidence of a rise in offending, violent crime included, among females aged 10–25 years. An alternative self-report data source, the MORI Youth Survey, commissioned by the Youth Justice Board on an annual basis between 2001 and 2005 and covering 11- to 16-year-olds, similarly found no increase in the proportion of girls (consistently one-fifth) reporting offending during the previous 12 months (Youth Justice Board, 2006). Unless we are to assume that young women became less inclined to tell the truth in surveys, it seems that something other than behavioural change was responsible for their new visibility in the recorded crime statistics.

... or subjected to new forms of criminalisation?

If we turn our attention from girls' lawbreaking to youth justice responses to it, there is good reason to believe that recent developments in youth crime processing, notably changes in policing practice at the 'front end' of the youth justice system – including the introduction of a National Crime Recording Standard (NCRS) and targets to increase the number of sanction detections or 'offences brought to justice' (OBTJ) – have resulted in an artefactual inflation of offending girls, and 'violent' young women, in particular.

The NCRS was implemented in 2002 to improve the integrity and geographical consistency of police recording. It sought to make universal the prima facie rather than evidential criterion for recording offences, with the result that the police are now required to record *any* notifiable offence reported to them, even in the absence of any other supporting evidence.[19] This has led to more petty offences resulting in formal police action, and hence more (often similarly petty) offenders being charged. Arguably of greatest importance, the previous New Labour Government, in a drive to close the 'justice gap', introduced targets to increase the number of OBTJ from 1.025 m in 2002 to 1.25 m in 2007/08. The target was exceeded, largely via the expansion of out-of-court summary sanctions imposed on children,[20] or 'punishment[s] without prosecution', as Morgan (2009: 65) has referred to them. The OBTJ target had no regard to the age or sex of the offender or to the seriousness of the offence, and sanction detections were increasingly used for behaviours that would previously have been dealt with informally or ignored altogether, rather than prosecuted (Bateman, 2008b; Morgan, 2008, 2009). The criminalisation of girls and young women accelerated apace following the introduction of OBTJ targets because, as discussed earlier, their offences are predominantly non-serious: petty theft and minor assaults, for example, constitute a considerably higher proportion of girls' than boys' offending. Accordingly, as Bateman has argued, a steep rise in detected female youth crime in England and Wales in the mid-2000s – according to *Criminal Statistics*, detected offending by females under 18 rose by just over 31 per cent between 2003 and 2006 – was a 'predictable outcome of a decline in informal responses to female misbehaviour' (2008b: 4), and not the result of girls' behaviour deteriorating (see also Arnull and Eagle, 2009).[21]

There is a further possibility that the police may be used increasingly as an agency of last (or earlier) resort in relation to parents' inability to control their teenage daughters, such that girl 'victims' who retaliate physically or lash out in response to physical victimisation or parent-initiated combat are arrested as perpetrators of violence. North American researchers have identified a trend towards a growing number of women being arrested as domestic violence perpetrators, due in part to mandatory arrest policies which may fail to recognise the context and the severity of the abuse, as well as the fact that the woman arrested may have been acting in self-defence. The reconstruction of girls' arguments with their parents as violent crimes – a practice referred to as 'bootstrapping' – has been documented in several recent US studies (Acoca, 1999; Buzawa and Hotaling, 2006; Davis, 2007, *inter alia*). Acoca's study of nearly 1,000 case files of probation-involved girls in California revealed that, of the 34 per cent of the young women who had been charged with 'person' (violent) offences, 'most of these charges were the result of nonserious, mutual combat situations with parents', and in many cases, 'the aggression was initiated by the adults'. Acoca goes on to describe a typical case of a girl whose 'father lunged at her while she was calling the police about a domestic dispute. She (girl) hit him' (1999: 7–8).

There are indications that similar trends might be emerging in the United Kingdom (Sharpe, 2009; see also Chapter Five). Research in the north-east of England has identified a recent increase in arrests of adult women for domestic violence (Hester, 2009), with women abusers three times as likely as male abusers to be arrested, despite the fact that they are the perpetrators in substantially fewer, and less serious, incidents. In contrast to social services or other family welfare agencies, the police do not operate an eligibility threshold. Consequently, the response of the police to calls for assistance may be perceived by families in crisis to be more dependable and speedy than that of social welfare agencies. In addition, police officers may be more likely to accept the version of events presented to them by an adult complainant than an agitated 'violent' teenager. Others have argued that the police are similarly being used as 'disciplinary back-up' in residential child care institutions (Morgan, 2006).

Evidence from the United States further supports a 'policy change' rather than a 'behaviour change' hypothesis in respect of increases in officially recorded violence by girls. Steffensmeier *et al.* (2005) found that the marked increase in female youth violence visible in official crime statistics during the 1980s and 1990s was not mirrored in unofficial longitudinal sources,[22] and thus contend that the rise is not an indication that girls are getting worse, but rather an artefact of zero tolerance policies towards youth violence in general, as well as the 'upcriming' of minor misdemeanours into violent offences, both of which have a disproportionately net-widening impact on young women (see also Feld, 2009; Sprott and Doob, 2009).

By contrast, Chesney-Lind and Irwin argue that it is not net-widening that has increased the number of girls in the US juvenile justice system, but rather that the way in which informal institutions of social control – schools, families and peer groups – monitor girls has changed:

> Egged on by the media hype about a supposed increase in girls' aggression and violence, adults in these settings are intensely monitoring girls, recognizing their misbehaviors (which are usually minor), and then sending them into the juvenile justice system in increasing numbers because of the 'aggression' and 'violence' they have 'discovered'.
>
> (2008: 4–5)

The gendered net-widening and criminalising consequences of shifts in policing and youth sentencing on the one hand and intensified and more formalised monitoring and surveillance of the girls' 'misbehaviour' on the other are not, however, mutually exclusive. On the one hand, misplaced notions of 'equal opportunities' and a decline in chivalry in favour of a gender-neutral, or gender-blind, 'search for equivalence' has arguably resulted in an increase in the number of girls and women being criminalised (Worrall, 2000, 2002). On the other, there has been a marked influx of 'violent' young women into the courts due to a shift away from governing young women through welfare mechanisms in favour of governing through crime (Simon, 2007) – and this includes the 'upcriming' of disputes in the playground or in residential care, as well as the relabelling of family disputes as girl violence. This may in turn have led practitioners and sentencers – whose attitudes towards young women charged with violence have long been censorious (Worrall, 1990) – to the commonsensical conclusion that young women today *must* be more violent, simply by virtue of their increased visibility in the traditionally male domain of the youth court (Sharpe, 2009; see Chapter Seven). For girls who are charged to court, the sentences they receive may also be influenced by media hype suggesting that crimes committed by young women are spiralling out of control and thus require a 'tough' penal response.[23]

Young women in penal custody

The toughest response is, of course, incarceration. Although they constitute a small minority – around 5 per cent – of the juvenile custodial population, the number of young women sentenced to penal custody in England and Wales rose substantially during the 1990s and until 2008, and at a much faster rate than the imprisonment of young men. As I noted in Chapter Two, the Crime and Disorder Act 1998 created a new custodial disposal, the Detention and Training Order (DTO), the latter 'training' half of which is served under supervision in the community. The Act also extended the sentencing powers of the Youth Court, allowing them to impose a custodial sentence of two years on a young defendant, doubling the previous maximum. The DTO had a disproportionately negative impact on girls, who have traditionally been considered in need of 'protective' incarceration (Cox, 2003), as well as particularly suitable subjects for supervision (Webb, 1984). Within just two years of its implementation in 2000, the proportion of girls in custody had risen from 3.9 per cent to 7 per cent of all incarcerated youths (Bottoms and Dignan, 2004: 107). The introduction of the DTO does not by itself explain the dramatic growth in female youth custody, however. Between 1990 and 2000, prior to the implementation of the new custodial sentence, the number of young women aged 15–17 years sentenced to immediate custody had increased fourfold, from 100 to 400 individuals (Home Office, 2001). Later, in the three years between 2002/03 and 2005/06, there was a further 25 per cent increase, from 498 to 623, in the number of girls and young women aged 10–17 years who were imprisoned, subsequent levels remaining stable for the next four years (see Table 3.4).

There are at least three explanations for the rise. Perhaps the most significant is that the number of incarcerated girls has risen in line with the burgeoning population of young women entering the youth justice system and being sentenced in court, as opposed to diverted from it.[24] The second explanation relates to the increased criminalisation of 'violent' girls, discussed earlier. A larger proportion of incarcerated young women than young men have committed violent offences. According to a profile of 300 children aged 10–17 years held in custody in the last six months of 2008, the primary offence of 28 per cent of the girls, but just 19 per cent of the boys, was violence (Jacobson *et al.*, 2010). It is thus likely that the disproportionate increase in arrests and convictions for violence committed by girls has played a part in the growth of young women's imprisonment. When 'violent' girls involved in playground fights or minor altercations in residential 'care' institutions are being dealt with by way of a criminal conviction or an ASBO, there are arguably few sentencing options left short of incarceration for genuinely violent young women. A third likely reason for the increase is that girls are being fast-tracked into custody for breach of a community order. As illustrated in Table 3.4, an upsurge in the number of young women sent to custody in England and Wales from 2002 was entirely attributable to an increase in short DTOs of just four months' duration, the number of longer custodial sentences remaining stable. Interestingly, this trend was not in evidence among young men (Sharpe, 2011). The fast-growing number of girls sentenced to community orders

Table 3.4 Custodial sentences imposed on girls and young women under 18, England and Wales, 2002/03–2008/09

	2002/3	2003/4	2004/5	2005/6	2006/7	2007/8	2008/9
DTO of 4 months	165	184	244	263	272	295	284
DTO of 4 months to 2 years	297	260	284	330	324	290	300
Custodial sentence > 2 years[a]	36	32	26	30	25	27	35
Total sentenced to custody	498	476	554	623	621	612	621

Source: Youth Justice Annual Workload Data 2002/03–2008/09.

Note

a Includes detention under sections 90–92 of the Powers of Criminal Courts (Sentencing) Act 2000 (murder and other grave crimes punishable by 14 or more years' imprisonment in the case of adults over 21 years), and sections 226 (detention for public protection) and 228 (extended sentence for serious violent or sexual offences) of the Criminal Justice Act 2003.

was discussed earlier. Concerns have been voiced in England and Wales over the number of conditions attached to community penalties (Morgan, 2009), making compliance more difficult. Indeed, the rate at which young women have been sentenced for non-compliance with a statutory order increased by 134 per cent in just five years between 2002/3 and 2007/08, and breach is now the third most common reason why young people (of both sexes) are serving a custodial sentence (Ministry of Justice, 2010f).[25] Almost one in six young people in breach of a statutory order in 2007/08 was sentenced to custody which, according to Hart (2010), accounted for more DTOs in that year – 26 per cent of the total – than any other offence category. Furthermore, girls in prison are more likely than boys to have been sentenced for breach of a statutory order as their primary offence: in 2008/09, 21 per cent of girls compared with 15 per cent of boys in custody had been sent there for breach (ibid.).[26] It is possible that short DTOs are being imposed on girls who have been returned to court for non-compliance with a community penalty in order to 'teach them a lesson', or because community penalties are not tailored to girls' needs.

Similar patterns in young women's imprisonment have been identified in the United States and Canada. The number of female juveniles (under 18) in custody in the United States increased by 52 per cent between 1991 and 2003 (Snyder and Sickmund, 2006). However, while the number of female 'status offenders' – those charged with 'offences' such as running away from home, truancy and 'ungovernability' – fell by 38 per cent, the number of girls incarcerated as 'delinquent' offenders increased by 96 per cent – a far sharper rise than among boys.[27] Sprott and Doob's painstaking analysis of arrest and court trends in the United States and Canada demonstrates that, in spite of both countries' efforts to deinstitutionalise status offenders,[28] the creation of new 'failure-to-comply' offences has permitted the incarceration of increasing numbers of girls for violating judicial authority. This includes cases where the original court order was imposed for non-criminal behaviour. In Canada in 1999 and 2000, for example, 34 per cent of custodial sentences handed down to girls – twice the proportion given to boys – were for failure-to-comply (Sprott and Doob, 2009: 145). In the United States, too, obstructing-justice or 'constructed' offences, such as violation of a valid court order, account for around 30 per cent of girls (compared with 20 per cent of boys) sentenced to custody, despite constituting approximately equal proportions of the court intake for both sexes (Snyder and Sickmund, 2006). Sprott and Doob argue that failure-to-comply cases are taken particularly seriously where girls are concerned, and conclude that girls continue to be incarcerated on 'welfare' grounds, and that contemporary obstructing-justice cases are effectively 'status offences in disguise' (2009: 122).

Conclusion

It is often suggested that girls' participation in crime may have increased in recent decades because their behaviour is subject to less informal policing by their families and by teachers than it used to be, and because their leisure time is no longer confined to 'bedroom culture' (McRobbie and Garber, 2000), but they are spending more time in the public arena, drinking more and taking more drugs. Despite the obvious appeal of these arguments, the available evidence suggests that changes in youth justice system *responses* to young women behaving badly – and not an increase in the volume or seriousness of their lawbreaking – have had the greatest influence on rising female juvenile crime rates in England and Wales. Minor youthful transgressions, which make up the vast majority of young women's offences, were formally policed at an unprecedented rate during the 2000s. Moreover, there are indications that behaviours which arise in the context of familial disputes and distress are increasingly likely to result in police action, rather than (or perhaps in addition to) welfare support. Such a blunt response to a complex and contextualised problem may even be criminalising victimisation. While the informal policing of girls may have lessened (a contentious claim in itself), a drive to be seen to be preventing crime by increasing sanction detections, or 'upcriming', combined with the criminalising interventionism of the 'new' youth justice system, has had a devastating impact on the number of British girls and young women labelled criminal and violent, on those deemed non-compliant with supervision and, ultimately, on the number of young women sentenced to custody. Recent government policies, in combination with police practices, have served to construct a new and expanded population of offending girls, and propelled them deeper into the youth justice system than previously.

As both the current chapter and Chapter Two have shown, definitions of female delinquency as well as the legal profile of offending girls in England and Wales have changed considerably over the course of recent decades. During the major part of the twentieth century, girls were frequently classified as 'delinquent' on account of sexual misbehaviour or because they were judged to be 'in moral danger'. By contrast, today's 'offending' girls are most likely to have been involved in theft or fighting. There is some evidence that girls whose behaviour would previously have been likely to attract a welfare response are now being dealt with as offenders within a crime prevention-oriented and correctionalist youth justice system. Although claims that Britain is in the throes of an unprecedented girlhood crime wave do not stand up to rigorous scrutiny, the increased visibility of young women in the criminal statistics has undoubtedly encouraged the *belief* that 'girls are getting worse'. This misconception is evident not only in media (mis)representations of unruly girls but also in youth justice practice, as I discuss later in the book.

4   Researching new offending girls

Despite the considerable popular attention young women's lawbreaking in Britain has received in recent years, there is a paucity of empirical research examining the 'new' young female offender, and even less analysis of contemporary youth justice responses to offending girls 'on the ground'.[1] Moreover, the beliefs and perceptions of youth justice professionals regarding the nature of girls' offending have not been examined empirically for over two decades,[2] when a substantial proportion of girls both in penal institutions and subject to community supervision had been charged with sexual delinquency (see Chapter Two). Since then, enormous social changes have taken place. Young women in general have more choices and opportunities but fewer structures of support, and those who do not 'play the game' – lawbreakers, single teenage mothers, school dropouts – are held personally responsible for their failures. Family structures have changed such that increasing numbers of young people are now growing up in female-headed lone parent households. Economic restructuring has meant that in entire neighbourhoods, third or fourth generations of residents are experiencing unemployment or underemployment. And consumption has become increasingly significant in young people's identity construction. In the policy and practice spheres, the ascendancy of managerialism and the dominance of risk and prevention imperatives have substantially altered the terrain of youth justice in England and Wales in the twenty-first century. Simultaneously, child welfare and support services, as well as community leisure facilities, have come under sustained attack – unless they cater for young people 'at risk of offending' (see Chapter Eight). In light of these far-reaching social-structural and penal changes, this study seeks to examine who is the 'new' offending girl and how does she differ from her twentieth century counterpart?

A central aim of the research was to analyse the contrasting perspectives of young female lawbreakers and criminal justice professionals regarding the nature and causes of contemporary female youth offending and the suitability and effectiveness of the 'new' youth justice system vis-à-vis girls. A further objective was to examine the extent to which young women's individual narratives or biographies are embedded in the social structures which delimit their opportunities, both criminal and non-criminal, according to gender, generation, class and ethnicity.

To this end, I asked the following five broad questions:

1   Who are the girls and young women in the contemporary youth justice system and what is 'new' about their behaviour and about the social and material conditions of their lives?
2   How do today's young female lawbreakers account for their pathways into crime?
3   What are the causal beliefs of youth justice and related professionals about girls' pathways into and out of crime, and what are their perspectives on the interpersonal aspects of working with girls and young women who offend?
4   To what extent, if at all, do youth justice practitioners believe that young women's behaviour has changed, or 'got worse', in recent years?
5   How do criminalised young women and youth justice professionals conceptualise youth justice for girls in the twenty-first century and, related to this, what 'works' for young women who offend, according to whom, and with what implications for youth justice policy and practice?

Research rationale and design

I decided to interview only girls, rather than to examine sex differences in offenders' or professionals' accounts.[3] Stanley and Wise (1993: 31) have cautioned that '[s]tudying women separately may lead to a "ghetto effect", because if "women" are separated-off in this way then feminist work may be seen as having no implication for the rest of the social sciences'. Gelsthorpe, too, has contended that an exclusive focus on girls risks 'abandon[ing] boys to their fate' (1990: 95), a concern which is notably absent in most studies of males. While these are undoubtedly valid concerns, I concur with Cain that women (and girls) 'do not need to be compared with men [or boys] in order to exist' (1990: 8); moreover, as Cain further notes, male–female comparison studies – especially where females represent a numerical minority as pronounced as in samples of adjudicated offenders – run the risk of 'othering' females and asking how they are different from an implicit male norm.

I chose to study young women and professionals involved in all stages of the youth justice system, rather than girls who have offended (and perhaps not been caught) or only girls in custody (who represent a small and statistically anomalous group). This was to allow a greater degree of representativeness of young women *in the youth justice system*, in order to analyse, among other things, current responses to young female lawbreakers, the vast majority of whom do not receive custodial sentences. Two Youth Offending Teams (YOTs) were initially sought to take part in the study, in order to ensure a reasonably sized (purposive) sample of girls. Fieldwork was also conducted at a third site, a secure training centre (STC), since this opportunity presented itself during the course of my YOT fieldwork (see below).

Theoretical framework

My interest in the subjective meanings of female offending and in offending girls' own motivational accounts, as well as practitioners' perspectives on young women's lawbreaking, led me to the qualitative approach of semi-structured interviews. Largely as a result of my own background as a youth justice social worker, it did not occur to me *not* to interview girls themselves.[4] My decision to undertake qualitative interviews was also influenced by feminist theory – in particular, the standpoint that women's and girls' experiences engender particular knowledges (Skeggs, 1997) – and by an existing body of feminist criminological research which foregrounds the voices of female lawbreakers.[5] Although there is no research technique, nor any epistemological position, that is distinctively 'feminist', feminist methodology tends to be characterised by the following features: a grounding in women's experiences;[6] attention to reflexivity in the research process and to power relations in the production of knowledge; political commitment; and locating the researcher in the same critical plane as the researched (Harding, 1987a; Ramazanoglu and Holland, 2002). On this latter point, while the 'objectification' of research participants has been rejected as 'morally unjustifiable' (Stanley and Wise, 1993: 168), complete avoidance of objectification is extremely difficult in practice, as it is researchers who have the power to define.[7] Moreover, as Skeggs notes, '[t]he working class are constantly aware of the dialogic other who have the power to make judgements about them' (1997: 167).

In exploring the meanings and interpretations of young women and youth justice professionals, my analytical framework was further influenced by symbolic interactionism[8] – the belief that people create meaningful worlds in the course of their social interactions. The research aimed to analyse how girls' 'vocabularies of motive' (Mills, 1940) interact with, or derive from, their social-structural position, their accounts being an integral part of their identity and the world that they describe, rather than simply representations of the external world (Hammersley and Atkinson, 1983: 107).

My method of data collection and analysis broadly followed the grounded theory approach (Glaser and Strauss, 1967; Strauss and Corbin, 1998), which emphasises the generation of theory from data, rather than the testing of prior hypotheses. This is not to say that I approached the fieldwork without any prior theoretical ideas, expecting to simply 'discover' theory from my emerging data in a theoretical vacuum. The daunting, as well as naïve, prospect of 'unjustifiably assum[ing] the existence of theory-neutral facts' has been well argued by Bottoms (2008: 98), who notes that the theories we inevitably bring to the research situation affect what we find there. The study was partially motivated by a desire to explore historical continuities and changes in perceptions and definitions of offending and troublesome behaviour by young women, and how these perceptions shape, and are shaped by, welfare and justice system responses to them. Given these considerations, my approach to fieldwork was in line with adaptive theory (Layder, 1998). Layder, outlining the key tenets and strengths of the approach, contends that attempting (only) to investigate individuals' subjective accounts means 'foregoing the possibility of understanding the systemic [...] aspects of society and social life and how they are intertwined with the everyday lifeworld' (1998: 8). He further argues that allowing a role for prior theory at the fieldwork stage means:

> abandoning the claim that theory should only be about representing people's everyday lives (the intersubjective understandings, meanings and reality negotiations of interpersonal conduct) [and instead] accept[ing] that theory should equally be about representing and/or depicting the social settings and contexts (system elements) that provide the social environment of people's lives.
>
> (Ibid.: 41)

To this end, in addition to drawing on previous research, I extracted data from each girl's case file,[9] documenting her past and current circumstances and experiences relating to her family, living situation, education and employment history, health and behaviour. I thereby hoped to include some relatively 'objective' data,[10] not least in order to situate the girls' narratives socially in an attempt to counter the theoretical risks posed in biographical interpretation 'of underplaying the significance of structure and of taking young people's interpretations at face value' (Furlong and Cartmel, 2007: 7).

Accessing the research sites

I wrote to the managers of six YOTs in England, introducing my proposed research and inviting their teams to participate. After receiving little response,[11] I telephoned each manager to reiterate my request and to explain the aims of the research and the likely demands on their team's time. One YOT, hereafter referred to as Midshire, agreed to be involved. My request coincided, serendipitously, with the management team's development of a new casework allocation policy for female clients (see Chapter Seven), so provision for girls was high on their agenda. Several weeks after I began fieldwork in Midshire YOT, the manager suggested that I contact Castleshire YOT, which was managed by a friend and former of colleague of hers. My (by then) established reputation in Midshire, as well as Castleshire YOT manager's personal interest in youth justice practice with young women, facilitated access to Castleshire, too. Contact with the STC was also fortuitous. I met the STC's deputy director at a regional youth justice training event, where I, together with Castleshire YOT's Manager, was leading a group about working with girls and young women. She suggested that I should interview some girls at the STC, with the Youth Justice Board's permission, which I obtained shortly afterwards.

I suspect it was no coincidence that all three senior managers who allowed me into their respective YOTs and STCs, advocated for me with their staff and offered substantial support and encouragement with the fieldwork, were women;

moreover, all three openly expressed a personal interest in, and an ideological commitment to, working with girls. My background as a qualified youth justice social worker also proved very beneficial in gaining their trust and credibility, as well as that of their teams.

Fieldwork for the study took place over a period of 13 months. I interviewed young women and practitioners in Midshire between June and December 2005, in Castleshire between February and June 2006, and in the STC in May and June 2006.

Background information about the research sites

Midshire

The English county of Midshire includes several large urban areas, while other districts are predominantly rural. At the 2001 Census, the shire county's total population was 629,676, of whom 68,701 (10.9 per cent) were aged 10–17 years. Midshire's population is predominantly white: 95.1 per cent of residents are white, significantly higher than the English average of 90.9 per cent. The proportion of both Asian/Asian British (2.0 per cent) and black/black British residents (1.2 per cent) is around half the average for England (4.6 per cent and 2.3 per cent, respectively). Employment levels in Midshire are somewhat higher than the English average (67.1 per cent cf. 60.9 per cent).

Castleshire

Castleshire, also a shire county in England, and with a number of similarities to Midshire, has several large urban areas, and is otherwise rural. The county's population was 505,860 at the last Census, including 51,349 children and young people aged 10–17 years (10.1 per cent). Castleshire's population is 95.6 per cent white, also significantly higher than the English average; 2.8 per cent of residents are Asian or Asian British, and just 0.4 per cent are black or black British. Castleshire also has an above average employment rate of 67.6 per cent of residents.

Secure Training Centre

Imprisoned girls and young women in England and Wales are held in one of three types of secure setting, according to their age and assessed vulnerability: young offender institutions (YOIs), STCs and secure children's homes.[12] STCs are purpose-built institutions for young offenders aged 12–17. Four STCs, all mixed sex and all in England (Oakhill in Bedfordshire, Hassockfield in County Durham, Rainsbrook in Northamptonshire and Medway in Kent) house girls aged 15–17 and each establishment holds between 58 and 87 remanded and sentenced children. All four STCs are run by private operators under contract to the Youth Justice Board of England and Wales. The staff-to-prisoner ratio is higher than in

YOIs but lower than in secure children's homes. Thirty-two girls, of whom one third were on remand and two-thirds under sentence, were held in the study STC when they agreed to be involved in the research. No further demographic details about the STC are included here in order to preserve its anonymity.

Sample selection

I interviewed 52 girls and young women with current or recent involvement in the youth justice system. Demographic details about the study participants are provided in Appendix 1. As detailed in Table 4.1, I made contact with 24 girls via Midshire YOT, 20 girls via Castleshire YOT and eight girls at the STC. Forty-four of the young women were either subject to YOT supervision or incarcerated in the STC when I interviewed them. A further eight had been subject to court orders which had ended before I met them, seven of whom had completed their orders within the previous six months. The eighth had completed a detention and training order (DTO) 13 months earlier, following two years of YOT involvement.

To select the interviewees in the two YOTs, I obtained a list of all the girls and young women whose cases were 'open', before approaching the relevant supervising officers to discuss the possibility of interviewing their female clients. I did not select a sub-sample of cases, but made attempts to interview *all* young women who were on the 'caseload' of each YOT. In addition to the girls they were currently supervising, several workers suggested that I contact other young women who had recently completed YOT interventions, typically urging me that '*X* would be a good person for you to talk to'.[13]

I had little influence over the selection of interviewees in the STC. It was agreed that I would not interview girls on remand, since this is a particularly vulnerable time for imprisoned individuals and I did not want to exacerbate feelings of uncertainty and distress. The deputy director also took the decision to exclude from the study those girls whose release was imminent, to allow time for me to gain the appropriate consents[14] and to book appointments for interviews. Consequently, several of the eight girls who I interviewed in the STC were serving longer than average custodial sentences.

Table 4.1 Sample location

Area	n	%
Midshire YOT	24	46
Castleshire YOT	20[a]	38
STC	8	15
Total	52	100[b]

Notes
a One girl recruited via Castleshire YOT was in custody when I interviewed her, but in a different establishment from the main STC fieldwork site.
b Percentages have been rounded.

Table 4.2 Young women's demographic characteristics

	$n = 52$
Age	
13–14	7 (13%[a])
15–16	32 (62%)
17–19	13 (25%)
Ethnicity	
White	45 (87%)
Black	2 (4%)
Asian	1 (2%)
Mixed	4 (8%)

Note
a Percentages have been rounded.

The mean age of the sample was 16.3 years, and almost two-thirds were 15 or 16 (see Table 4.2). The majority (45) were white, including 93 per cent of the 44 YOT-involved girls, consistent with the relatively low black and minority ethnic (BME) population in the two counties in which they lived. Four of the seven minority young women in the sample – two of black origin and two of mixed heritage (both white and black Caribbean) – were incarcerated. In addition, the one Asian girl I interviewed had initially received a custodial sentence, although this had been commuted to a referral order on appeal.[15] The four imprisoned minority young women were serving relatively long custodial sentences due to the offence(s) they had committed (which included manslaughter, robbery and assault occasioning grievous bodily harm), or to institutional racism, or perhaps both.

The absence of any national data combining the gender and ethnicity of young people receiving a criminal justice disposal in England and Wales (both are available separately) impedes analysis of differential treatment at the intersections between gender and 'race'; not even the most basic information about the presence of BME young women at different stages of the youth justice system is published. In a recent survey of young prisoners by Her Majesty's Inspectorate of Prisons which included 95 per cent of the young women incarcerated in the four female YOI units (54 out of a total population of 57), 21 per cent were from BME backgrounds (Tye, 2009). However, the proportion of BME girls – of which the largest number (13 per cent) was of 'mixed' heritage – varied considerably between the four establishments. Monthly 'snapshot' data obtained from the Youth Justice Board for the period April 2008 to May 2009 (personal communication) indicate that an average of 19 per cent of the young women in custody in England and Wales are from BME backgrounds.[16] Data provided by the study STC in April 2006 indicated that, at that time, three black and eight mixed parentage girls were held there, together comprising 34 per cent of the establishment's population of 32 young women.

Criminal histories

Around half of the sample (52 per cent) had been criminalised by the age of 14, although their own accounts generally revealed a slightly earlier criminal début of 12 or 13 years.[17] It is important to keep their youthfulness in mind when considering both their motivations for offending and their perceptions of their treatment by youth justice and other state officials. Broadly consistent with national trends, theft and handling, violence, criminal damage and public order offences appeared most frequently, in that order, on their criminal records, and those whose previous charges displayed a discernible pattern had most often committed both theft (usually shoplifting) and common assault. In addition, the sample included 12 young women who were serving, or had recently served, custodial sentences; these were usually for violent offences of a more serious nature, including manslaughter (in two cases) and robbery. The group as a whole had a mean of eight recorded offences, although this ranged from just one to thirty-four.[18] One-third of the girls (31 per cent) had three or fewer previous recorded offences, and two-thirds (67 per cent) had fewer than ten offences on their records.

Table 4.3 shows the most recent disposal received by the young women. Most commonly, they were subject to a referral order (37 per cent) or a community penalty (35 per cent), followed by custody (23 per cent), with the remainder (6 per cent) having received a final warning.

It is difficult from the available national data to determine how representative my sample is of girls in the youth justice system as a whole, since there exists no national 'snapshot' of young offenders subject to different disposals at any one time. National youth justice data coinciding with the fieldwork for this study indicate that six out of every ten girls who offended were dealt with pre-court, the majority of these receiving a reprimand,[19] and just 1.4 per cent were sentenced to custody (Youth Justice Board, 2007). The study sample therefore under-represents girls in the pre-court stage of the system and over-represents those at all other stages, most notably in custody or on the community (post-release) supervision portion of a custodial sentence. A direct comparison cannot, however, be made with the national figures cited above, since the majority of the sample young women who were serving custodial sentences or subject to community penalties had previously also received 'lower tier' disposals, often just months or even weeks earlier. Indeed, a number of girls who were subject to final warning interventions when I made initial arrangements to interview them had 'graduated' to a referral order by the time the interview took place. Since the majority of young people receiving final warnings are offered just one appointment – a 'one hit wonder', as one police officer put it[20] – or no intervention at all, it proved particularly difficult to access this very transient, and for the most part probably criminally inexperienced, population. It is not my aim in this study to generalise – from a relatively small sample of young women recruited from just two YOTs and one STC – about *all* criminalised girls, but to provide a rich and contextualised analysis of 52 young women's pathways into the youth justice system and of their accounts of their lawbreaking.

Table 4.3 Most recent disposal of the sample young women

Disposal[a]	Midshire YOT	Castleshire YOT	STC	Total	System stage (%)
Final warning	3			3	Pre-court (6%)
Referral order	9	10		19	First tier (37%)
Action plan order	3	1		4	Community (35%)
Supervision order	6[b]	5[c]		11	
Community rehabilitation order[d]		1		1	
Community punishment order		1		1	
Community punishment and rehabilitation order	1			1	
DTO	2	2	6	10	Custody (23%)
Section 85 detention[e]			1	1	
Section 91 detention[f]			1	1	
Total	24	20	8	52	52 (100%)

Notes

a Four girls were further subject to an anti-social behaviour order (ASBO) in addition to the disposals tabled here, and a fifth young woman received an ASBO shortly after I interviewed her.

b One young woman subject to a supervision order in Midshire YOT was concurrently subject to a community punishment order. For the sake of simplicity, only the supervision order has been recorded in this table.

c One girl subject to a supervision order in Castleshire YOT was concurrently subject to a reparation order. For simplicity again, only the supervision order is included in the table.

d The community rehabilitation order, community punishment order and community punishment and rehabilitation order were replaced in the Criminal Justice Act 2003 by a single community order, which has been available since 4th April 2005, to include one or more of 12 requirements, including supervision, unpaid work and attendance at accredited programmes. The Criminal Justice and Immigration Act 2008 further 'simplified' community penalties for under-18s by introducing a single community order, the youth rehabilitation order, which came into effect in November 2009.

e One young woman had been sentenced under section 85 of the Powers of Criminal Courts (Sentencing) Act 2000, which provides for the licence period of a custodial sentence to be extended in the case of violent or sexual offences. This particular (black) young woman received a three-year sentence – 12 months in custody followed by 24 months on licence in the community – for an offence of assault occasioning grievous bodily harm.

f One young woman had been sentenced to five years in custody for manslaughter under section 91 of the Powers of Criminal Courts (Sentencing) Act 2000. This subsection, previously known as 'section 53' (of the Children and Young Persons Act 1933) provides, in the case of a young offender aged under 18, for a period of detention longer than the 24-month maximum allowed by a DTO, and can be imposed in respect of offences punishable in the case of a person aged 21 or over by a period of imprisonment of 14 years or more. Interestingly, another young woman I interviewed at the STC received only an 18-month DTO for manslaughter. The former girl was black and the latter white.

Interviewing the girls and young women

The legal status of young people as minors necessitates gaining the consent of various gatekeepers before a young person may be interviewed.[21] Several YOT workers I approached about their female clients told me that it was 'not appropriate' for me to interview them. I suspected that in some of these cases, YOT workers (or a residential care establishment and a mother, in two instances) feared what they might have perceived to be external scrutiny and did not want to risk giving girls the opportunity to talk negatively about them to an outsider. In other cases, YOT workers repeatedly 'forgot' to mention my research to their female clients. In practice, this meant that some young women were denied the opportunity to participate in, or even to be informed about, the research. However, I was able to invite the vast majority of the girls on practitioners' caseloads to be interviewed. Often this meant a YOT worker telephoning one of her supervisees and, if the young woman indicated her agreement, asking her permission to pass on her telephone number to me. I then called each young woman to introduce myself, explain the purpose of the interviews and to arrange an appointment.[22] In the meantime, I mailed each girl and her parent(s) or guardian(s) (unless she was living independently) an information sheet outlining the study, assuring the anonymity and confidentiality of all participants (with the usual caveats regarding child protection and serious harm to self or others) and giving my contact details and a consent form to sign. It was not possible to speak to the girls in the STC before interviewing them, although STC staff gave them the information sheet and consent form.

The majority of the interviews with the young women accessed via the YOTs took place in public venues, usually cafés or fast food restaurants, but also on occasion at the girls' homes and, in two instances, in a private room at the YOT offices following a scheduled supervision appointment. I collected each young woman from her home address by car and took her home after the interview, which lasted between 40 minutes and two and a half hours (most lasted between 75 and 90 minutes).[23] I did not use a tape recorder due to the public location of most interviews, although I took notes throughout, in full view of the young woman, sometimes asking her to add to or clarify what I had written down. I typed my notes and observations as soon as possible after the meeting, usually later that day. I did not pay the girls, although I bought them a meal, unless the interview took place at their home or the YOT office. I paid for the young women in custody to have a takeaway meal, arranged by the deputy director of the STC, to thank them for their involvement.[24]

I interviewed most of the girls on their own, but four individuals asked to be interviewed in pairs, both pairs being friends as well as co-offenders, and several others brought along a friend, boyfriend or sibling. Although this sometimes disrupted the interview, I considered it important for the young women's sense of safety and control that others should be present during the interview if they so wished.[25] At the start of each interview, I reiterated assurances of anonymity and confidentiality and explained to each young woman that I was keen to hear what she had to say about her experiences of offending, her life more broadly and her views of the youth justice system. I gave her a further copy of the information sheet which included this information and explained that she was free to 'opt out' of the research at any time during the interview or subsequently.[26]

As a middle-class woman with no criminal record, I differed in many respects from the young women I interviewed. Two of the interviewees at the STC were from the Midlands city where I lived at the time of the fieldwork, so we shared some geographical reference points; however, the majority were not. Miller and Glassner note that social distance between interviewer and interviewee can be beneficial, since

> the interviewee can recognize him- or herself as an expert on a topic of interest to someone typically in a more powerful position vis-à-vis the social structure [… thereby] facilitat[ing] respondents' recognition of themselves as experts on their social worlds.
>
> (2004: 132)

Moreover, my status as a geographical outsider, unfamiliar with the towns, estates and villages where the girls lived and had grown up, perhaps served as a (small) leveller, enabling them to act as local guides and, as passengers in my car, to direct me to somewhere suitable to eat and talk. Many of the young women knew each other and word circulated that I was 'alright', thus facilitating my acceptance by potential interviewees.

My choice of semi-structured, open-ended interviews (some interviews were rather less structured than others and included chatting in my car en route to or from a café) presented a further dilemma. While this method was chosen to give girls more power in setting the research agenda and in defining the issues *they* considered to be important, as well as in deliberate contrast to the more common use of direct questioning in child–adult interactions (see Burman *et al.*, 2001), the perception that one is *obliged* to disclose information about oneself can leave interviewees feeling exposed. Several girls were moved to tears when they recounted experiences of victimisation or parental neglect or disinterest. Thus, at times I felt the 'real exploitative potential in the easily established trust between women, which makes women especially vulnerable as subjects of research' (Finch, 1984: 81).[27] While I was initially concerned that I might be seen as yet another adult asking them to tell their story, the vast majority of the girls were very eager to discuss their personal lives, and articulate in doing so, sometimes at length and in great detail. Finch has further described the ease with which women will often talk to a female interviewer, and her own ambivalence about trading on her identity as a woman in order to get other women to talk. Her assertion that a feminist researcher 'of course will be "on the side" of the women she studies' (ibid.: 85) is complicated when the women being studied are offenders, some of whom have harmed other women. Whether or not I *was* on their side was clearly a real concern for a small number of girls who, despite my assurances of confidentiality, expressed fears that I might disclose what they had told me (especially self-reported offending) to the police, their YOT workers or other professionals.[28]

Interviewing professionals

I interviewed youth justice and related professionals, as well as girls and young women involved in the youth justice system, for several reasons. First, I wanted to contrast practitioners' beliefs about young women's pathways into crime with those of criminalised girls. In addition, I aimed to examine the degree to which (if at all) contemporary 'moral panics' about girls' lawbreaking, and particularly girlhood violence, are reflected in professional discourse, and also how gender informs professionals' beliefs about young female offenders' needs and about how they respond to youth justice support and control. As highlighted earlier, no British empirical work has been conducted in this area for over 20 years, and significant changes have taken place during the intervening period in the legislative framework governing youth justice, as well as in the broader socio-political climate that influences penal policy and practice (see Chapter Two). I thus hoped to identify continuities and changes in perceptions of girls who offend, and to examine how broad social, cultural and ideological shifts in expectations, as well as changes in youth justice policy, have been accompanied (or not) by shifts in professional youth justice discourse in relation to girls and young women.

I interviewed 48 practitioners and managers – 32 women and 16 men – working with young offenders or young people 'at risk of offending'. The majority of the professionals were employed by Midshire and Castleshire YOTs (21 and 18 individuals, respectively), and a further nine worked in other agencies, usually in partnership with one of the two YOTs.[29] With the exception of one black British man, all of the practitioners were white British. Interviewees were selected to reflect the range of professional backgrounds of workers in the contemporary youth justice system; I also chose individuals who had direct experience of working with girls and young women.[30] As illustrated in Table 4.4, just under two-thirds (30) of the professionals were case-holding practitioners, one quarter (12) were team leaders or senior practitioners (who supervised staff with case-holding responsibilities), and one eighth (six) were strategic-level managers. All of the team leaders and managers had previously been employed as practitioners undertaking direct work with young people in youth justice or a related field.

Practitioners came from a variety of professional backgrounds – including social work (most commonly), probation, police, education, health, youth work, careers guidance and the prison service – and had between 1 and 23 years' experience of working with young offenders.

My being a relatively young female student was a mixed blessing with regard to interviewing professionals. YOT managers and the STC's deputy director consistently introduced me to their colleagues as a student, which, though entirely accurate, may have suggested someone younger than I actually was. While being female and appearing young had advantages in terms of what staff were prepared to share with me (because I may have been perceived to be naïve and unthreatening), some older male staff, for example, went to great lengths to explain, rather paternalistically, the workings of the youth justice system. This happened several times even after I explained that I had previously been employed as a YOT

Table 4.4 Role of the professional interviewees

Professional role	YOT/STC area			
	Midshire	*Castleshire*	*STC*	*Total*
YOT/operations manager	3	2		5
Team leader	3	3		6
YOT officer	3	6		9
Probation officer	1	1		2
Police officer	4	1		5
Education officer/manager	1	1		2
Substance misuse worker	1	1		2
Mental heath worker	1	1		2
Connexions worker	1	1		2
Sessional worker	1	1		2
Accommodation manager	1			1
Victim liaison worker	1			1
YISP worker/manager[a]		5[b]		5
Police youth justice process marker*	1			1
Voluntary sector partner	2[c]			2
STC unit manager			1	1
Total	24	23	1	48

Notes
a 122 YISPs, jointly funded by the Youth Justice Board and the Children's Fund, have been established in England and Wales. Their aim is to prevent antisocial behaviour and offending among 8- to 13-year-olds who are considered to be at high risk of offending. YISPs include representatives from a range of agencies, including the police, education, health and social services. See http://www.yjb.gov.uk/en-gb/yjs/Prevention/YISP/. The aims and functions of YISPs are discussed in greater detail in Chapter Eight.
b Interviewed as a group of five.
c Interviewed as a pair.
* See note 29.

officer and regularly undertaken court duty. On one occasion, having rung the doorbell of the office Midshire YOT shared with one of their voluntary sector partners, a middle-aged man opened the door, looked me up and down, and asked me which worker I was there to see, clearly assuming I was a client.

Interviews with professionals lasted between 40 and 90 minutes. Most were conducted in private rooms at YOT premises or at the interviewee's usual place of work. Thirty-eight interviews were tape-recorded and transcribed in full, and for the remaining five, I took brief notes during the interview and more extensive notes immediately afterwards.[31] The semi-structured interviews followed an outline schedule designed to encourage conversation about practitioners' beliefs about young women's pathways into crime, their perceptions of girls' needs, experiences of working with girls, their views as to whether girls' behaviour is 'getting worse' and their opinions about young women and desistance from crime. My regular presence in the YOT offices (although not those of other agencies) and frequent contact with practitioners to arrange interviews with their female clients led to many additional informal conversations with YOT professionals.

Analysing the data

There are numerous difficulties associated with analysing interviews. First, the interview process itself inevitably fractures individual stories, through the asking of questions, interrupting, eliciting clarification and so on. Coding processes – categorising extracts of text or 'talk' – further risk fragmenting and decontextualising interview narratives. However, accounts are, by their very nature, fragmented, and it would be naïve to assume that, in the course of one-hour-long interview, it is possible to obtain a person's complete and unabridged life history (see Plummer, 2001). The notion of 'authentic experience unmediated by interpretation' (Burman *et al.*, 2001: 454) is also something of a fallacy, since individuals' stories and accounts are inevitably, in the telling, 'edited, rewritten, and interpreted away from the social relationships in which they occurred' (ibid.: 454). And such interpretation and editing is not solely the researcher's prerogative; interviewees themselves inevitably rewrite or reconstruct their activities, in order to create biographical consistency and coherence in their narratives, to present a 'good' image or, more prosaically, due to memory lapses. Accounts, or 'self-stories', are interpretive acts that 'represent ways in which people organize views of themselves, of others, and of their social world' (Orbuch, 1997: 455). The narrator of an account is thus actively involved in the post hoc construction of the meanings of her actions; moreover, her narrative can function to structure her *future* actions by actively constructing an identity she desires, the pursuance of which may mediate her subsequent behaviour (Maruna and Copes, 2005). Since (certain types of) lawbreaking is widely perceived to be socially undesirable or even immoral when engaged in by girls and women,[32] it is unsurprising that some of the young women's offence attributions (see Chapter Six) took the form of rationalisations, minimisations, excuses and other 'techniques of neutralization' (Sykes and Matza, 1957).[33] The social desirability of attributions themselves may also vary according to the social-structural positioning of the account-giver and to the behaviour that is being accounted for.

A further difficulty with analysing accounts and endeavouring to represent actors' meanings faithfully – which Becker (1967) famously referred to as the taking of sides – is the question of whether taking sides introduces so much bias into our work as to render it useless, invalid or at least substantially distorted. Moreover, as radical social constructionists have asked, can what goes on during an interview tell us anything about truths or realities in the interviewee's social world beyond that particular interview? On this latter issue, I concur with Miller and Glassner, who have argued that narratives which emerge in the interview context are nonetheless situated in social worlds. Noting how the adolescents they have interviewed experience their identities – including dimensions of age, gender and ethnicity – regardless (and in spite) of being interviewed, Miller and Glassner assert that the assumption 'that realities beyond the interview context cannot be tapped into and explored is to grant narrative omnipotence' (2004: 129). Readers are referred to the endnotes for further details of my analysis of the interview data.[34]

5 Pathways into crime and criminalisation

The behaviour of the 'new' girl criminal presented in popular discourse tends to be devoid of any contextual background behind the immediacy of her hedonistic acts of aggression and alcohol consumption. Her private life – her family and educational circumstances and other life experiences – is rarely discussed. Rather, she is represented simply as acting like a boy. However, when we look carefully at offending girls' lives, it becomes clear that a raft of adverse life circumstances can precipitate, or accelerate, young women's pathways into lawbreaking and that both the experience of such adversities and their impact are cross-cut by gender, class, race and generation, to varying degrees in different contexts.

This chapter examines the background circumstances of the 52 girls and young women[1] in the study, drawing on information imparted by the girls in interview and also gleaned from documentation in each of their case files. While each young woman's life circumstances were unique, three important and interrelated themes emerged. The first of these was *troubled families*, characterised by unstable living and care arrangements, experiences of familial abuse, bereavement and loss, as well as strained mother–daughter relationships. The second was *trouble at school*. In contrast to the popular story that girls are excelling in the classroom, entering university in unprecedented numbers and that, provided that they work hard and are ambitious, educational success is theirs for the taking, youth justice system-involved young women, and particularly those from lower-income families living in disadvantaged neighbourhoods, are not doing very well at all at school and face considerable structural obstacles which mark them out early on as school 'failures'. Finally, the *coping strategies* that the young women employed, usually in the absence of any formal support, as a means of escaping or resisting the various domestic and educational adversities in their lives – involvement in alcohol or drug use, self-harm or becoming pregnant – frequently resulted in their criminalisation.

The picture presented in this chapter is one of a highly disadvantaged population of young women, many of whom had experienced multiple and significant adversities, and whose lives were frequently characterised by disconnection, disruption and exclusion. Social and educational exclusion were often exacerbated by the girls' status as minors and by their financial hardship, which together limited their capacity for active citizenship. Perhaps of greatest interest, given both the far-reaching social changes that have taken place, as I outlined at the beginning of Chapter Four, and also in light of contemporary constructions of young women's lawbreaking as a 'new' and growing social problem (see Chapter One), offending girls' socio-biographies and the material circumstances of their lives have changed surprisingly little during recent decades.

Troubled families

The family as a source of stress and as a major precipitating factor underlying girls' pathways into crime has been a recurrent theme in research about criminalised young women,[2] and the findings of the current study lend further support to the conclusions of previous research. Precious few of the young women in the sample had escaped some form of familial upheaval, violence, loss or conflict and precarious and disrupted domestic arrangements featured prominently in their lives. Where they lived and with whom, and who was available to care for them – both practically and emotionally – often changed frequently and were the sources of considerable anxiety and uncertainty. Very few individuals ($n = 9$) were living with both parents, while over two-fifths ($n = 22$) no longer lived with either of their parents (see Table 5.1). Significantly, 11 of the 12 girls who had ever been in custody lived with neither birth parent, despite their mean age of under 17 years. This stands in stark contrast to national trends: 23 per cent of British children live in lone parent families, while just 1.5 per cent either do not live with a parent or live in a 'communal' setting, such as a children's home (Office for National Statistics, 2009).

Almost half of the young women ($n = 24$) had experienced disruption in their living arrangements, including multiple foster or residential placement changes,

Table 5.1 Current living situation[a]

Living situation	n	%
With mother	13	25
With both birth parents	9	17
Living independently	8	15
With another relative	5	10
With mother and stepfather/mother's partner	4	8
With father	4	8
In residential care	3	6
With boyfriend and his parent(s)	2	4
Homeless/no fixed abode[b]	2	4
With foster carers	1	2
With friends	1	2
Total	52	100[c]

Notes

a The living situation of the girls in custody denotes their situation prior to being incarcerated.

b Notably, both of the homeless girls were in custody when I interviewed them, and both felt it highly likely that they would be homeless on release.

c Percentages have been rounded.

temporary stays on friends' sofas and moves between family members due to bereavement or family conflict.[3] Multiple moves and placement 'breakdowns' had disturbed the domestic lives of all 10 of the young women with histories of local authority care (19 per cent of the sample). Fifteen girls (29 per cent) had experienced homelessness: several had been turned out of the family home as soon as they turned 16; others had chosen to move out because they disliked their mother's new partner or because they (and sometimes their mother) had been victimised by a male member of the household.[4]

Grace had escaped the turbulence of family life by leaving home and moving in with her older sister when she was just 11, after witnessing regular and escalating violence by her father towards her mother throughout most of her young life. Although her parents eventually separated and her father left the family home, Grace decided that she could no longer cope with her mother's alcohol abuse, from which she was now dying. Grace recounted her distress at watching her mother – who was 'that ill, she just watches the mess grow in her house' – steadily deteriorate due to liver failure. Another older sister, who had Down's Syndrome as well as a hole in her heart, was still living with Grace's mother; however, the family had recently learned that this sister's health was declining, which had driven their mother further into alcoholism.

Toni, the only gang-involved girl I interviewed, was 17 when we met and had lived in hostels for two years before being imprisoned three months earlier. In her grandmother's care from birth, Toni had later moved between the homes of her father, her aunt and, most recently, her mother. No one had visited Toni since she had arrived at the secure training centre (STC) and she had not had any form of contact with her mother. Toni attributed this to her own offending, and believed that, 'if I started doing all the good stuff I'm supposed to be doing, she'd probably be interested in me again'.

Backgrounds of domestic abuse and victimisation

Home was not a safe place for many of the girls. Fifteen girls (29 per cent) had been physically abused and eight (15 per cent) had been sexually abused or raped. One quarter ($n = 13$) had witnessed domestic violence in the family home: in each case, either the girl's father or her mother's partner was the assailant (see Figure 5.1). A further two young women had been victims of domestic violence perpetrated by their own boyfriend or partner, and eight reported that they had been bullied at school, physically and/or psychologically. These figures almost certainly underestimate the true extent of victimisation among the sample: case file documentation relating to the young women in the STC was often incomplete; moreover, young women may not have wished to divulge abuse to YOT or STC workers, or indeed to me, especially if they feared the consequences of disclosure.

Theoretical accounts of the associations between girls' and women's abuse experiences and their offending were reviewed in Chapter Two, where I emphasised that the intervening mechanisms between victimisation and offending are

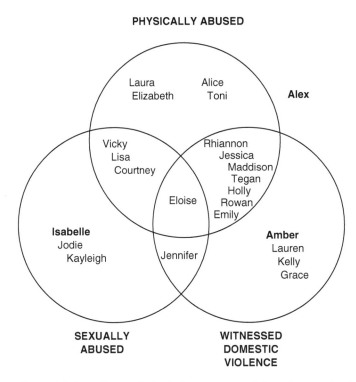

Figure 5.1 Prevalence of physical abuse, sexual abuse/rape and witnessing domestic violence in the family home.

Note: Names in bold denote young women who had also been victims of domestic violence themselves.

poorly understood. While the 'typical' young female offender, according to US feminist analyses, is a girl who is sexually abused by a stepfather or another male relative, who then runs away from home to escape the abuse, and consequently engages in illegal activities as a survival strategy (Giordano *et al.*, 2006: 22), Giordano and colleagues have suggested that girls' victimisation experiences 'are most often catalysts for delinquency involvement when they occur in tandem with other traditional predictors of delinquency' (ibid.: 32), such as poor parental care and control, poverty and associating with delinquent peers. This analysis implicates class as an important intervening variable. In other words, the highly gendered experience of intimate abuse may interact with other, more generic, risk factors, such as poverty, having criminal associates and receiving poor parental care and supervision, to ultimately culminate in offending (see Giordano, 2009).

The majority of the young women I interviewed had friends who offended, sometimes as co-offenders. Experience of victimisation, coupled with a lack of attachment to school, may for some have constituted an indirect pathway into offending, for example, through girls spending more time on the streets in order to avoid school as well as violence at home, running away from abusive situations, or through homelessness resulting from abuse. Thus an individual girl's victim-to-offender trajectory might variously be conceptualised as a coping mechanism, a response to feelings of anger and distress following victimisation or as a side effect of alcohol and drugs consumed as a means of escaping the stresses and strains of daily life. Affluent, well-supervised girls who have a stable place to live and are engaged in full-time education are relatively unlikely to turn to crime as a consequence of being abused.[5] By contrast, the girls in the current study – most of whom lived in poverty, spent a large amount of time 'hanging around' in public space for want of anywhere else to go and a lack of money to pay for commercial entertainment, had frequently been excluded from school and felt that they had little to gain from formal education – may have found delinquent means of dealing with the emotional distress and trauma caused by victimisation.

Offending girls' greater vulnerability, compared with their male counterparts, to familial and partner abuse and sexual exploitation, may additionally render them subject to more intensive criminal justice scrutiny and control, in a misguided attempt to constrain their sexuality and/or for their own 'protection', rather than address the patriarchal structures that allow girls and women to be victimised with impunity (Sharpe, 2009). Such individualised censure and control ignore the hyper-sexualisation of girls in a contemporary culture in which young women might easily be forgiven for believing that their sexual capital is their greatest asset and in which young female bodies are ubiquitously displayed as objects for male consumption.[6]

Bereavement and loss

Bereavement and other losses of significant relationships emerged as a recurrent theme in both the girls' narratives and their case file documentation. As Figure 5.2 shows, 60 per cent of the sample had lost contact with at least one close family member, most often their father. Twenty-seven per cent had experienced one or more significant bereavements, including the death of a parent (in five cases), grandparent or other family member, to suicide, homicide, overdose or alcohol-related illness.[7] In addition, Aimee, whom I met when she was 14, and six months pregnant – her third pregnancy, the other two having resulted in miscarriage – gave birth three months later to a stillborn child, while Anna was involved in a car crash shortly after we met in which her sister, the driver, was killed.

Emily was living with her mother when we met, having spent the previous two years in numerous foster placements in four different counties. She declared that her mother was threatening to beat her, which was why she had initially been taken into state care, but that her social worker 'can't be bothered coming round mine every week' to work with her and her mother. Emily, who was on a mornings-only curriculum at school and on the brink of permanent exclusion, believed that her mother cared little what she got up to. She had only met her father once, commenting that 'he said he doesn't want to get to know me till I'm sixteen, so he don't have to pay for anything'.

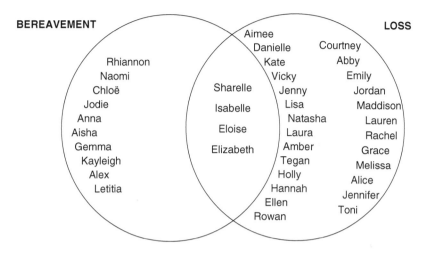

Figure 5.2 Prevalence of bereavement and loss among the study young women.

Many young women recounted how a member of their extended family – often a grandparent, and typically a grandmother or another female relative – had performed a substantial caring role during their childhood, and been a dependable adult providing support and encouragement that was otherwise lacking in the parental home. Loss of a grandparent in such circumstances was particularly devastating. Letitia's experience of bereavement was exceptional for a girl of 14. Her mother died of a drugs overdose when she was just one year old, after which Letitia was cared for by her paternal grandmother, until she, too, died when Letitia was 12 – the same age at which she reported starting offending. According to a pre-sentence report, her grandmother 'was effectively her mother and a stabilising influence in her life'. Letitia's maternal grandmother, aunt and two female cousins had also subsequently died: her aunt was hit by a car, one cousin died of spina bifida and the other overdosed on drugs. Following the death of her paternal grandmother, Letitia's father, a heavy drinker with no previous experience of parenting his children, became her primary carer. Prior to being sent to the STC, where we met, for 'glassing' another girl who had stolen from her father, Letitia had spent several months in a children's home, as her father could no longer manage her behaviour. She now feared that he, too, would die and leave her orphaned. Perhaps by virtue of her age, Letitia appeared to have little insight into the impact of these numerous losses on her life and her behaviour; however, when I prompted her, she pondered whether the fact that she 'always used to be angry'– to which she attributed much of her violent offending – might be connected in some way to her grandmother's death.

Researchers examining the backgrounds of persistent and serious young offenders have documented similarly high levels of loss and bereavement.[8] Although a large body of psychological research has linked childhood bereavement with negative outcomes, including an increased risk of developing a range of psychiatric problems, such as depression, anxiety and attachment disorders (Black, 2002), criminological theory has rarely addressed its often devastating effects. Quantitative research examining the links between bereavement and subsequent behaviour has produced mixed findings: a review by Rutter and colleagues concluded that there is evidence of only a 'minimal' association between parental death and a child's risk of antisocial behaviour (1998: 185), while Ribbens McCarthy and Jessop's (2005) literature review concluded that there is some evidence supporting the idea that bereavement may be a risk factor for offending, in particular where drug-related or serious crime is concerned. And although feminist criminologists have made much of the connections between victimisation and offending among women and girls (see Chapter Two), bereavement – which may, like victimisation, result in feelings of grief, depression, post-traumatic stress disorder or anger (Bowlby, 1973), and in turn lead to alcohol or substance misuse – has been neglected in feminist (as well as mainstream) theories of offending. There are, however, indications that coping styles following bereavement may be gendered. Sweeting and colleagues' (1998) longitudinal study of 1,000 young people in Scotland found that young women bereaved of a parent were more likely than any other group to be engaged in poor health behaviours – including smoking, drinking and drug use – during their teenage years, while Reinharz and colleagues (1993) found evidence of an association between being bereaved of a parent and major depression in later adolescence among girls but not boys.

The intervening mechanisms between bereavement and loss and offending, if indeed one accepts the association at all, are undoubtedly complex. The great majority of young people experience bereavement, most commonly the death of a grandparent, and bereavement is usually managed without professional help and without the child experiencing enduring adverse effects. However, individuals who are already vulnerable by virtue of living in chaotic and distressed families within disadvantaged neighbourhoods may, when confronted with the additional potentially disruptive experience of a significant bereavement, be exposed to a 'double jeopardy' (Ribbens McCarthy and Jessop, 2005: 63). Bereavement that co-occurs, or interacts, with the emotional effects of poverty and social isolation, school problems, and perhaps a parent traumatised by their own loss and unable to provide much in the way of emotional support, may render young women particularly vulnerable to 'coping' through self-harm or substance abuse.

The losses of family relationships, in addition to the bereavements, that many young women experienced have been included here not only because they featured prominently in the girls' biographies, but also because the perception that 'nobody cares' was cited by many – particularly those who had grown up in state 'care' – as a reason for their lawbreaking (see Chapter Six). Perhaps more accurately, such individuals felt that they were not inhibited from offending by the informal familial controls that often proscribe other young people's lawbreaking. In addition, feeling 'given up on' by a parent during childhood was sometimes mirrored in the young women's later experiences of welfare and youth justice professionals, who, as discussed in Chapter Eight, they often believed had 'abandoned' them or 'dropped their case' without explanation.

Trouble with mothers

Fractious relationships with mothers also featured frequently in the girls' narratives. Almost two-thirds ($n = 33$) of the sample had a poor relationship with their mother, according to either their own account or their case file, which they themselves most often attributed to their mother moving in with a new partner, or to her alcohol abuse. Several girls recounted arguments between themselves and their mother – often concerning boyfriends (the girls' own or their mothers') – which affected their mood for a prolonged period, rendering them especially susceptible to behaving aggressively if subsequently provoked or irritated by others. Kayleigh explained that she had offended 'just out of spite and to be a little bitch to my mum. I know it pisses her off. Because I know it annoys her, I'll just go and do it'. Similarly, Emily understood her lawbreaking as 'payback' to her mother, to 'prove a point' to her mum and to 'get my own back'. Emily, referred to earlier, had spent several years in foster care after being physically abused by her mother, who, Emily was at pains to point out, was just 17 years her senior. Her mother had been a victim of domestic violence at the hands of various boyfriends in the past. Back home following the breakdown of a recent foster placement, Emily's relationship with her mother had once again reached crisis point, as I rather uncomfortably observed at first hand when I took her home. Emily conceptualised her own offending as 'justice' towards her mother, declaring, 'she's been so nasty, I thought, I'll just teach her a lesson'.

Evidence from previous criminological and psychological research lends some support to the young women's perspectives. Cernkovich and Giordano (1987) found that girls in general experience greater levels of conflict with parents than boys do – perhaps, as the authors also discovered, because girls also communicate more with their parents. A later Canadian self-report study (LeBlanc and Bouthillier, 2002, reported in Lanctôt and LeBlanc, 2002) found that adjudicated adolescent females tend to rebel against their families and behave aggressively towards their parents more often than males do, with girls in step-parent families rebelling against their families most frequently. Carol Gilligan (1989), reviewing historical evidence that girls suffer more, or 'face a psychological crisis', during adolescence, suggests that this 'suffering' is of a relational nature because girls and women live intensely in relationships. Elsewhere, Gilligan has proposed that:

> [I]t is in close relationships that girls are most willing to argue or disagree, wanting most to be known and seen by those to whom they feel closest and also believing that those who are close will be there, will listen, and will try to understand.
>
> (Gilligan, 1991: 20)

Terri Apter's work on mother–daughter relationship conflicts extends earlier feminist psychological and psychoanalytical theories of female development, such as those of Gilligan, through empirical scrutiny of *both sides* of the mother–daughter dyad during adolescent conflict. Apter contends that teenage daughters are at a period in their lives when they undergo a process of individuation and that a girl's need for recognition and appreciation of her newly forming self underlies many mother–daughter fights, the younger woman 'seeking a sign that her developing self is validated through [her mother's and father's] (positive or negative) responses, or legitimized through their admiration and understanding' (2004: 242). When considered from such a perspective, a certain level of mother–daughter conflict can be understood as adaptive, enabling daughter and mother to maintain relationship with one another. Observing how negative labels such as 'lip', 'back talk' and 'disrespect' may in fact mask genuine and healthy attempts at communication on the part of teenage daughters, Apter cautions that '[i]f a mother punishes or threatens a daughter who asserts her sense of difference … a daughter is likely to heighten her opposition' (2004: 51). Moreover, when a daughter's oppositional behaviour is reported to the authorities, she may find herself criminalised, rather than supported. As I argued in Chapter Three, the relabelling of girls' arguments with their parents as violent crimes appears to have resulted in the criminalisation of increasing numbers of girls for 'domestic' issues, such as assault and criminal damage in the home. This trend has perhaps been further accelerated by the retrenchment of welfare services for adolescent girls and their families, such that criminal justice responses to crises have, for some families with teenagers, become more predictable than welfare assistance in the twenty-first century. In the current study, seven of the girls (13 per cent) had convictions for offences against their mothers or against substitute carers, and a further six (12 per cent) had 'offended' in similar ways but not been charged. These transgressions related to criminal damage to mothers' or carers' homes or property ($n = 7$), theft of cash or cash cards ($n = 5$) and assault ($n = 5$).[9]

Fifteen-year-old Kelly was in her fifth foster placement in six months when I met her, having been removed from the family home for stealing money from her stepfather to fund her 'alcohol problem'. She was now living directly across the road from her mother's house. Although her mother had refused to have any contact with Kelly on account of her daughter's behaviour and the company she was keeping, Kelly could see her from her window. Kelly, who had started drinking at 13 due to 'family problems' (she particularly disliked her new stepfather), had recently been charged with assault and criminal damage. Her YOT worker described in a court report how Kelly had returned home one night after spending the day drinking with friends, which led to a drunken altercation between Kelly and her mother and sister:

> … [A]s the argument got more heated she clenched her fist in anger, seeing this her sister went to hit Kelly, but Kelly hit her sister first. Her sister then phoned the Police to report the assault, and Kelly was subsequently arrested.

A second offence, committed four days later, was similar: Kelly had returned home drunk and her mother had told her to go to bed, after which another argument ensued. As the exchange became more heated, Kelly smashed various items in the kitchen, whereupon her mother phoned the police who arrested Kelly for criminal damage.

I did not interview the girls' mothers, and so I cannot comment on their 'side of the story'. It is, however, important to note that the white middle-class perspective of writers such as Gilligan and Apter neglects consideration of the impact of such factors as (young) age at childbirth, stress caused by poverty, mental health problems, alcohol and drug misuse, and her own experiences of abuse and violent victimisation on a mother's ability to maintain a positive bond with her adolescent daughter as the younger woman begins to assert her new yet fragile identity. Mothers who are struggling to cope with troubles of their own (and there was evidence that a significant proportion of the study girls' mothers were, or had been, victims of domestic violence) may experience their teenage daughters' relentless criticism, rage and even apparent hatred of them as overwhelming, which may lead them either to disengage emotionally or to intensify conflict in an attempt to hold on to some degree of maternal control. Just a quarter of the sample young women lived with their father and many had no relationship or contact with their father at all. In such circumstances, young women may project feelings of anger – at being compelled to live with a stepfather not of their choosing, or towards absent fathers – onto their mother, as the 'last one standing'. Some of the girls had perhaps turned feelings of hurt and distress outwards against mothers who had failed to protect them from abuse by stepfathers or other male relatives. Moreover, the psychological impact on a daughter of her mother, as her primary (and often sole) carer, calling the police and having her arrested in the context of what she may perceive to be an 'equal' fight, is likely to be considerable. At the same time, when girls (and boys) break the law, the disciplinary gaze, as well as public and political condemnation, frequently falls on their mothers (Holt, 2008), many of whom are now subjected to criminal justice sanctions on account of their children's lawbreaking,[10] despite the fact that these mothers are frequently 'the very same parents who have been denied assistance and support from state agencies' (Goldson and Jamieson, 2002: 91).

Trouble at school

National debates about the educational underachievement of young people underwent a dramatic gender shift in the 1980s, when the gender gap in attainment began for the first time to favour girls (Walkerdine *et al.*, 2001). Indeed, today young women, whose 'highly visible bodies are now marked by the possession of grades, qualifications and occupational identities' (McRobbie, 2009: 73), are imagined not only as the foremost beneficiaries of social change in the educational sphere but also as the 'ideal flexible subject of the new economy' (Harris, 2004: 37). While many traditionally 'male' working-class jobs in the manufacturing industry have all but disappeared, the growth of the service sector has been accompanied by a dramatic rise in female employment, albeit frequently poorly paid and insecure. However, as Walkerdine and colleagues have shown, the discourse of female 'success' and credentialism – and, conversely, male failure – ignores persistent class differences and evidence that young women's educational and employment trajectories diverge increasingly with age according to their class position. Despite the considerable gains of middle-class women in the higher echelons of the labour market, young women who leave school early remain heavily concentrated in a handful of insecure occupations whose prospects and rewards are extremely limited (Biggart, 2002; Furlong and Cartmel, 2007).

The educational backgrounds of the youth justice system-involved young women in this study contrasted markedly with the prevalent public discourse about young women's educational achievement and ambition. Many of the girls had fallen, or been pushed, off the path to educational success at an early age. Thirty-two (62 per cent) had left school before reaching the statutory leaving age;[11] this number was split more or less evenly between those who had left 'voluntarily', by 'voting with their feet', and those who had been formally excluded. Twenty-nine girls were still below the school leaving age when I met them (although this did not necessarily mean they were attending school) and it seemed highly likely that several of these would follow the older young women out of the school gates prematurely. Nineteen of the school-aged girls were engaged in some type of statutory education although, for six, this involved short timetables at (variously) a pupil referral unit (PRU), a special unit attached to a children's home, a special education project for young mothers with an on-site crèche, or another 'education otherwise than at school' project.[12] Nineteen of the early school leavers – 37 per cent of the total sample – had been permanently excluded from school at least once,[13] and another two were on the brink of exclusion. Seven of the twelve girls who had ever been in custody (58 per cent) had experienced permanent school exclusion. Educational exclusion was sometimes associated with social exclusion more broadly: Kate and Amber both recounted positive experiences of mentoring projects they had been involved in at school, although mentoring had ceased for both of them when they left school prematurely. For Anna, who lived in a small village, school exclusion was accompanied by automatic exclusion from her youth club, which was located on the school grounds. Although a small number of girls who were not attending school were (or had been) enrolled on some form of alternative educational provision, such as a PRU, most were receiving no formal education.

National statistics indicate that girls comprise just one fifth of permanently excluded pupils in England and Wales. In 2005/06, 0.5 per cent of the total female school population aged up to and including 17 years was excluded, permanent exclusions peaking at 13–14 for both sexes (Department for Education and Skills, 2007). Thus the girls in this study constitute a small and particularly marginalised group. Despite substantial gender disproportionality in school exclusions and underperformance, the gender gap appears to be minimal among the young offender population. In one survey of girls in custody in England and

Wales, 89 per cent of the young women (and 88 per cent of young men) reported that they had been excluded from school and a similar number had truanted. Thirty-eight per cent of young women (cf. 40 per cent of young men) had left school at age 14 or younger (Tye, 2009).

Just nine of the 23 young women in the sample who were above school leaving age had any General Certificate of Secondary Education (GSCE) qualifications – often only one pass at grade C or above – although several others had gained CLAIT, NVQ or AQA accreditation.[14] The majority did not meet the entry requirements for training courses or employment. Ironically, the quantity of education the incarcerated girls were receiving at the STC (25 hours per week, at least in principle) far exceeded the number of hours' schooling they had received from the education system in recent years, given that so many were excluded or non-attenders.

The sheer amount of time the young women spent telling me about the problems they had experienced at school – including bullying, fighting and their treatment by teachers – attested to the social and emotional significance of schooling (or lack thereof) in their lives. Informal exclusion, or self-exclusion, from school was often related to experiences of bullying, which several individuals felt had not been taken seriously by their teachers.[15] Many girls considered formal education to be irrelevant to their everyday lives. Danielle, for instance, told me that she 'learnt more from my mates on the street than I did at school', while Laura was 'too busy getting paralytic to go to school – it was much more fun'. The role of school in credentialism or upward mobility was rarely mentioned, and few of the girls demonstrated any attachment to school beyond its social benefits: to Erin, for example, school was 'more like a social event than anything', and Rachel compared her PRU to 'a little youth club'. Twenty-three young women (44 per cent) actively disliked school, and just seven (13 per cent) had *anything* positive to say about it.

The girls tended to personalise their negative school experiences and talked about teachers in very similar ways as they did about police officers (see Chapter Eight). Several felt that they had been excluded from school unfairly – stating, for instance, that friends or acquaintances had not been excluded, despite having behaved in the same way as themselves. This frequently led girls to the conclusion that their school 'just didn't like me', or 'had it in for me'. Others pointed to their family's 'bad name' as a reason for their unfavourable treatment by teachers, as well as by the police. Anna felt that she had been excluded from school simply because of her 'reputation' (her parents were both heroin addicts), while Rosie and Amber explained that their respective family names were infamous at school, which meant that they were singled out by teachers as 'trouble'. Others, conversely, thought teachers had ignored their requests for help or failed to confront pupils who had bullied them.

These negative perceptions of authority figures, combined with an absence of attachment to both work and to a daily routine, did not augur well for the girls' future careers. Some young women's criminal records ruled out certain education and employment opportunities: a significant proportion had wanted to be teachers or work in the caring professions. Dionne and Lisa both found themselves ejected from child care courses due to their respective convictions for common assault and affray. Others highlighted the negative impact of various upheavals on their school attendance and achievement: the disruption caused by frequent changes of residence, by pregnancy and, most commonly, by their involvement in the criminal justice system, particularly if they were in custody. While none of the young women explicitly stated that bereavement or caring responsibilities had affected their education, it is likely that these, too, had adverse effects on their schooling.

Considerable research attention has focused on girls' behaviour, and responses to it, within the school walls (Crozier and Anstiss, 1995; Lloyd, 2005; Osler and Vincent, 2003, *inter alia*); however, the relationship between young women's behaviour at school and their offending or antisocial behaviour in the community, as well as between educational and social exclusion, has been neglected.[16] This is a considerable oversight, given that the *majority* of young offenders in England and Wales are classified as 'NEET' – not in education, employment or training – and since, as Stephenson has contended, '[e]ducation and youth justice [policies] are increasingly converging in the politics of behaviour where zero tolerance is promoted on the streets and in the classroom' (2006: 220). Evidence of a culture of intolerance resonated throughout the sample girls' accounts of their (often parallel) experiences at school and in the youth justice system. Moreover, the majority lacked attachment to school and felt that teachers did not care about them, the psychosocial impact of which may be considerable. On a more mundane level, girls whose days are unstructured by attendance at school are particularly susceptible to boredom and, when non-attendance combines with victimisation, bereavement or other losses, to heavy alcohol and drug use.

The association between education and offending is well documented (Audit Commission, 1996; Stephenson, 2006), although evidence from the small number of (North American) studies that have paid attention to gender, education and delinquency appears to indicate that the relationship between academic performance and delinquency is weaker for females than for males (Payne *et al.*, 2009). However, attachment and commitment to school as well as good school performance are important protective factors inhibiting offending (ibid.) and dislike of school may have particular criminogenic implications for girls: Graham and Bowling (1995), for example, found that offending was much higher among girls who did not like school or who thought that their school work was average or below average for their age, although these factors were not associated with boys' lawbreaking. Excluded and low-attaining girls are a particularly marginalised group, who may be sidelined by the education system as well as by employers. They may also opt out of employment altogether by choosing motherhood (Phoenix, 1991).

Coping strategies

The young women in the study employed strategies (pregnancy), or engaged in activities (self-harm, alcohol and drug use), that might be characterised as means of escaping, or resisting, their troubled family and school lives. However, girls who become teenage mothers and those who consume 'unladylike' quantities of alcohol in public have been singled out as having disordered relationships with reproduction or consumption (Griffin, 1997) and are, as a consequence, particularly vulnerable to state surveillance and control. In the remainder of this chapter, I examine the place of these 'coping strategies' in the young women's lives, as well as the public discourses that have been constructed around teenage pregnancy and young women's alcohol consumption, in particular.

Pregnancy and motherhood

As Chapter Two showed, twentieth-century critiques of 'delinquent' girls exposed the role of the juvenile justice system in policing and regulating girls' sexual activity, most visibly through the legal category of 'moral danger'. This particular mode of moral policing no longer (explicitly) goes on via criminal justice mechanisms (although see Chapter Eight), since the care and control functions of the juvenile and family courts were separated in 1989, the term 'moral danger' having disappeared from child welfare legislation several years earlier.[17] There have also been profound shifts in recent years in normative Western expectations about young women and sexual activity, with the result that female youthful (hetero)sexual activity today is generally tolerated – at least up to a point and provided that it keeps within certain bounds. However, while both lone motherhood and reconstituted families have become increasingly commonplace and socially accepted, not least due to high divorce rates in all class groupings, the *teenage* single mother is the subject of unprecedented vilification. Middle-class girls in Western liberal democracies in the twenty-first century are expected to regulate their fertility and plan (and certainly postpone) parenthood, so that it does not under any circumstances interfere with their academic achievement or with the accrual of the economic advantages of employment and occupational identity (McRobbie, 2009: 85). The dominant message is that while unmarried sexual activity may be (more) acceptable,[18] teenage procreation is not.

As the antithesis of the 'can-do' middle-class credentialled female young subject (Harris, 2004) who delays motherhood (but must be careful not to leave it 'too late'), the teenage mother is imagined as a reckless 'welfare scrounger' – financially dependent on the state, rather than on a male partner or the maternity benefits provided by her employer. She is also constructed both as a member of the underclass and as the mother of a future criminal underclass (Dwyer and Wyn, 2001). The previous New Labour Government's introduction in 2007 of a US-style *Family–Nurse Partnership* programme targeting young, low-income, first-time mothers attracted the newspaper headline, 'unborn babies targeted in crackdown on criminality' (Ward, 2007) and was parodied thus by another journalist:

> What a wonderful boost to the confidence of a first-time mother! Barely four months pregnant and already the recipient of a fasbo, a foetus asbo,[19] for her unborn child plus a weekly visit from a health visitor until the age of two to

ensure that the potential criminal in the womb doesn't begin nicking baby rattles before teething is done.

(Roberts, 2007)

Four of the young women in the sample were mothers, each of one child under one year old, and a further three were pregnant.[20] Their (expected) age at childbirth ranged from 14 to 19. Of the four infants, one had been removed into state care and the remaining three were being looked after at home by their mothers. Most of the pregnancies had been planned and, in contrast to and in spite of widespread public condemnation of teenage parenthood, motherhood was proving to be a positive experience for all four of the mothers. Maddison saw her pregnancy as a turning point in her life, which had also strengthened her resolve to desist from crime. She elucidated:

> I'm definitely not getting in any trouble again. Nothing! … I've got my baby to think about now and I don't want my baby to be in and out of care because of me. I've got something positive in my life for once. And no-one can threaten me with taking it away unless I get in trouble.

Pregnancy had not been a wholly salutary experience for Maddison, however. She had tried repeatedly to enrol on training courses while pregnant, and was turned away on 'health and safety' grounds. Ironically, for several other girls still of statutory school age, pregnancy had acted as a springboard onto otherwise hard to access education and support services, perhaps on the grounds of preventing crime among their future children.

All but one of the seven mothers and expectant mothers had experienced the loss of a significant relationship including, for five of them, being forced to leave home before they were 16 due to parental rejection or severe family discord. Although each of the four pregnant young women was still in a relationship with the father of their unborn child, none of the young mothers was, their respective boyfriends and partners all having left, or 'abandoned' them, once the child was born. Lisa, though not pregnant, desperately wanted to become a mother. She told me how she and her boyfriend of five weeks had discussed moving in together and having children, and stated that, 'if I was pregnant tomorrow I'd be over the moon. I just want to give the TLC[21] and the love to a baby that I want'. Lisa had been living independently in a shared house from the age of 15, and had a very poor relationship with her 'dad' (not her biological father). She had repeatedly run away from home since the age of nine. She had recently been physically and sexually abused by a friend's parents, and also badly bullied at school, as a result of which she chose to leave before taking her GCSE exams. Lisa saw 'settling down' with a partner and a child as a means of proving to others, and indeed to herself, that her life was different now, and that she had a brighter and more loving future ahead of her.

Nationally, teenage pregnancy rates among the most deprived 10 per cent of wards are four times higher than in the least deprived 10 per cent (Wiggins *et al.*, 2005), although the stereotypical association between teenage pregnancy and economically marginalised areas has frequently been exaggerated.[22] Young women from neighbourhoods characterised by poverty and constrained opportunities may view motherhood as one of few realistic and (legally) achievable options open to them. Some writers have argued, from a psychosocial perspective, that teenage pregnancy may be 'not so much the "rational choice" of motherhood and a council flat for an educationally failing young woman, but a complex emotional response to the fear of failure' (Walkerdine *et al.*, 2001: 203). Walkerdine and colleagues suggest that through teenage motherhood – a practice largely confined to the working classes – young women effectively self-regulate in order to keep themselves in their (classed and gendered) place: a place of female fecundity, in contrast to the careerism frequently preferred by their middle-class counterparts. Teenage motherhood may be less difficult and painful for working-class girls than '[c]rossing over to the other side' (ibid.: 210) of upward mobility or the 'masculine' professions, since to take such a step would be an unknown and fearsome quantity. Moreover, a dependent child confers symbolic capital on its mother, as well as introducing a degree of predictability into an otherwise uncertain future.

Positive stories of young women's own experiences of motherhood are unlikely to attract widespread sympathy in a political climate that considers young single mothers to be near-criminal as well as bearing considerable responsibility for a crisis in state welfare spending. Far from being a marker of status, for some, the pregnant belly of a teenage girl is the very embodiment of pathology. In March 2010, then shadow Children's Minister Tim Loughton, commenting on an increase in pregnancies among 12- and 13-year-old girls, went so far as to suggest that pregnant girls (not unlike their grandmothers who were deemed to be 'in moral danger') ought to be subject to criminal sanctions:

> We need a message that actually it is not a very good idea to become a single mum at 14. [It is] against the law to get pregnant at 14. How many kids get prosecuted for having underage sex? Virtually none. Where are the consequences of breaking the law and having irresponsible underage sex? There aren't any.

When asked whether there *should* be prosecutions, Loughton replied: 'We need to be tougher. Without sounding horribly judgmental, it is not a good idea to be a mum at 14. You are too young, throwing away your childhood and prospects of developing a career' (Ramesh, 2010). Quite aside from the dubious deterrent potential of criminalising teenage pregnancy (and it is difficult to envisage how 'underage' sex might be proven among anyone other than pregnant girls and teenage mothers), Loughton's position appears to suggest that pregnancy and motherhood inevitably and necessarily have a profoundly negative impact on young women's lives and on their future life chances.

Self-harm

Twenty-one young women (40 per cent of the sample) had self-harmed and/or attempted suicide on at least one previous occasion, according to their case files or self-reports. The injuries they had inflicted upon themselves ranged from cutting wrists and arms (the most common form of self-injury) to self-poisoning by overdosing on paracetamol or drinking bleach.[23] Around three times as many females as males in the general population self-harm deliberately (Hawton *et al.*, 2000). Harrington (2001: 55) asserts that:

> Deliberate self-harm in young people is usually precipitated by stressful life problems. The most common are arguments with parents, other family problems, rejection by a boy or girl friend, or school problems such as bullying. These events often occur against a background of long-standing difficulties concerning family, school and behaviour [. . .]. Some of them, particularly those who repeatedly harm themselves, have been abused.

Many of the girls in the current study were distressed, angry and depressed about their domestic circumstances, and there were some indications that individuals blamed themselves, and particularly their lawbreaking, for their predicament. Many had also been the victims of abuse. Harrington further suggests that success at school or in other areas of life can protect young people from the effects of adverse life experiences. Examples of personal successes and achievements were, unfortunately, conspicuous in their absence from the lives of the young women I interviewed, and seemed rarely to have been actively encouraged by adults who were important to them.

Alcohol and drug (mis)use

Consistent with numerous research studies that have identified very high levels of alcohol and drug misuse among girls who offend,[24] regular intoxication was commonplace among the young women. Indeed, just six girls (12 per cent) reported no substance use during the preceding month, including Aimee and Naomi who were pregnant and Aisha, a Muslim. As shown in Table 5.2, alcohol and cannabis were the girls' drugs of choice, the vast majority of the sample having recently consumed both. In addition, around half of the young women reported ever having used ecstasy or cocaine.

Rarely did girls consider their substance use to be problematic. Probably on account of their age, few had experienced significant alcohol- or drug-related health problems, although paradoxically, intoxication was prominent among their attributions for their lawbreaking (see Chapter Six). For many young women, getting drunk was imbued with cultural and social expectations – which resonate throughout wider contemporary British society – that excessive alcohol consumption is a necessary prerequisite for enjoying oneself, or at least for behaving in ways that have become expected, even encouraged, among young women. Angela McRobbie has argued that a new female figure – whom she refers to as the 'phallic girl' – has recently emerged. The phallic girl, embodied in the figure of the so-called 'ladette', is encouraged by consumer culture, as well as by magazines, 'trashy' television and the tabloid press as though in the name of sexual equality, to overturn the old double standard and emulate the assertive and hedonistic styles of sexuality associated with young men ... particularly ... in the context of the UK city centre leisure culture which has developed around late night drinking and the relaxation of laws in regard to the consumption of alcohol.

(McRobbie, 2009: 82)

I discussed in Chapter One how media representations of increases in officially recorded violence by girls in recent years have tended to blame 'binge drinking' and 'ladette culture' – the adoption of that type of female 'phallicism' that McRobbie has identified, which appears to be simultaneously encouraged (as entertaining spectacle) and disparaged (as a symbol of declining 'feminine' standards). However, as Jackson and Tinkler have noted, '[p]opular discourse on the ladette ... masks the complexity and causes of women's behaviours. The identification of hedonism as the driving force within ladette culture obscures other motivations for drinking, smoking or having casual sex' (2007: 268), as well as sidelining the real problems that young women face. Moreover, claims that girls who drink to excess are simply 'acting like boys' fail to acknowledge girls' greater vulnerability to sexual exploitation and their unique capacity to

Table 5.2 Self-reported substance misuse (*n* = 51)[a]

Substance	Ever used (n)	%	Used in past month (n)	%
Alcohol	49	96	43	84
Cannabis	48	94	35	69
Skunk[b]	38	75	26	51
Ecstasy	27	53	15	29
Cocaine	25	49	14	28
Poppers	23	45	6	12
Amphetamines	22	43	8	16
Solvents	17	33	8	16
Magic mushrooms	13	26	4	8
Prescribed drugs	10	20	1	2
Crack	9	18	3	6
Heroin	6	12	2	4
Ketamine	6	12	1	2
Other substance(s)	6	12	1	2
LSD	5	10	1	2
Methadone	4	8	2	4

Notes

a Each young woman, at my request, completed a self-report exercise with the aid of prompt cards, disclosing whether she had ever used any of a list of substances and, if so, how many times during the previous month. Girls interviewed in the STC were asked to report their substance use during the month prior to their most recent reception into custody. The data presented in this table relate to just 51 young women. I met Alex with her probation officer at Alex's home. Alex proved rather difficult to track down, and I did not manage to meet her again to complete the self-report exercise.

b Skunk is a potent form of cannabis plant.

become pregnant. They also ignore class and age differences in patterns of consumption, which complicate the 'unbridled excessive consumption [that is] portrayed in media images of youth at play' (Measham, 2004: 319). Tabloid newspaper photographs of the revelries of glamorous female TV celebrities in expensive bars and nightclubs, for example, bear little resemblance to the street-corner drinking habits of marginalised teenage girls. Several of the young women I spoke to were well aware of social pressures to 'keep up with the boys' in their leisure pursuits; however, nearly all lacked the financial means, and were too young, to consume alcohol in pubs and clubs, and instead drank on the streets or in parks where they were particularly vulnerable to police surveillance.

The consumption activities of lower-class teenage girls, which take place in public space outwith the confines of the privatised leisure industry, are both disproportionately policed and the subject of intense media scrutiny. Vitriolic condemnation of the (purportedly) violent 'ladette' is overwhelmingly focused on a female member of the 'underclass', who is, in common parlance, 'uncouth' and 'cheap'; and her sexual activities, whether alcohol-fuelled or not, are most vilified when they result in procreation or do not conform to heterosexual norms. Moreover, the 'phallic girl' who shows herself to be 'up for it' is also frequently 'the target of old-fashioned insults and hostility from the men she seeks both to please and to emulate' (McRobbie, 2009: 85). By contrast, greater tolerance is shown towards the antics of female (usually middle-class) university students, whose alcohol-induced 'high jinks' are either licenced or ignored since they are considered an acceptable means of letting off steam and quite compatible with their trajectory through educational success into economic productivity and consumer citizenship.

Conclusion

As this chapter has illustrated, the backgrounds of the 52 girls and young women in the study were frequently characterised by disconnection, disruption and exclusion relating to their domestic and school lives. What was particularly striking was how little personal control the study young women had over their life trajectories. The many family-related adversities they faced included being forced to live independently at an early age (in some cases as the sole carer of a dependent child), as well as experiencing abuse and violent victimisation, bereavement and loss. When these various precipitating circumstances arose in the girls' lives, formal help was rarely forthcoming and the support of parental figures – the adults on whom most children and young people rely – was inconsistent or lacking. However, it was often possible to identify points in individual young women's lives where support or 'preventive' help – particularly within school – might have steered them along quite different pathways.

A central question here is what has changed since previous research in this field? Several decades have passed since early feminist studies first examined the lives of offending girls and women (e.g. Carlen, 1983, 1988; Chesney-Lind,

1986, 1989), and substantial social and cultural changes have taken place during this time, both in terms of normative expectations about what it means to grow up 'girl', and in relation to family structure, young people's education and employment trajectories, and young women's reproductive and consumption patterns and choices. However, evidence from the current study indicates that the socio-biographies of offending girls in the twenty-first century are in fact very similar to those of their mothers and grandmothers.

What *has* changed significantly in recent years is the nature of both normative expectations and public discourse surrounding young women. While young women in general are frequently championed as subjects of capacity in the spheres of education and employment, in particular, the lived realities of working-class girls appear to have changed little in the course of a generation, and the reality behind the rosy picture of 'girlpower' and feminine success is that the life chances of criminalised girls continue to be heavily constrained and circumscribed by their class and gender, much as they ever were. Importantly, there are indications that girls who do not achieve the successes in education and employment that are now expected of them, those who become teenage mothers and, above all for the purposes of this book, those who find themselves on the wrong side of the law, are constructed as even bigger failures than their forebears. Certainly, the likelihood of young women being criminalised for stepping out of line increased substantially in the early twenty-first century, as Chapter Three showed. Culturally, too, broad changes have occurred in relation to the normalisation of alcohol consumption and the rise of consumer culture, which I discuss in detail in Chapter Six.

I argued in Chapter One that the widespread repudiation of feminism in the twenty-first century has contributed to a tendency for young women's collective problems to be individualised or reconstructed as 'bad' personal choices, and for the constraints associated with their gender, class, age and ethnicity to be underplayed or even ignored. Indeed, it has been routinely claimed in popular rhetoric about youth crime and punishment that a 'new' girl criminal has emerged, whose behaviour and the motivations underlying it are scarcely distinguishable from that of her male counterparts. This myth ignores the realities of young female lawbreakers' lives. Many offending girls have been the victims of family violence and of educational neglect, and often it is only when their own 'coping' strategies pose risks to others or to the social order that adults show an interest in them.

To counteract such myths, it is important to consult offending girls themselves in order that we might gain insight into the shared contexts in which their offending occurs. In the following two chapters I examine, respectively, the accounts of the 52 young women, and those of professionals who work with them, of young women's pathways into crime and their motivations for offending. A central concern in my analysis is the degree to which the adverse experiences and life circumstances discussed in this chapter feature (or not) within the young women's and the professionals' narratives, as well as the extent to which girls' 'problems' are constructed, variously, as personal troubles and as collective – gendered, generational, classed and raced – experiences.

6   Accounting for trouble

The girls' perspectives

In Chapter Five, I discussed the young women's pathways into crime, noting that their backgrounds were characterised by disruption, disconnection and exclusion in their family and school lives. I also highlighted the girls' responses to such strained circumstances, some of which led them into conflict with the law. This chapter expands my analysis of the young women's demographic circumstances and backgrounds. Here I consider their attributions for their lawbreaking. I pay special attention to the ways in which gender, class and generation structured the social and cultural attributions the girls offered for their lawbreaking, as well as to the central role played by feminine consumption in contemporary young women's identity construction, as well as in their lawbreaking.

The young women's offending accounts were diverse and varied according to the type of behaviour under discussion. Generally speaking, however, they referred to their lawbreaking not as criminality, but as 'getting into trouble'. The use of this terminology is telling in two ways: first, it implies they did not take their offending particularly seriously, but rather they conceptualised it as 'naughty', or youthful silliness, in contrast to what they understood to be the conduct of 'real' offenders; second, as I discuss in Chapter Eight, most girls believed that the *real* trouble they were in stemmed as much, if not more, from being apprehended as from their own behaviour.

Everybody else is doing it

Many of the young women's lives were unstructured by school or work, and the majority had few opportunities for (legal) participation in social life, due to their age, their limited or non-existent personal finances and, in some cases, their geographical isolation. As Chapter Five showed, experiences of abuse, domestic violence and unstable residential and care arrangements were commonplace and were highly likely to have motivated some young women to spend as much time as possible outside the home. Their adverse life experiences also appeared to have led many to seek a sense of purpose or belonging – often lacking at home or at school – from other similarly situated young people. Thus the majority of the girls spent their considerable quantities of spare time hanging around the streets or in parks. In these public spaces drinking, drug-taking and occasional (and, for a minority, regular) lawbreaking provided temporary relief from tedious lives in deprived neighbourhoods depleted of community resources, and from the emotional strains of family and school life.

I noted in Chapter Four that in accounting for their offending, the young women often employed various techniques of neutralisation (Sykes and Matza, 1957). Their offending attributions must be understood not only in the context of the marginalised and impoverished neighbourhoods in which many of them had grown up, but also in terms of their age and maturity: some of the girls I interviewed were only 13. The sheer ordinariness of offending among peers, family members and neighbours was a recurrent theme in their accounts: two-fifths ($n = 21$) stated that other members of their family, usually siblings, had been in trouble with the law,[1] and half ($n = 25$) attributed at least some of their lawbreaking to their 'mates', or to 'getting in with the wrong crowd'. There was a general acceptance that getting into trouble is just what young people do – at least young people like themselves whose social and leisure opportunities are constrained by their age, class and place of residence. Getting into trouble, almost always presented as spontaneous rather than planned, tended to be viewed as a side effect of having fun, alleviating boredom, attracting attention, gaining recognition or simply escaping the stresses of their daily lives.

Many of the girls disliked their local estate or neighbourhood and several commented on its notoriety. Naomi, aged 16 and six months pregnant, did not want her baby to grow up in her local area, fearing that he would 'get in with the wrong people' if he did. Grace recounted how others referred to her neighbourhood, where there had been several recent shooting incidents, as a 'ghetto'. Somewhat amused by this description, Grace stated that she was used to (and hence unshocked by) violence because her father used to hit her mother, 'so I've been brought up with that'.

While a few young women felt they had been coerced into offending or had taken the blame for other people, as described in more detail below, a more common view was that getting into trouble with friends, including 'bad' friends, is a question of personal choice, rather than a matter of being led astray. Melissa, 16, was serving her fifth custodial sentence for breaching a community order which had been imposed for robbery with an imitation firearm – an offence committed while drunk, and from which the proceeds were five pounds. Melissa, who had previous convictions for further robberies and driving offences, explained:

> [E]veryone just thinks it's like your friends and that, but it's me that wanted to do it [. . .]. I am a young offender. I shouldn't be driving, selling drugs and that, but I still do it.

Similarly, Anna (15) emphasised her own agency:

> The way we see it is people you're with might get into trouble, but at the end of the day, it's *your* decision. […] It's your fault if you get into trouble. It's *you* that's doing it.

Melissa's and Anna's acknowledgements of personal responsibility for their actions challenge traditional pathologising discourses constructing female offenders as devoid of agency, unable to control their actions either because of the scars of prior victimisation experiences (Daly, 1998) or because they are emotional and irrational (Allen, 1987). On the other hand, their self-blaming language perhaps suggests that they had internalised the responsibilising discourse of the courts.

One of the lads?

Being led astray by older males has long been considered a common pathway into crime for girls. However, in the current study, offending due to encouragement or coercion by males was rare and, perhaps significantly, this was largely restricted to girls who had been convicted of very serious offences. As a group, the imprisoned young women had committed rather more serious offences than the sample average: both Elizabeth and Sam, for example, had been convicted of manslaughter, and both had been jointly charged with older males. Sixteen-year-old Elizabeth was serving a five-year custodial sentence; she was convicted when she was 14 and her male co-defendant/boyfriend was some eight years older. Elizabeth had been found guilty by association due to her presence in the room when her boyfriend stabbed a man – a drug dealer to whom he owed money – in the chest. When she tried to call an ambulance from a nearby telephone box, her boyfriend stopped her and, being intensely scared, Elizabeth did not make the call. She explained that at no time had it been alleged that she had played an active part in causing the victim's death. Sam, also 16, was convicted of manslaughter at 15, together with three male co-defendants, two of whom were 16 and the third 17. Sam attributed some of the 'other trouble' she had been in (but not arrested for) – which included 'egging' cars, riding in stolen vehicles and breaking windows – to her hanging around mainly with a group of boys. She reflected that, unlike herself, 'none of the girly girls are in trouble now'. Three more young women who expressed similar views had been involved in pastimes such as climbing trees, 'having a laugh' or 'being daring' (which sometimes included lawbreaking) in the company of boys because it was exciting. Rosie (14) explained that 'the girls where I used to live just sit there and smoke drugs all the time, and I just got fed up with it'.

Aisha's offending had clearly not been of her own choosing. While she was sitting in the passenger seat of the car of an older male 'friend' as he dealt drugs from the window, her 'friend' gave her 30 packages of crack cocaine and heroin to hide on her person when he saw a police officer approaching. Aisha, a 15-year-old Asian girl, was charged with supplying Class A drugs; however, the man was not charged, since no drugs were found in his possession when he was searched.[2] Coercion by others was not restricted to older males. Jessica (16), who had mild learning difficulties, had pulled an emergency telephone off a wall in a police station and, later the same night, dropped lit toilet paper through the window of a second police station, setting fire to blinds inside, which led to her being charged with arson. Jessica told me that an older female acquaintance she was with had a knife and had threatened to kill her if she did not start the fire.

There is little consensus about the sex of girls' co-offenders. While the majority of young offenders' joint lawbreaking takes place in same-sex pairs or groups, there is some evidence that older male/younger female co-offending is more likely to occur when female co-offenders are encouraged to offend by male 'recruiters' (namely individuals who commit crimes with a large number of co-offenders who are usually younger and less criminally experienced than they are) than when no such 'recruitment' has taken place (van Mastrigt and Farrington, 2011). This lends some support to the 'bad boyfriend' hypothesis (Caspi *et al.*, 1993; Warr, 2002), at least for some young women. Giordano (2009) has suggested that the 'bad boyfriend' hypothesis is more adequate for explaining the conduct of girls on the margins of criminality than those involved in more serious offending. However, girls and women involved in abusive relationships with men, as both Elizabeth and Aisha appeared to have been, may be at increased risk both of being coerced into offending and of being criminalised for offences that were in fact committed by their boyfriends or partners.

One of the girls: offending as social recognition

Social acceptance and 'fitting in' are of special importance during adolescence, when a teenager's developing self-image is likely at times to be fragile. A key concern for many young women was the impression they created among their friends and associates, and it was of great importance to them to maintain their reputation in front of their 'mates', both male and female.[3] Sometimes lawbreaking was considered a necessary means to the end of such image-maintenance: 60 per cent of the young women ($n = 31$) talked about how their behaviour made them look in front of other young people. Given many of the girls' limited opportunities for gaining respect or status – or indeed any sort of positive recognition – at home or at school, it is not difficult to understand why looking good (or not looking stupid) in front of their friends was so highly prized. Vicky (18) recalled her desire to be 'just one of the lads', which tended to involve heavy drinking sessions, when she had moved to Midshire and found herself in a homeless hostel the previous year, while Kayleigh (14) thought that she had got into trouble 'through showing off and stuff like that in front of my mates', and 'trying to be someone that I'm not'. April (17) had recently been charged with robbery: she and a female friend had robbed another girl, but her friend had not been charged, April believed, because the victim's parents knew her friend's parents. April attributed her part in the offence to a 'lack of self-confidence': she had 'gone along with my friend and been worried that she'd think I was a twat if I didn't'.

I interviewed Toni (17) in the secure training centre (STC), where she was serving a six-month sentence for robbery. Toni had lived alone in hostels since she was 15, after moving between the homes of her grandmother, aunt, father and mother throughout her short life. Toni was the only self-confessed gang member in the sample, and belonged to the junior branch of a notorious street gang.[4] She did not elaborate on her own activities within the gang, although she had previous convictions for violence, including assault occasioning grievous bodily harm and violent disorder, as well as several more robberies. Toni, of mixed white British and black Caribbean ethnicity, explained that gang membership was 'normal' and almost expected among young people in her neighbourhood. I asked her whether a young person *has* to be in a gang to gain acceptance or approval where she lives; Toni explained that 'you don't *have* to be, but if you want to rep it, you have to rep it properly'. Gaining status, or working up the ranks, in Toni's gang, involved 'reppin' the higher ones' which, she elaborated, meant that 'if someone asks you to do a job for them, you're there to do it'.[5] Toni aspired to be a 'proper' gang member (a member of the main gang) when she was older, but stressed that 'I don't want to be one in a bad way. Bad ones are stupid'. 'Bad ones', she elucidated, shoot other people 'for no reason'.[6]

Less frequently, the attention and esteem of peers came as a consequence of young women's involvement in the criminal justice system. Rachel committed two robberies at the age of 15, for which she received an 18-month prison sentence. She had attracted a great deal of attention both inside prison, where she was the youngest inmate and 'mothered' by the older women, and also after her release: her now somewhat infamous status as a female ex-prisoner was accompanied by a certain kudos – or 'respect', as Rachel saw it – due to the rarity of imprisonment among girls of her age. Rachel recalled her excitement at a party she had recently been to, still sporting an electronic tag on her ankle, where 'it was all about me'. In Laura's case, her violent reputation had become an integral part of her social identity. Laura was renowned locally for 'battering' other young people, usually young women, and almost always while intoxicated. She recounted in detail the time when she had 'battered a copper', and her subsequent amusement and delight when her solicitor 'embarrassed' the (very tall) policeman when he gave evidence against her in court. Laura's reputation – which had earned her the nickname 'Mad Bird'[7] – did not appear to have waned despite that fact that she had not been arrested for some time. Laura, a very personable young woman who was popular among her peers, clearly enjoyed this positive recognition, and the soubriquet, while implying that Laura was unpredictable and out of control, was also used with affection.

Violence: provocation and the (gendered) defence of respect

In accounting for their violent offending, the young women generally blamed provocation or victim precipitation: somebody 'starting' on them or offending them. The 16 girls (31 per cent of the sample) who represented their violent offending in this way typically perceived themselves to have been in situations where no realistic alternative course of action was available, and where violence was a necessary and legitimate means of defending self-respect or 'saving face'. From a psychological perspective, people who react with verbal aggression or physical violence towards someone who has (apparently) 'started' on them have been characterised as misinterpreting social cues or manifesting a lack of social information-processing skills (Crick and Dodge, 1996). However, young women's violence must be understood within the context of a normative climate that is supportive of (a certain level of) violence by girls as well as boys. In other words, by fighting (back), young women are standing up for themselves in accordance with the norms and practices of the neighbourhoods in which they live.[8]

The perceived legitimacy of physical retaliation (and perhaps also pre-emptive strikes) was well illustrated by Rachel. When I asked her whether she thought she was likely to get into trouble again, Rachel replied, '[i]f the wrong person comes up to me, yeah, I probably would. But if people keep their distance ... ' Rachel gave examples of others not keeping their distance as people 'starting' on her or bumping into her in a nightclub, which sometimes resulted in her 'losing it'.

Girls' violence may involve a complex interplay of historical experiences of victimisation as well as the more immediate and context-specific exercise of agency in the face of provocation, as well as anger, fear or even boredom. While the emotions that give rise to girls' violence – rage, perceived disrespect, defiance and so on – to a large extent parallel those of their male counterparts, the contexts in which feelings of disrespect arise are characterised by unequal gendered power relations and by 'the negative consequences of the sexual double standard that is a feature of adolescent peer culture' (Miller and White, 2004: 184). Consequently, media representations of violent girls acting 'like boys' and, conversely, representations of violent females as hapless victims of abuse and oppression 'whose lawbreaking is presented as symptomatic of their victimization' (Maher, 1997: 200), are equally deficient.

Friendships play a pivotal role in many girls' lives (Girlguiding UK, 2007; Griffiths, 1995; Hey, 1997) and female peers can act as a source of support; however, they can also judge and disapprove, particularly where matters of sexual reputation are concerned (Lees, 1993). Indeed, the motivational accounts of the majority of the young women who had been arrested for violent offending generally focused on reacting to slurs about reputation – either their own or that of a close friend or family member. Fights commonly arose from insults relating to sexuality (such as being called a 'slag') or slurs about the weight, physical appearance or sexual reputation of female friends or relatives – typically their own mothers.

Jordan and Sophie had both been arrested several times for assaulting other girls 'over lads' (Jordan), or following insults directed at friends and family (Sophie). Both girls saw themselves as essentially non-violent *except* in situations where violence was called for:

> I've got a short temper, so anything can trigger it off, really. I don't go, like, *looking* for trouble. It's only when it comes to me. [...] I'm not really a fighting person. I don't like fighting. It's just when I have to. [Jordan later added that next time she *should* walk away from similar situations] but ... I wouldn't stand there and let someone hit me. I'd hit back.
>
> (Jordan, 15)

I don't think, like, that I'm violent or anything.

(Sophie, 15, who had recently been charged with
GBH for assaulting a girl who called her a 'slag')[9]

Since both provocation and victim precipitation were widely perceived to justify, and even necessitate, the use of physical violence, the expression of remorse was usually superfluous.[10] Laura (19) had served a custodial sentence a year before we met for assault occasioning actual bodily harm: she had thrown a toaster at the head of a girl who she discovered *in flagrante* with her boyfriend. Although she had not been arrested again since being released from custody, Laura was adamant that she would 'do it all over again' if a similar situation arose in the future.

Looking for trouble

There's nothing at all to do. So we just get into trouble.

(Charlie, 15)

We don't see it as getting into trouble. We see it as having fun.

(Anna, 15)

The words of Charlie and Anna were echoed in the accounts of the majority of girls who had been involved in petty or 'nuisance' offending, including acts of criminal damage, public order offences and fighting – all of which they commonly referred to not as crimes, but as 'messing about' or 'having fun' – as entertainment or diversion to dispel boredom, which was often enhanced by drug and/or alcohol use. Many of the girls lived in deprived housing estates on the outskirts of towns and cities[11] where social cohesion and 'community spirit' had been slowly eroded (if indeed they had ever existed), and local shops and post offices had gradually disappeared for reasons of 'economic rationalisation', while unemployment and drugs had taken their place. Few individuals were involved in any sort of structured activities or sports, and a number expressed annoyance that their local youth club did not open regularly, or not on the days it was supposed to, with the result that they sometimes forgot it *was* open so did not go there.

Danielle (16) depicted the children in her local area as casualties of such community disintegration. Of her home town, where the impact of de-industrialisation was clearly visible, she explained:

Danielle: If you drive about these streets at night, I bet you'll see kids from the age of eleven or twelve with cans of cider.
GS: What else is there for young people to do around here?
Danielle: Nothing. Either get wrecked or smoke draw. It's shite. Nobody likes it here.

And those streets were where, on the spur of the moment, 'trouble' would often be initiated. In the absence of anything better to do, Danielle described, young people from her estate would congregate in public to have a drink and a laugh, and 'end up getting wrecked and having fights'. Indeed, girls' very presence on the streets, desperately bored and in the company of other similarly bored and aimless young people, increased the likelihood that disputes or fights would occur, as Letitia and Sophie explained:

> When you're out in the street, it'll be boring and you just get into a *bit* of trouble, and then it escalates ... [typically, Letitia described, someone 'starts', someone else 'retaliates', and then] all of us just join in.
>
> (Letitia, 15)

> When I'm with my mates and my mates start [...], I jump in [...] because I'm bored. [...] I come to their rescue!
>
> (Sophie, 15)

When I asked how they spent their spare time, many girls stated that they would simply 'walk around' or 'look for trouble' during their (usually considerable amounts of) free time, drinking alcohol and sometimes taking drugs. Once intoxicated, they were at risk of taking things 'too far', as Natasha described:

> We just mess about ... I mess about more. I have to go a bit further than they [friends] do ... And then I end up getting nicked [arrested].

Being out on the streets, looking for trouble, renders young people particularly vulnerable to heavy-handed policing: working-class youthful sociability has become increasingly criminalised in England and Wales, largely via new technologies of control introduced under the umbrella of the 'anti-social behaviour agenda' (Crawford, 2009a; see Chapter Three). I interviewed two friends and co-offenders, Anna and Abby, respectively aged 15 and 16, together in a fast food restaurant. Abby explained that a combination of boredom, a lack of money and there being nothing (affordable) to do locally often meant that they got into trouble 'for stupid things', to alleviate boredom or to acquire funds to pay for an evening out. The two girls had recently been arrested with another friend, Susi, aged 17 (another study participant), for selling fake raffle tickets from door to door in their small, predominantly middle-class, village. Both Anna and Abby were excluded from the village youth club and lived 11 miles from the nearest town, from which the last bus departed at around six o'clock in the evening and a taxi-ride home was well beyond their means. The pair conceptualised getting arrested largely as an unpleasant side effect of their creative responses to resist the structural constraints of boredom and poverty[12] which, in turn, were a function of their age, class and geographical isolation.

A minority of the young women ($n = 8$) stated that they enjoyed the excitement that offending provided. Jennifer (17) was serving 18 months in custody for robbery, and had previous driving convictions. While adamant that she would not offend again, she conceded that, 'knowing, at the age of fifteen, you can get into a car and drive it away, it's an amazing buzz'. Young women in general, and those who are excluded from school in particular, have few opportunities to experience feelings of power and control in their everyday interactions, and they tend to be socialised to eschew risky situations in order to avoid personal victimisation (Batchelor, 2007b). Batchelor has argued that the risk-taking activities of young women who have experienced family backgrounds characterised by adversity, abuse, 'care' and disruption – as was the case for many of the girls in the present study – may be understood as a means of 'permit[ting] the young women to construct an enhanced sense of self and self-efficacy', and thus reasserting their identity (ibid.: 220). Jennifer's description of her typically 'male' offence of car theft, combined with her young age at the time, indicates such a sense of accomplishment and thrill (cf. Katz, 1988).

The adrenaline rush achieved through crime had implications in relation to ambivalence about desistance, too. Holly (16), who had stopped all but occasional offending on account of her boyfriend's disapproval of her past violence (which, though he condoned male violence, he felt was not 'ladylike'), expressed regret about her new-found 'boring' lifestyle: Holly was now largely drug-, alcohol- and crime-free. Her account of giving up, and now missing, both offending and drugs illustrated her ambivalence about leaving crime behind. She assured me that she would go back to crime if she split up with her boyfriend because it was fun: 'I didn't stop because I *wanted* to. I stopped because he *made* me'. There was no evidence of any 'cognitive transformation' (Giordano *et al.*, 2002[13]) in Holly's (or, perhaps more accurately, her boyfriend's) decision to stop offending, and she implied that her abstinence might be short-lived.

It was clear that some delinquent activities provided excitement and stimulation as well as social status in the context of otherwise tedious lives, in which the young women's social participation was constrained by their youth and poverty and also, in many cases, by virtue of being excluded from mainstream education and youth provision. While 'buzz' offending was by no means universal, the accounts of Laura, Jennifer and Holly demonstrate that some young women derive considerable excitement from engaging in illegal risk-taking, reflecting the fact that youthful offending, for girls as well as boys, is often 'shot through with adventurous exploits that are valued for the stimulation they provide' (Matza and Sykes, 1961: 713).[14] Such stimulation was rarely available from other sources, with the notable exception of alcohol and drug consumption.

Disordered consumers? Alcohol, drugs and girls' lawbreaking

As I argued in Chapter One, contemporary British concerns about unruly young women have converged on the purported emergence of a 'new' violent girl, who is commonly assumed to be a hedonistic, feckless (and usually) working-class white binge-drinking 'ladette'. Indeed, it often appears that young women have replaced young men as the public face of binge drinking and that they have been represented as displaying particularly disordered patterns of alcohol consumption.[15]

Increases in recorded female youth violence in Britain have been greatly exaggerated and, as Chapter Three showed, are largely the result not of significant changes in girls' behaviour, but of zero tolerance policies towards youth 'violence' and disorder enacted within a crime prevention paradigm, combined with police targets to increase sanction detections. Artefactual increases in girls' officially recorded violence may in turn have had the self-fulfilling effect of encouraging professionals to 'notice' more 'violence' in young women (Chesney-Lind and Irwin, 2008), and thus to be more inclined to respond to 'unruly' girls via criminal justice (as opposed to informal) mechanisms, thereby propelling them in greater numbers into the youth justice system. Although girls' violence appears not to have risen, there is clear evidence (in the British context, at least) that alcohol consumption among young people of both sexes *has* increased significantly in recent years. Indeed, Britain has become notorious as a binge-drinking bastion of Europe (Measham and Østergaard, 2009): frequent drinking, binge drinking and drunkenness are more common among 15- and 16-year-olds in Britain than in most other European countries, and the gender gap in alcohol consumption – which narrowed significantly between 1995 and 2007 – is much smaller (Hibell *et al.*, 2004).[16] And despite indications of a decline in British young women's drinking during the 2000s, there was, during the preceding 20 years, a substantial rise in young women's alcohol consumption (Plant, 2008), as well as a widespread 'normalization of determined drunkenness' (Measham, 2004) among both young women and young men in the British night-time economy. This has led some authors to suggest that 'a normalized culture of intoxication is now central to many young people's lives' (Griffin *et al.*, 2009: 457).

Unfortunately scholarly research has largely neglected to analyse in any detail the relationship between alcohol use and offending by girls and young women, despite the fact that a raft of research studies has identified particularly high levels of alcohol and drug misuse among girls who offend. The incidence of drug and alcohol use among the sample young women was documented in Chapter Five, where I noted that alcohol and cannabis were the girls' substances of choice, although the consumption of 'harder' drugs was not uncommon. Half of the young women ($n = 25$) believed that alcohol use was a causal factor in their past offending, or at least that lawbreaking was incidental to their alcohol use, and around one-third ($n = 17$) felt that drug use had precipitated their offending. This relationship was often very direct: the thefts of at least 16 of the young women (31 per cent of the sample) were related to the consumption of alcohol and/or drugs. They had either stolen alcohol itself – usually from a large supermarket chain – or sold other stolen goods in order to finance the purchase of drugs or alcohol. However, and in contrast to popular discourse, the majority of the girls described their alcohol and drug use not as problematic, 'risky' or 'anti-social', but as a 'normal' group activity among their peers and in their local neighbourhood – a means of providing excitement, and sometimes structure, in their lives, as well as temporary respite from the boredom of poverty and exclusion. Laura and Jodie, for example, described how they spent their time on an average day, in the absence of any education or employment commitments:

> Get up, go to Asda, rob a bottle of vodka, get wrecked, and see what trouble we can cause.
>
> (Laura, 19)

> Get up, get stoned, watch telly, eat, get stoned, eat more, get high, go home.
>
> (Jodie, 15)

Jodie and Ellen, two years her senior, had grown up in the same street and were regular partners in crime. The pair had recently been apprehended wheeling a trolley filled with electrical goods – including a plasma screen television, DVD player and a computer – out of a large supermarket towards the parked car of an older woman who was waiting to drive them away. They had done this on several previous occasions without being caught. Ellen explained that they always shoplifted goods to sell, spending 'every penny' of the proceeds on 'hash'. It was apparent that there was a receptive black market of adults waiting to purchase (and perhaps order more of) the girls' stolen gains. Jodie declared that they 'kn[e]w whose door to go to' to sell stolen goods locally. With no intention of giving up cannabis and no foreseeable means of earning the money to pay for it (the girls had recently found casual employment in a local fish and chip shop but lasted only two hours because they were not quick enough at the job), they saw shoplifting as a reliable way of obtaining money to buy cannabis. Both girls explained that they smoked cannabis heavily on a daily basis – usually becoming 'stoned' by lunchtime – due to a lack of anything else to do in the 'boring' town where they lived. Both Ellen and Jodie had not been to school since year nine (aged 13 or 14), when Jodie was excluded for fighting while Ellen was regularly sent home for arriving late and eventually stopped attending. They had filled their days subsequently with shoplifting and smoking cannabis.

The widespread use of alcohol and drugs among her peers, combined with boredom and social and economic marginalisation associated with living in a poor family in a neighbourhood deprived of resources, underpinned Natasha's feelings of ambivalence about reducing her alcohol consumption. She explained that, 'I go out with my friends and it's not boring if we're drunk. If we're not drinking, there's nothing to do and we just sit there'. Consequently, Natasha questioned whether the efforts of her YOT workers would help curb her offending, which she attributed to heavy alcohol use:

> They [YOT staff] can't help me. I can only help myself, really. I ain't gonna stop drinking, 'cause everyone else is drinking. I ain't gonna sit there sober on my own.

Laura, a lively and talkative white 19-year-old, was no longer under youth justice supervision when I met her but had a string of previous convictions for stealing alcohol, usually vodka, from supermarkets. Laura, whose background is discussed in more detail below, had spent most of her life in 'care', interspersed with several years of moving to and fro between bail hostels, and sleeping rough or on the sofas of friends, with whom she would 'get wrecked'. Now living in her own flat, which Castleshire YOT had helped her to obtain, with her two-month-old baby daughter, and conviction-free for the past two years, Laura had recently moved to a new town and acquired new friends. She explained that her 'old mates' were now 'all on smack' (heroin). A can of lager in her hand, Laura told me that she used to drink a bottle of vodka every day, but had reduced her alcohol consumption two or three years earlier. Prior to this, her daily routine (she had left school at 13) revolved around stealing alcohol, drinking and fighting. Were it not for her small daughter, Laura was sure that she would still 'go out and get paralytic' on a regular basis.

Erin generally consumed around half a bottle of vodka every Friday and Saturday night. She explained, 'I won't go out unless I can have a drink ... It lightens you up, and you don't feel embarrassed'. Most of the young women I interviewed, like Erin, Natasha and Laura, described their alcohol and drug use in terms of either boredom or 'social facilitation'.[17] However, the frequency with which they had experienced trauma and loss complicated the distinction between social drinking and alcohol or drug use in response to psychological distress or depression, as a means of temporarily numbing the pain of their everyday lives. Experiences of victimisation, bereavement, neglect and family dysfunction had for some young women resulted in a low sense of self-worth, such that they no longer cared about themselves nor, in some cases, about what they did to other people. While the girls' accounts of their drinking habits frequently reflected the 'normalization' of alcohol use in youth culture generally (Parker *et al.*, 1998), for some, alcohol appeared to have become a 'drug of solace' (Pavis *et al.*, 1997).[18] Hannah, for example, had only been arrested when intoxicated. She had started drinking in order to forget about her body. Hospitalised for four months with anorexia nervosa, then 'kicked out' of home by her mother shortly after she was discharged, and two days after her 16th birthday, Hannah explained that her escalating alcohol use enabled her to blank out feelings of anxiety and distress. Alcohol abuse had brought its own problems, however: on a number of occasions in the recent past, Hannah had woken up in a police cell with no recollection of how she had got there.

Sociocultural and psychological motivations underlying substance use may also coexist or overlap. Rachel began 'sleeping around' shortly after she turned 13, consuming large quantities of alcohol and drugs and 'kicking about' with 'loads of people' in a 'gang' – activities that she attributed to her poor relationship with her mother at the time. Rachel fell pregnant three times in the subsequent two years, resulting in two miscarriages and a termination. By the time she turned 15, she had been permanently excluded from school and evicted from home by her mother. I met Rachel when she was 17, a few weeks after she had been released from prison after serving nine months of an 18-month custodial sentence for robbery. She felt that prison had prevented her from becoming an alcoholic: before being incarcerated, she would drink non-stop from Friday to Sunday, stealing alcohol from shops, asking her father for money or buying it with the money she earned working part-time in a fish and chip shop. While asserting that she is by nature a quiet and calm person, Rachel commented that she feels 'less shy', 'more loud around boys' and 'more confident in myself' when drunk, and less inclined to get upset if people insult her. She also reported 'lov[ing] the feeling when I don't know what I'm doing' when high on drugs or alcohol.

Several of the girls' accounts that detailed the context of their alcohol use implied that they had effectively set out with the intention of becoming excessively drunk – a kind of 'controlled loss of control' (Measham, 2002) – in order to see what would happen or, as Laura, quoted earlier, put it, to 'see what trouble we can cause'. However, other young women's attributions for their offending relied on a post hoc rationalisation of the influence of alcohol and drugs, which enabled them to dissociate themselves from their crimes and thereby maintain an essentially non-criminal self-narrative by attributing their lawbreaking to an episode, or episodes, of temporary disturbance or psychological absence due to intoxication. Twenty-two young women (42 per cent) described their past offending as out of character and not their 'real' selves, for which alcohol was most frequently blamed (by one quarter of the girls[19]): these young women frequently described being drunk or high on a particular occasion and then regretting their actions when they had sobered up. Rhiannon (17) had recently served a custodial sentence for a serious assault which involved her cutting her ex-boyfriend's face with a scalpel blade out of jealousy over his new girlfriend. She was heavily intoxicated at the time, although her use of a blade indicated a degree of planning. Rhiannon struggled with the dissonance between this particularly unpleasant act and her self-concept as an essentially kind and good person, stating that 'I'm not capable of doing that, and I actually did something that I'm not capable of doing ... I don't like violence'. Alcohol does of course provide individuals with a ready-made post hoc defence should their revelries culminate in lawbreaking. Intoxication is popularly used as an excuse or rationalisation for a range of behaviours, including lawbreaking; indeed, it may even be our 'favourite excuse' (Rumgay, 1998). Rumgay contends that offenders continue to offer 'the intoxication excuse', not because it has any factual validity, but *because they can*, because it works, and because the excuse is 'immediately accessible, widely available, readily intelligible, and, indeed, personally meaningful as an explanation for moral infractions' (1998: 205).

Nobody cares: offending in the context of neglect and disconnection

While sociocultural attributions were most prominent in the girls' accounts of their offending, in many cases these overlapped considerably with the psychological legacy of adverse life events, including loss and bereavement, neglect and frustration or powerlessness relating to past experiences of victimisation. Sixteen young women – 31 per cent of the sample – said that they offended because no one cared about them and because they did not care about themselves. This attribution was most marked among those no longer living with their birth parents, in particular girls who had been brought up in 'care', such as Laura.[20] In addition to enjoying the excitement of being drunk and the exploits – including fighting – that often ensued, Laura simultaneously blamed her offending on the fact that, prior to the birth of her daughter, she had cared about nothing and no one, since she believed that no one cared about her. As I documented in my field notes:

> Laura has been in care for most of her life. She was born in Newcastle, but moved to Midshire at an early age. She was in foster care from age two, and adopted when she was nine (has two surnames – reverted to original one). Adoptive parents kicked Laura out when she was 11 years old – she said they phoned the police and said that she'd run away. She has no contact with them now. Between the ages of 11 and 13 Laura stayed with various friends [. . .]. She went to a children's home when she was 13 until she was 16, when she spent about a year in bail hostels, with mates, and in shared houses. Laura is under a care order until she is 21. As to why she offended (so much), Laura said: 'I had nothing to care about. My family didn't give a shit. I was in a children's home. If I went to prison I wasn't bothered. I had no-one to care about me and no-one to tell me off'.

For Laura, the psychological legacy of childhood neglect, disruption and disconnection was perhaps effaced by the feelings of excitement and power she experienced during drunken fights. By regularly drinking to excess and fighting, Laura was able to both blot out painful memories of neglect and abuse by significant adults in her life and also to achieve positive recognition and respect from her peers.

Vicky and Naomi had been diagnosed with attention deficit hyperactivity disorder (ADHD), and both blamed their lawbreaking on their refusal to take their prescribed medication. Naomi (16), for example, attributed much of her past offending to not taking her Ritalin tablets:

> I didn't use to take my medication, and when I don't take my medicine I don't care about anything or anyone.[21]

The high incidence of bereavement and loss among the sample was discussed in Chapter Five, where it was noted that two thirds of the girls had experienced the loss and/or bereavement of a significant person in their lives. Bereavement featured prominently in a substantial number of the girls' narratives, with 19 of those interviewed (37 per cent) making some connection between their experience of loss and their offending, most often in terms of not feeling themselves which had caused them to behave in a manner that was out of character and inconsistent with their 'normal' or 'real' self. Gemma's mother had died of cancer just a few weeks before we met, following a long period of illness and physical deterioration. Gemma reflected at length about her mother, who had suffered from long-term depression before her death, and explained that she now felt 'lost' without her. Gemma explained that, at the time of her recent offence (she had been arrested for criminal damage after being dared to climb on a car by a group of young people who were calling her names), she was 'really down because of problems at home, and I lost my head'. Aisha, discussed earlier, had been charged with supplying Class A drugs while in the company of an older man. She was arrested shortly after her grandmother's death, which followed a prolonged period during which she was badly bullied at school. Aisha told me that she 'went mental' for a time because of these events, and that she had been in the 'wrong place, wrong time and getting into the wrong crowd' when the offence took place, and 'was took advantage of'.

In contrast with bereavement, very few girls made any direct link between their victimisation experiences and their offending, despite the frequently documented incidence of abuse and neglect in their case files (see Chapter Five). They may of course not have wanted to talk about such personal issues with a researcher they had only just met. Another possible explanation is that, due to their young age and limited life experience, as well as to pervasive cultural stereotypes constructing sexual assault victims as blameworthy (Lees, 2002), girls who experience physical and sexual violence or emotional neglect at the hands of adults may understand their experiences not as *abusive*, but as *normal* or *deserved*, unaware that not all girls are treated similarly.

The effects of victimisation may be indirect: for example, drugs and alcohol may be used as a means of self-medication to temporarily erase distressing memories or flashbacks, which in turn may lead to expressive or acquisitive offending to fund a habit or addiction. Rumgay (2004a) has suggested several additional mechanisms through which women's victimisation experiences may be translated into offending behaviour. These include impaired moral reasoning due to increased stress, and poor mental health outcomes associated with post-traumatic stress disorder and other manifestations of psychological distress, including increased irritability and the propensity to 'explode' aggressively if provoked (Shapiro, 1999). Although few of the young women in the current study explicitly associated past or current abuse experiences with their lawbreaking, they did frequently discuss offending in the context of feelings of pent-up anger and rage.

Angry young women

Twenty girls (38 per cent) attributed their lawbreaking to anger or 'losing it'. Sometimes their anger related to specific incidents or disputes; however, for those girls who had been rejected by their families, or had experienced abuse, neglect, or unstable residential or care arrangements, anger and frustration were sometimes more deep-seated. Jodie (15) was living in a children's home when we met – her tenth placement since entering 'care' when she was seven. She had recently been prosecuted by the children's home for damaging cars and for breaking a member of staff's manicured false nail, for which she was charged with (and, remarkably, convicted of) common assault. Jodie spoke very negatively about the children's home and what she perceived to be its unfair rules.[22] She told me, 'I have a very short temper, and I just go mad'. One of the triggers that prompted her to 'go mad' and which led to her recent arrest (significantly, Jodie had only ever been arrested for 'offences' committed at the children's home) was when 'people piss you off, and it's the only way to let your anger out'.

Not infrequently, angry outbursts had led to girls being charged with damaging their own homes, and to fights with other girls or public order offences. For two of the girls in the STC, the venting of anger had much more harmful consequences: both were serving sentences for assault occasioning grievous bodily harm. Toni, aged 17, attributed her anger to 'things that I've seen when I was little ... I'm normally all right, but when I get angry, nothing can calm me down. I just see black'.[23] Sharelle's recent offences had followed arguments with her 21-year-old boyfriend, who got jealous if Sharelle, five years his junior, talked to other boys: 'sometimes I just do it [assault people] because I'm angry and I just take it out on other people'.

Tegan (13) lived with her grandmother, who was undergoing chemotherapy for cancer. Tegan's mother, whom she had previously lived with, had decided that she could no longer cope with Tegan's aggressive and violent outbursts. Tegan had long-standing psychological problems and she described herself as 'the devil's daughter'. She recounted how, aged five, she had broken her cousin's leg, tried to stab her and put bleach in her drink, and concluded that she [Tegan] 'must have been a twisted little girl'. Referring frequently to her angry and distressed state of mind, Tegan was very concerned that neither she nor anyone else had been able to identify the cause of her anger, which she suspected was biological: 'there's definitely something up with me. There has been since I can remember'. Tegan apparently blamed herself for her erratic behaviour, while simultaneously searching for a label to excuse (or at least explain) it. Although many girls talked about generalised feelings of anger or psychological distress, they were rarely able – I suspect largely on account of their young age – to account for the origins of such deep-seated feelings. Rather, several girls, most of whom were serving a custodial sentence, saw their anger or 'quick fuse' as an immutable character trait over which they had little or no control.

Several of the young women's accounts, like Tegan's, were contradictory in the extent to which they accepted or denied personal responsibility for, and control over, their violent acts. Throughout their accounts of anger and 'venting', the girls tended to represent their subsequent aggression as expressive, rather than instrumental – a means of 'letting your anger out', as Jodie described it, or a loss of control. While such an analysis fits well with the young women's descriptions of *generalised* anger and subsequent explosiveness arising from feelings of frustration and powerlessness, most accounted for the physical fights they had been involved in – which were most often against female opponents and rarely involved weapons – in more agentic terms. These fights generally arose due to righteous indignation or provocation, as discussed earlier.

Consuming desires: shoplifting and the female subject

Ornamental consumerism has become increasingly significant in identity construction and status-acquisition among today's young people. At the same time, the availability of credit – as well as the burden of debt – has increased, resulting in a degree of democritisation in the acquisition of material possessions and the narcissism that frequently accompanies their display. Hall *et al.* (2008) have contended that the precipitous rise of conspicuous consumption (Veblen, 1994) in recent decades has been accelerated by the demise of traditional forms of identity-provision and status-enhancement, most notably those anchored in work-based forms of production. They further argue that the pervasiveness of consumption in contemporary social life, combined with a loss of those solidarity-promoting institutions that have traditionally been associated with more predictable patterns of work, family and social life, has highly criminogenic consequences, leading them to conclude that consumerism deserves much greater attention as a primary issue in contemporary criminological theory.

While acknowledging the generational impact of consumer culture, Hall and colleagues are rather inattentive to its gendered implications, beyond their confident statement, which is largely unsupported by empirical evidence, that their 'central thesis would be proven correct by data gathered by streetwise female researchers' (2008: 20). This ignores the fact that women's relationship to production and, in particular, their relationship to reproduction, has traditionally been rather different to that of men. Moreover, the recent rise in consumer culture has had particular gendered implications for the identity construction of teenage girls in the twenty-first century. Young women, no longer (only) 'assumed to be headed towards marriage, motherhood and limited economic participation' (McRobbie, 2009: 58), have emerged as a powerful economic force in consumer society and a consumer group of unprecedented importance (Aapola *et al.*, 2005). A new hyper-visible feminine consumer culture has emerged in recent years, the terms of which, according to Angela McRobbie, are career success, glamour and sexuality (2009: 26–8). This culture pervades every area of young women's lives, from the female celebrities who are ubiquitous everywhere from television to the tabloid press, to 'celebrity' gossip magazines and fashion monthlies, to the nail bars and tanning parlours that are now a staple feature of most high streets and suburban shopping parades, even – and perhaps especially – in relatively poor areas.

The association of feminine consumption with young women's offending is of course not a new idea; shoplifting has long been considered the archetypal female crime. Thirty years ago, Anne Campbell observed that consumables are of substantial symbolic value in women's self-definition, which renders them particularly vulnerable to a 'consumer fetishism' that may encourage acquisitive crime (1981: 93–131). Campbell reported that 66 per cent of girls in 1959 stole clothes or cosmetics;[24] today, although just one quarter of youth arrests for theft and handling involve girls (Povey *et al.*, 2010), shop theft substantially outstrips all other recorded offences committed by young (and older) women and features more prominently in their punishment: more than one third of custodial receptions of sentenced women – double the proportion of men – are for theft and handling (Ministry of Justice, 2010a). Eighty-six per cent of the young women in the current study reported having committed retail theft, and theft and handling appeared most frequently on their criminal records.[25]

Nowhere is consumerism's gendered and generational impact more pronounced than in the contemporary fashion and beauty industries. McRobbie (2009) contends that a key feature of the 'aftermath of feminism' is the rise of the symbolic power of the fashion–beauty complex (Bartky, 1990), itself a hallmark of the reinstatement of traditional gender hierarchies at a time when traditional gender boundaries in the workplace have become somewhat blurred. Images of femininity are marketed back to young women – symbolic images of glamorous, individualised girlhood (Harris, 2004), which further encourage girls and women not only to consume, but to display themselves as conspicuously 'feminine' *objects* of consumption. Due partly to the selective appropriation of second wave feminist discourse emphasising empowerment and choice, young women are being sold a narrow image of hyper-feminine, hyper-sexualised attractiveness, such that

> having them wear spindly stilettos and 'pencil' skirts [and, I would add, for the young women I interviewed, thickly applied make-up and manicured nails] does not in fact mean entrapment (as feminists would once have seen it) since it is now a matter of choice rather than obligation.
>
> (McRobbie, 2009: 65–6)

Natasha Walter's recent popular text, *Living Dolls: The Return of Sexism* (2010), similarly argues that consumer culture has seduced girls and young women into believing that anything from pencil cases bearing the Playboy bunny logo to lap dancing to prostitution are the product of women's 'empowerment', and that, increasingly, careers in the sex and pornography industries are portrayed in the media as positive 'lifestyle' career choices for young women – in particular, working-class and poorly educated young women with few alternative avenues of employment. From the late twentieth century, there has been a somewhat unlikely alliance of consumer culture and a particular (distorted or conservative) variety of female 'empowerment' or 'girlpowered' feminism, such that young women are now encouraged to be aggressively individualistic as well as self-monitoring in all areas of their lives – from education and employment, to sexual relationships and childrearing to self-presentation (McRobbie, 2009). And pressure to be glamorous and to 'have it all' – or at least to look like one does – even as a teenage girl has undoubtedly accelerated what was already a buoyant female consumer market. It has perhaps also rendered shoplifting more acceptable, or even necessary, among young women with limited financial means who, ironically, are increasingly encouraged, even pressured, to consume without restraint at the same time as they are excluded from other forms of civic participation by virtue of their age.

Zoë was described to me by her YOT worker as an anomalous young woman whose involvement in offending defied explanation. Eighteen years old and living with both parents – employed and relatively economically advantaged professionals who owned a large house in a desirable village in Castleshire – Zoë insisted that she had no 'problems' which might have led to her lawbreaking. Zoë's shoplifting career had begun in year seven, the first year of secondary school,[26] and had escalated to the point where she was stealing from shops on a daily basis by the age of 16. She was now 'banned' from most of the shops in her local town and also from the shopping precinct. Despite having been 'well scared' when she first tried it, shoplifting had become increasingly 'normal' for Zoë. She explained: 'I don't think twice about it. It's just sort of, like, instant reaction'. Zoë likened her shoplifting habit to what she described as her 'drink problem', accounting for both in terms of her 'addictive personality': 'once I've tried it, I can't get enough of it'.

Zoë's account of shoplifting was not simply one of 'sneaky thrills' (Katz, 1988) experienced in avoiding detection. Nor were her thefts acts of rebellion. Rather, she was motivated above all by the desire to consume and the excitement of acquiring a constant supply of new clothes, shoes, make-up, hair straighteners and other 'stuff I really want'. She explained that if she forgot to take her foundation[27] out with her, she would simply steal a new one, and she regularly stole large quantities of make-up from a high street pharmacy chain – mostly for her own use, but sometimes to give away to friends as presents. Attractive and glamorous, smartly dressed with thickly applied make-up, Zoë's shoplifting habits had significant symbolic significance and enabled her to achieve the persona of the glamorous young woman, without the financial means: she had started a part-time job in a pub a few days before we met, and prior to this had been unemployed for a number of months.

The 'feminine' ideals of fashionableness and physical attractiveness are unattainable via legal means for many young women growing up in poverty. As Chloë (15), subject to a referral order for stealing make-up, explained, 'make-up's really dear [. . . around] ten pounds a piece'. Nonetheless, they are still highly prized goals. In the absence of any legitimate income, the rational choice many girls described was to take their chances and steal the items they 'needed'.[28] Half of the young women had stolen items of clothing, make-up or jewellery for their own use.[29] Discussion of shoplifting – the offence with which the girls had most frequently been charged – was conspicuous by its absence during the interviews. Indeed, with the exception of robbery (for which eight young women had previous convictions), their stories rarely focused on acquisitive offending at all, despite the fact that their offending 'careers' had commonly begun with the theft of small items for their own use. It was as though most of the girls considered shoplifting to be too mundane and ordinary to be worthy of mention, and not serious enough to be a real crime.

Some young women appeared to have come to the conclusion that the benefits of shoplifting outweighed the costs, for the time being, at least; indeed, the threat of being caught and of unpleasant consequences ensuing was rarely discussed. Several girls expressed surprise at having been apprehended for sho-plifting at all, having got away with it so many times in the past. Zoë, for exam-ple, had not come to the attention of the police until she was 16 – five years after her shoplifting début. With the increased threat of a custodial sentence now that she was 18, Zoë acknowledged this danger but could not imagine her life without shoplifting and was clearly adept at (usually) avoiding apprehension: although she had four previous convictions and had received a string of penalty notices,[30] she estimated that she got caught only around one time in ten. However, she had recently been 'forced' to shoplift in a nearby city, since she was too well-known to local police and security staff. Rather than give up her habit, Zoë had chosen to be 'really, really, really, really careful', by avoiding security guards and shops where she was likely to be recognised. Zoë was insis-tent that she would never steal from a person (and she had no record of so doing), but felt that stealing from shops was 'not, like, personal'.

Naomi, aged 16 and six months pregnant, reported that she had stopped offending a year earlier after previously shoplifting regularly, often stealing alco-hol to sell, 'because I could get away with it'. Although she was proud of her new crime-free lifestyle and adamant that there was 'no way on earth' that she would shoplift again, Naomi found it ironic that she now *chose* to pay for things which she 'could nick anyway'.

Courtney, a 15-year-old white girl living in a residential children's home, came into the reception of Midshire YOT office, where we had arranged to meet, 10 days before Christmas, a Dior handbag dangling from her wrist and clutching an expensive new mobile phone. Courtney had started shoplifting when she was 12 or 13 years old. Her criminal record included burglary, street robbery, assault and stealing a car, but shoplifting featured most prominently. Courtney explained that, while she was trying hard to abstain, she was finding her new (relatively) theft-free lifestyle difficult: having become used to the instant gratification of obtaining the clothes she wanted, she now had to save three weeks' pocket money to be able to afford a new pair of jeans. Although adamant that she was desisting, Courtney had recently stolen a bottle of fake tanning lotion because she felt 'very white' [pale]. She also admitted that if she really wanted something, she would 'push herself' to steal, sometimes drinking alcohol beforehand to 'psych herself up'. However, her current favoured means of obtaining the clothes and cosmetic items she desired was by threatening her grandparents, with whom she stayed every other weekend, that she would resort to theft if they refused to buy her what she wanted. They usu-ally gave in, fearful of the consequences for their granddaughter of further arrest.

Courtney explained that most members of her family were involved in crime: two uncles were serving long jail sentences for armed robbery, and both her par-ents had spent time in prison. Courtney had recently re-established contact with her father after his release from custody and had resolved to 'hit him for money now'. Somewhat unusually among the young women in the sample (see Chapter Eight), Courtney spoke very highly of her social worker, primarily on account of the fact that she apparently bought her 'everything I want', including new clothes and manicures.

Like Zoë, Courtney saw her age as a shield against (serious) punishment but felt that, once she turned 16, she would probably face imprisonment if she continued to offend. Courtney had recently told her incarcerated mother about her own shoplifting exploits and said, of her reaction, 'she weren't mad, but she told me I could only do it until the New Year'. Other young women's accounts, too, suggested that the fear of further criminalisation rarely acted as a significant deterrent against further shoplifting. Indeed, several girls naïvely believed that they were protected from the full weight of the law due to their age, and sometimes their gender: a number of individuals recounted their attempts to put on a 'sob story' to (usually male) police officers if they were arrested – for example, affecting temporary pathology caused by conflict at home or period pains in their defence. All, however, commented that such ploys had not proved effective!

Young women, including those who lack opportunities to gain status or esteem through work or the achievement of academic qualifications or indeed through the support and encouragement of their families, are increasingly urged by a raft of popular media, reinforced by female celebrities, that their 'image' – the way they look, what they wear and how sexually attractive they are – is either more important than employment in 'feminine' identity construction and/ or a means of securing employment (as objects of male consumption) in the expanding sex or glamour industries. Moreover, exclusion from mainstream services may mean that shopping/shoplifting is one of the few leisure opportunities available. Thus girls' shoplifting can be understood as an inclusionary strategy which enables them to participate in a consumer-driven society, as well as being status-enhancing through the bodily display of clothes, make-up, false nails and other such symbols of glamour. It is likely that some of the young women in this study who, due to their youth and their excluded status, had no job and no school place, did not have sufficient social capital to consider that they had much to lose by continuing to offend. During their teenage years, the girls may well have considered the cultural and symbolic capital they were able to acquire (only) through shoplifting – in the form of cash, clothes and sexual attractiveness – to be too valuable to give up.

Conclusion

As Chapter Five showed, many of the young women were the victims of exclusionary educational and social practices which, exacerbated by their youth and financial hardship, limited their capacity for active citizenship. Let down or given up on by adults, they found their own means of alleviating boredom, escaping the stresses of their daily lives and gaining recognition from peers. This often involved hanging around the streets and drinking or using drugs: indeed, many of the girls considered their lawbreaking to be incidental to having fun. The girls' offending attributions, which were by no means homogeneous, were context-specific, and the salience of gender, class and generation in their accounts differed according to the type of lawbreaking they were accounting for and the social context in which it took place. Their accounts did not reflect dominant popular stereotypes that offending girls are simply or always acting like boys.

In this chapter, I have argued that the rise of consumer culture in contemporary society plays a central role in girls' lawbreaking. For young women, far more than for young men, consumption is embodied. Young women in the twenty-first century are invoked to imagine themselves as consuming subjects; the acquisition of material goods and the consumption of personal grooming services are seen as positive lifestyle 'choices', which in turn are essential to attaining the glamorous and 'successful' self-image that is so important in contemporary young women's identity construction. Advertising campaigns communicate to women and girls that buying a new pair of shoes will increase their self-esteem, and that wearing expensive make-up will make them feel more attractive and confident. It is, of course, costly in both money and time to live up to what are perhaps increasingly narrow and idealised normative expectations about 'feminine' self-presentation and attractiveness. The power of the feminine fashion–beauty complex and cultural pressure to make oneself sexually attractive exerted considerable influence over some of the study young women's perceived 'need' to steal clothes and cosmetics. Certainly few of them were likely – given their current educational (non-)status – to earn sufficient wages in the foreseeable future to enable them to legitimately acquire the trappings of a glamorous feminine lifestyle: most of those who had any future employment aspirations wanted to be hairdressers.

The motivations underlying many of the young women's violent acts echoed themes identified in young men's violence, most notably that violence is frequently employed in the defence of respect or in the face of provocation. In addition, the emotions that gave rise to the girls' acts of violence – rage, perceived disrespect, defiance and so on – were broadly similar to those that might have motivated their male counterparts. However, the contexts in which such emotions originate are characterised by unequal gendered power relations: violence was frequently employed in response to sexual slurs and insults to their own (or their mothers' or female friends') femininity and sexual integrity. Importantly, the girls' accounts of their violent behaviour challenge the popular claim that a 'new breed' of violent girl has emerged in British society in recent years. Indeed, their stories were, in many ways, reminiscent of historical accounts of the street brawls of 'rough' girls or 'scuttleresses' in Victorian times (Davies, 2008; Godfrey, 2004). Then, as now, female violence was relatively rare, although young women were (and are) quite capable of resorting to violence when they felt it was justified and necessary. One might also assume that expressive violence – the venting of pent-up rage and frustration at having been left to deal, without support, with the emotional legacy of bereavement, abuse and neglect – existed long before reports of the contemporary so-called 'ladette', and is not unique to recent times.

What *has* undoubtedly changed for criminalised young women, compared with their counterparts a generation ago, is the salience of alcohol and drug consumption, as well as consumer culture more broadly, in their social and public lives. While there is, again, no shortage of evidence that female drunkenness is not a new phenomenon, nor that it has only recently been considered a serious problem of order and morality (see, e.g., Zedner, 1991), normative generational expectations regarding alcohol and drug consumption in Britain – including among very *young* teenagers – have changed considerably in recent decades. In contemporary youth culture alcohol, as well as (perhaps less often) drugs, is increasingly considered a necessary ingredient of a good night out. The motivations the young women ascribed to their drinking habits are perhaps better understood from the perspectives of generation and class, rather than gender. However, their accounts of alcohol use complicated simplistic media representations of the hedonistic thrill-seeking 'ladette'. Rather, 'disordered' alcohol consumption – which almost always took place not in pubs and clubs, but on street corners or in parks where the girls were subject to increased adult surveillance – provided, at different times and in different combinations, structure and excitement in otherwise empty lives, a means of social facilitation, and solace from the emotional pain of victimisation and loss. Importantly, perceptions of, and responses to, youthful alcohol consumption *are* highly gendered. The public spectacle of a drunken young woman continues to be considered more shocking than that of an intoxicated young man, and such women, now as much as ever, are considered 'unfeminine', uncouth and disreputable.

7 The trouble with girls today

Professional perspectives on young women's offending*

Researching 'front line' perspectives (Robinson and McNeill, 2004) on the causes of crime and the needs and characteristics of offenders is extremely important. As street-level bureaucrats who enjoy a relatively high (albeit arguably decreasing) level of discretion and autonomy (Lipsky, 1980), youth justice and related professionals are, in a sense, policy-makers: the youth justice 'system' is shaped in part by their decisions and actions, including the extent to which they endorse and apply, modify, resist or even undermine central Government policies. In spite of the rapid increase of managerialism in criminal justice (Feeley and Simon, 1992; Muncie, 2008), in England and Wales it remains the primary responsibility of individual (usually) Youth Offending Team (YOT) employees to recommend the punishments they believe young offenders should receive, to determine the content of interventions and to enforce young people's compliance with community and custodial penalties.

In this chapter, I present findings from 43 interviews with 48 practitioners and managers working with girls in the youth justice system or 'at risk of offending'.[1] A central aim of the interviews was to explore the theoretical beliefs of professionals employed in youth justice and related fields about the causes of girls' and young women's offending in the twenty-first century. Additionally, I asked professionals whether or not they felt that changes have taken place in patterns of female youthful behaviour, in order to examine the extent to which contemporary 'moral panics' about female youth violence and criminality are reflected in professional discourse and practice. Finally, I set out to investigate how the needs and risks girls present are conceptualised and assessed by youth justice practitioners, including how they discussed the interpersonal aspects of working with girls and young women.

In the first part of the chapter, I discuss practitioners' beliefs about girls' pathways into crime.[2] Their accounts of the aetiology of girls' offending tended to prioritise individual and family factors over social–structural ones. Indeed, professional discourse very often reconstructed *social–structural* disadvantage – the obstacles which delimit girls' life chances and constrain their non-offending choices on account of their age, class and gender – as *individualised* problems or needs located within individual girls and/or their families. Furthermore, the micro-social contexts of offending in the company of peers, which were dominant features of the young women's accounts of their lawbreaking activities, as documented in Chapter Six, were often ignored or refuted with respect to girls' offending: 'peer pressure' was widely believed only to affect boys.

The second part of the chapter examines professionals' perspectives on the interpersonal aspects of working with girls and young women, including the importance (or not) of gender in client–worker relationships, an issue that was fiercely contested. I argue that professional discourse can serve to decontextualise behaviour by female clients that indicates gendered resistance – or, conversely, a plea for help and support – by constructing girls' actions as signs of 'difficult and demanding' behaviour.

In the third part, I analyse practitioners' perceptions of contemporary patterns of female juvenile lawbreaking and criminalisation, in order to examine the extent to which media-promulgated 'moral panics' about 'ladettes' and girl violence have infiltrated professional discourse. The resultant picture was complex and sometimes contradictory: interviewees frequently voiced uncertainty and confusion about whether the visible influx of female bodies into the youth justice system was the result of widespread behavioural change, or a social construct, driven (partly or entirely) by legislative and practice changes. Many of them were apparently attempting to reconcile popular stereotypes about 'bad' girls with their lived experiences of working with *vulnerable*, rather than dangerous or predatory, female clients.

The fourth and final part of the chapter explores professionals' beliefs about young women's pathways out of crime. Many practitioners thought that girls experience more guilt and remorse than their male counterparts on account of their lawbreaking and that they are consequently more motivated to leave crime behind, including by starting a family. However, the interventionist thrust of an 'intolerant' (Muncie, 1999) contemporary British youth justice system and the attendant – and lasting – effects of a criminal label make it increasingly difficult for young women to cast off the shadow of criminalisation. Moreover, those young women for whom motherhood provides a prosocial 'identity script' (Rumgay, 2004b) facilitating desistance from crime may find that the vilification and social censure which confronts them on becoming a lone teenage mother may be no less stigmatising than the condemnation directed towards them as young offenders.

Professional accounts of girls' pathways into crime

Conceptualisations of boys' and girls' offending and delinquent behaviour as essentially different have historically underscored a common assumption among youth justice professionals that girls' offending stems from individual or family pathology, as opposed to youthful immaturity or rebelliousness (Priestley *et al.*, 1977; Hudson, 1984; Gelsthorpe, 1989).[3] I thus set out to examine whether such gender-specific understandings have shifted in a contemporary climate where gender blindness or 'gender equality' (Chesney-Lind and Eliason, 2006) has come to dominate popular accounts of young women's lawbreaking.

Excess 'baggage': family pathology

The majority (38) of the professionals maintained that there is a close association between family dysfunction and youth offending. Moreover, while poor parenting, strained family relationships and family breakdown were frequently considered to have similarly negative consequences for young people of both sexes, a significant minority (over a quarter) of interviewees believed that family pathology was either more prevalent among, or that it had a distinctive psychosocial impact upon, their female clients. Girls were thus sometimes thought to be carrying a lot of 'baggage' resulting from their problematic family histories. As one probation officer put it:

> I think usually the girls' backgrounds tend to be more difficult and more in need. They usually have some sort of baggage that they're carrying, where the boys won't necessarily have as much.
>
> (Probation Officer, male, Castleshire YOT)

Underlying this notion of problematic backgrounds was a frequent assumption that girls and boys offend for different reasons, or, more accurately, that girls offend *for a reason*, whereas boys' lawbreaking is simply a symptom of immaturity, teenage rebellion or adventuresomeness, which thus requires no deeper explanation. By contrast, girls, due to a plethora of 'underlying issues', were frequently believed to be emotionally complicated:

> I feel girls are a lot more complex [...] Whereas lads, a lot of them ... they've just been out messing about with mates, and it's not really got anything to do with anything else in their lives, whereas girls, it seems to all be connected in some way. [...] Low self-esteem, things going on at home, friendships, relationships – it all seems to link in.
>
> (Drug and Alcohol Worker, female, Midshire YOT)

> The whole background to why [girls] are there is different. [Girls] tend to have more ... psychological or emotional problems ... you know? *Psychological* [is] too strong, but just kids who aren't coping on a deeper level than just boys who don't sleep and go out and offend. I just think it's far more complicated. [...] So although the girls are presenting with just anti-social behaviour ... the family situation behind is not normal, by any stretch of the imagination.
>
> (YOT Officer, female, Castleshire)

Several practitioners considered the association between familial adversity and offending to be particularly pronounced among girls who are more entrenched in the youth justice system. For instance, one YOT officer believed that while many girls 'get into a little bit of trouble' but soon 'sort themselves out', those who remain in the system:

usually have got really, *really* broken family backgrounds. [...] Always abused. Always very unstable. Always rubbish accommodation issues. [...] I'm trying to think of any girls who've had really supportive families, and I'm struggling to think of any, to be honest with you.

(YOT Officer, female, Castleshire)

The predominance of a family psychopathology paradigm has long been emphasised in studies of professionals' beliefs about young women's offending (Campbell, 1981; Hudson, 1984; Gelsthorpe, 1989; A. Hudson, 1989, *inter alia*); indeed, experiences of family disruption, discord and violence were common-place among the girls and young women in this study, as Chapter Five showed. Practitioners and managers frequently voiced complaints that 'preventive' chil-dren's services, notably social services, are too pressured to be able to undertake direct work with teenagers except in situations of extreme seriousness, and that they function instead as gatekeepers, restricting access to support for young peo-ple in need and their families. As I argued in Chapter Three, this filtering process is less available either to the police, who are increasingly required to respond substantively to all but the most petty of young lawbreakers (and sometimes these too), or to YOTs who, as agents of the court, may not reject court referrals. Experience of family-related adversities, combined with a lack of external sup-port, may result in some young women entering the youth justice system by default, when family relations have reached breaking point and parents or carers are desperate for help, as one YOT officer explained:

The girls that I've seen in [police] custody ... they're the ones who were there for self-harm, and they're doing things like criminal damage within the home in order to ... get into the system. Because the parents believe they can get into the system that way to get more help. In fact it's not true. It doesn't work like that. But parents don't know ... the difference. [...] I think parents don't know what else to do and therefore call the police ... So therefore when the girls [are] kicking off big time in the house, then they'll present with a criminal damage, when in fact that isn't the issue at all.

(YOT Officer, female, Castleshire)

Adolescent girls' refusal to defer to parental rules may of course be the result of lower levels of tolerance towards, and stricter tutelage of, daughters compared with sons (Wilson, 1980), as one team leader believed:

I think parents can be ... more restrictive, and have one set of rules for boys and one for girls. And then they'll break those rules, and they won't keep to their curfews, and then everything kicks off at home.

(Team Leader, female, Castleshire YOT)

A police officer in Castleshire YOT, whose responsibility it was to undertake final warning assessments, noted that almost all of the warnings he had recently dealt with involving girls had related to 'domestic-y-type assaults' resulting from 'domestic-y type angst' felt by the girls' parents, who had, in his view, 'come to the end of their tether with their daughter'. Such 'angst', in his opinion, frequently related to girls having older boyfriends of whom their parents did not approve. The criminalisation of girls' involvement in domestic disputes was discussed in Chapters Three and Five, where I suggested that, in the context of the increasing retrenchment of family welfare services, particularly those aimed at young people, troubled parents may have come to consider the response of the police to be more reliable and more speedy than that of social welfare agencies. Recent initiatives promoting a more proactive response to domestic violence may have also had the unintended consequence of criminalising girl 'victims' (Chesney-Lind, 2002). When a parent or carer calls the police in a situation of domestic crisis, the child may be constructed – by the parent or the police – as the offender, thus deflecting blame from the parent(s) and scapegoating the child for problems relating to the whole family.

(Still) pathologising offending girls ... and their families

Expectations that female conduct should be passive, docile and domesticated have long determined the types of female acts – principally aggression and untrammelled sexuality – that have been considered deviant. And when girls have contravened such expectations, their behaviour has tended to be understood not simply in terms of lawbreaking, but as indicative of more serious underlying trouble. Gelsthorpe's study of youth justice professionals two decades ago, for example, demonstrated that practitioners tended to view girls' problems as more serious than those of boys, and that girls were seen to have greater 'pathological potential' (1989: 120). One of the team leaders I interviewed highlighted how long-standing cultural beliefs among youth justice practitioners that girls' offending, by virtue of its relative rarity, requires a greater degree of explanation than that of boys, may introduce bias into YOT workers' assessment practices:

> It worries me that we will just sort of accept ... Oh well, yeah, he got into a fight. It's only a common assault. Move on. And yet we'd pick it apart with a girl. We'd be *very* concerned to look at the family situation.
>
> (Team Leader, female, Midshire YOT)

Several professionals linked girls' family 'baggage' and their consequently greater levels of need to their having caring responsibilities within the home, for mentally ill or substance-dependent parents, or for younger siblings. Such views are consistent with prevailing cultural expectations that women and girls should to be able to cope, without complaint, with looking after other family members as well as themselves, as one social worker explained:

> I think they have more needs because they're female, and females have to take more responsibility of more things, and be more independent at an early

age, whereas even the males that have that level of need, somehow ... we don't place such high expectations on them to manage by themselves.

(Social Worker, female, Midshire YOT)

Although a handful of interviewees (all of whom were female and themselves mothers) did acknowledge that such social and cultural expectations are likely to influence perceptions of girls' behaviour, the majority located girls' 'baggage' squarely within the family sphere, thereby engaging in a discourse of responsibilising families – or, more accurately, parents – for the crimes of their children (Donzelot, 1979; Rose, 1989). Youth justice practitioners are not alone in blaming families, and specifically poor parenting, for much of the youth crime 'problem'; indeed, a plethora of new guidance and legislation premised on this assumption has been enacted in recent years.[4] The punitive, as opposed to supportive, implications of the relevant legislation have attracted extensive academic criticism, most notably for disregarding the impact of poverty and structural disadvantage on parents' capacity to engage in stress-free parenting (Goldson and Jamieson, 2002; Arthur, 2005; Burney and Gelsthorpe, 2008, *inter alia*). Moreover, a historical and continued emphasis on *female* parents as the primary caregivers and moral educators of their children, combined with the fact that a large proportion of young offenders come from female-headed lone parent families, has meant that parenting orders have been imposed disproportionately on women (Holt, 2008).

Self-esteem

Professionals commonly considered low self-esteem to be a risk factor for female youth offending,[5] particularly in the context of alcohol consumption, as highlighted in the extracts below:

I'd probably say the main problem [leading to offending by girls] is self-esteem, I really would. Because that covers a multitude of sins anyway ... And emotional stuff that they can't handle. And therefore they're displaying it in another way.

(YOT Officer, female, Castleshire)

I think with the girls the alcohol is more of an issue ... if you look at the research that the links to alcohol, and issues with self image, and self-esteem and confidence ... [this] would [imply] that ... the underlying motivational factors for girls to be offending would be different to the boys.

(Drug and Alcohol Worker, male, Castleshire YOT)

While the girls I interviewed accounted for their alcohol use principally in terms of social facilitation or conformity to peer expectations (see Chapter Six), professionals tended to describe girls' (mis)use of alcohol as a form of stress relief or a drug of solace (Pavis *et al.*, 1997):

I think that there is probably more binge drinking. And I think a lot of that is some of the pressure that young people, and particularly young women, are under. And it's their escape route … I think society has become so pressured in so many ways, it's about where do youngsters find those sort of get outs now?

> (YOT Manager, female, Midshire)

In addition, young women's alcohol use was seen as a 'front' to mask a lack of confidence and low self-esteem that was believed to result from anxieties about school and relationships:

In the real world … I won't say 24/7, but certainly maybe 24/5 … then it's just the day-to-day school, relationship problems, you know … All sorts of things that are going on. And then … for the other two days or whatever, when they go out, they don't have to worry about it. And … drinking … gives them the confidence, you know, to be something they're probably not, really.

> (Police Officer, male, Castleshire YOT)

Further gendered implications of low self-esteem emphasised by professionals related to girls' sexuality, including their involvement in 'inappropriate' sexual relationships (with older and/or exploitative males), sexual risk-taking (engaging in sexual intercourse without using contraception) and teenage pregnancy. Practitioners rarely commented on sexual identity, however: just four interviewees highlighted the significance of sexuality, two of whom openly identified as lesbian/gay. Indeed, one manager was of the opinion that issues relating to young people's sexuality were generally 'over people's heads'. Another worker conceptualised (some) young people's offending as a means of externalising 'emotional internal trauma' relating to uncertainties about their nascent (homo)sexual identity in a culture which continues to view lesbian and gay individuals as deviant – a form of discrimination which is particularly deep-rooted in working-class communities.

While it was apparent from the professionals' narratives – as well as from my interviews with the girls and close examination of their case files – that many, if not the majority, of young women offenders *do* have low self-esteem or feelings of low self-worth,[6] the association between low self-esteem and female criminality is problematic, both theoretically and practically. Shoshana Pollack has argued that the association that is commonly made between girls' and women's offending and their low self-esteem

decontextualizes women from the social and political parameters of their lives [thereby] individualiz[ing] the experiences of women in conflict with the law by locating the cause of lawbreaking within women's psychology. As such, forms of oppression such as racism, classism and sexism are ignored and escape being understood as contributing factors in the lives of women in conflict with the law. Instead, the problem *and the solution* to the problem, lie within the individual woman herself.

(2000: 79)

Furthermore, conceptualising female offenders (only) as victims whose low self-esteem has been caused by neglect and abuse within or outside the family home leaves little space to acknowledge girls' and women's agency, thus leaving unanalysed both how victimisation experiences interact with agency (Batchelor, 2005) and how the exercise of agency may be constrained by oppressive social conditions. It is hardly surprising that young women in the youth justice system suffer from low self-esteem, given the damaging and exclusionary experiences that have so frequently blighted their young lives (see Chapter Five). Moreover, the accounts of both the young women and the professionals I interviewed repeatedly indicated that 'young offenders' are rarely deemed deserving of support from agencies outside the youth justice arena.

According to psychologist Carol Dweck, self-esteem is not a static entity or 'thing', but an incremental concept: self-esteem is increased by exerting effort to meet challenges, and is 'a way of experiencing yourself when you are using your resources well – to master challenges, to learn, to help others' (2000: 128). A key question with regard to criminalised girls and young women is how they can be encouraged to use their resources well – including their intelligence and their creative and interpersonal skills – if they are excluded, by virtue of poverty and/or their criminal records, from participation in mainstream educational, social and recreational opportunities. The direction of causality between low self-esteem and offending is by no means clear, and involvement in the criminal justice system – particularly for females, for whom the shame and stigma of having a criminal record may be especially strongly felt – might *cause*, or at least exacerbate, low self-esteem, rather than the converse. The feasibility of improving young offenders' self-esteem in a climate of increasingly exclusionary criminal justice policies which often serve to 'other', or even to *eliminate*, troublesome individuals (Rutherford, 1998; see also Muncie, 2006), is questionable.

The (criminogenic) impact of girlhood adversity: acknowledgement and silence

The majority of professional interviewees (63 per cent of the sample) believed that drug and alcohol use by young people (of both sexes) is significantly causally related to lawbreaking, and particularly violent offending, a point on which the young women in the study tended to concur (see Chapter Six). In contrast to the media attention conferred upon 'ladettes' and girl violence, professionals rarely voiced concerns regarding the risk of harm *to others* presented by inebriated girls; rather, girls' vulnerability, and principally their risk of being (sexually) victimised, gave rise to far greater anxiety:

I've got one that ... the concern's how much she drinks, over what she gets up to when she's drinking. And she's thirteen, and she's hanging round with seventeen, eighteen year old lads ... Seventeen, eighteen year old lads binge-drink ... So if your thirteen, fourteen year old girls are hanging round with them ... they drink as well.

(YISP worker, female, Castleshire[7])

Numerous practitioners voiced similar concerns about their female clients' sexual vulnerabilities, and they considered them to be at greater personal risk than their male clients in this respect.[8] However, most denied that there is any *causal* relationship between sexual victimisation and lawbreaking among young women. In contrast to the growing body of feminist literature that situates girls' and women's pathways into crime in the context of their victimisation experiences – the 'blurred boundaries' thesis (see Chapter Two) – professionals in just 11 interviews (26 per cent) suggested that girls' offending might be a consequence of their experiences of abuse. The significance of abuse in the aetiology of offending by young people of *both* sexes was, however, more frequently highlighted (in 40 per cent of the interviews), and a number of practitioners, while asserting that a large proportion of young offenders on their caseloads had been abused, rejected the notion that this might be a gendered phenomenon, stating, for example, that 'boys can be abused too'. Such views seemed to arise in part from a misplaced concern about 'equal opportunities', whereby to highlight a characteristic or need as being distinct to, or more prevalent among, girls was believed to constitute discrimination against boys. Moreover, denial that the impact of childhood abuse might be gendered contrasted markedly with the widely held belief, discussed earlier, that family pathology is more prevalent among young women offenders than among young men. Additionally, professionals rarely discussed their clients' experiences of bereavement and loss,[9] in spite of their frequent occurrence among the girls interviewed. Where abuse and bereavement *were* referred to, practitioners associated girls' subsequent offending with the expression of unresolved anger or distress, which had been 'bottled up', only to 'explode' in angry outbursts later on.

So far, I have argued that professional interviewees' beliefs regarding the aetiology of girls' offending tended to prioritise individual and family factors over social–structural ones. Their descriptions of the needs and characteristics of offending girls were replete with highly individualised references to low self-esteem and family-related 'baggage'. Indeed, professional discourse very often reconstructed social–structural disadvantage – the constraints which delimit girls' life chances – as *individualised* shortcomings or family pathology. In other words, while most recognised that the girls they worked with had numerous 'problems', there was limited acknowledgement of the social origins of their troubles.

Poverty was mentioned in just ten interviews (23 per cent) and many practitioners denied that poverty *causes* offending. On one level, this is of course correct, since the majority of people living in poverty do not become offenders; however, poverty serves to limit children's and young people's citizenship opportunities by denying them the means to participate in social life as consumers of goods and services. The exclusionary effects of material deprivation are highly likely to contribute to boredom and disaffection among young people, who are already over-represented among the United Kingdom's poor (UNICEF, 2005), by confining their leisure pursuits to public space, where they are particularly visible to agents of social control. Moreover, poverty appears to be more closely associated with female, than with male, offending (Carlen, 1988; Farrington and Painter, 2004).

Midshire YOT's (male) operational manager recognised the atypicality, in the contemporary criminal justice policy climate, of his own privileging of poverty as an explanation of offending – or, more precisely, as an explanation of why individuals' *non-offending* choices are severely restricted:

> People don't talk about poverty any more, actually, they talk about social exclusion. I have heard and seen references to child poverty and pensioner poverty [. . . but] only in the context of trying to raise particular standards and performance indicators and targets, rather than *explanations* for behaviour. [...] I know it's dead unfashionable, but I think poverty is a big factor ... it's a significant factor in young people, em, being drawn into, and having a lack of access to other options ... And I think that's the critical thing: rather than it being a driving force for them to *go into* crime, it's the lack of other options that means that the amount of decisions that they can make in another direction are constrained, more than for other people who aren't in poverty.

This manager's use of the word 'unfashionable' is revealing, and his terminology hinted at the broad neo-liberal shift that many have argued has taken place in recent years, whereby explanations of crime that prioritise social–structural disadvantage have largely been supplanted by individual and familial explanations (see, e.g., Garland, 1997; Muncie and Hughes, 2002). The advent of actuarialism in youth justice has arguably de-emphasised the individual offender and encouraged youth justice practitioners to conceive of young offenders as collections of 'criminogenic needs' or 'risk factors' (Kempf-Leonard and Peterson, 2000; Maurutto and Hannah-Moffat, 2007), thus serving to disconnect their needs and problems from the contexts and structures in which they originated. While poverty does feature to a greater or (usually) lesser degree in contemporary research and practice guidance on 'criminogenic' risk factors and youth crime prevention (Farrington, 1996, 2007; Anderson *et al.*, 2001), the most effective 'risk-focused prevention' interventions are said to include skills training, parenting education and pre-school programmes targeted at 'at-risk' children and their families (Farrington, 2007), rather than universal fiscal policies. Consequently, in the youth justice policy arena, poverty is effectively reconstructed as family and/or individual pathology.

Reporting on the preliminary findings of an organisational analysis of risk and need assessment practice in an English YOT, Phoenix has argued that

[b]oth the explanations and the generalised notions of 'risk' and 'need' [which ran through the discourses of the YOT practitioners she interviewed] can be characterised as highly individualised and pathologising accounts in which the responsibility of lawbreaking is located firmly within either the young person or their family.

(2006: 27)

As Phoenix further notes, this position is supported, if not created, by contemporary criminal justice policies based on a narrow (mis)reading of the 'what works' literature, which have resulted in an almost exclusive focus on dynamic risk factors, in particular factors which are considered to be modifiable through cognitive behavioural interventions.

Furlong and Cartmel (2007) have contended that life in late modernity is based on an 'epistemological fallacy', insofar as contemporary social theorists' accounts of processes of individualisation, risk and uncertainty (Giddens, 1990, 1991; Beck, 1992) have served to obscure the ways in which class, 'race', age and gender continue to act as impediments to advancement and achievement. In their view, 'although the collective foundations of social life have become more obscure, they continue to provide powerful frameworks which constrain young people's experiences and life chances' (Furlong and Cartmel, 2007: 138). Consequently, the authors maintain that

Individuals are forced to negotiate a set of risks which impinge on all aspects of their daily lives, yet the intensification of individualism means that crises are perceived as individual shortcomings rather than the outcome of processes which are largely outwith the control of individuals.

(Ibid.: 144)

There was evidence that many of the professionals I interviewed had subscribed to such an 'epistemological fallacy' by erasing the macro-social constraints that impinge upon the lives of their clients from their accounts of the causes of young women's offending. The fact that abuse, bereavement and poverty were so rarely mentioned by practitioners and managers in connection with the aetiology of girls' lawbreaking raises a number of important questions. While it is possible that workers were genuinely unaware of the prevalence of experiences of bereavement or victimisation among their female clients, this seemed unlikely, given the frequency with which the case files of the young female clients in each of the three study areas documented previous experiences of victimisation and loss. A more likely explanation is that professionals *were* aware that a high proportion of girls had been abused and bereaved but, traumatic and enduring as the effects of these experiences were, workers did not, in general, consider them to be (directly) relevant to the *causation* of offending and, perhaps most importantly, the emotional and psychological effects of abuse and bereavement are not obviously amenable to intervention through the criminal justice system, but may require longer term and more therapeutic support than YOTs are able to provide.[10] Conversely, alcohol and drug use – which practitioners and managers associated rather more closely with young women's offending and which are more popularly linked with offending in the public imagination (Rumgay, 1998) – were perhaps believed to be more feasible targets for change from within a criminal justice framework.

The Asset assessment tool, the use of which is mandatory in all YOTs, requires practitioners to indicate whether a young person has had 'experience of abuse', has 'witness[ed] other violence in the family context' or has experienced 'significant bereavement or loss'. However, these are but three 'tick box' factors out of ten in the 'family and personal relationships' section of the assessment. Substance misuse, by contrast, fills an entire section by itself. The assessment proforma alludes to poverty only briefly: practitioners are required to indicate whether a young offender lives in a 'deprived household' or has 'inadequate personal income'. Individual youth justice practitioners are all but powerless when it comes to addressing poverty and social exclusion, hence they might understandably be frustrated about apparently being expected to engage in the Herculean task of modifying or reducing such social–structural 'risk factors'. As one YOT police officer explained:

> [In t]he Asset … there's things like, where does this person live? Where do they go to school? […] Is it identified as a crime hotspot? Well, we can't change any of that. So … for that individual, that section of this assessment is useless.

Peer influences in girls' offending

The downplaying of social factors in young women's offending extended from the macro to the micro level, as revealed in professionals' views about the influence of peers in female youthful lawbreaking. While more than half of the practitioners (58 per cent) highlighted the significance of peers, or 'peer pressure', in youth crime *in general*, just three individuals suggested that peers are important in girls' offending specifically, and one quarter emphasised what they perceived to be the greater relevance of peers in crimes committed by boys:

> Because of the age we deal with, I think more of the guys run with the pack … they seem to work in groups. There's usually half a dozen of them, or a couple of them, you know what I mean? They're not working on their own.
>
> (Police Officer, female, Midshire YOT)

> The boys will be … more readily going along with peer pressure, and following the gang, and trying to blend in. I often feel that the girls aren't doing that blending, image thing. It's a lot more about, this is where I'm at. […] You've made me angry and I'm going to clobber you. Where the boys will … you're just going to be clobbered, because there is a clobbering going on, and we're expected to join in en masse.
>
> (Drug and Alcohol Worker, male, Castleshire YOT)

Participation in (group) offending was understood as a normative and expected activity among teenage boys from certain sociocultural backgrounds, which functions as a rite of passage facilitating the acquisition and maintenance of respect or reputation – acquired, in some cases, by serving time in custody. But not among girls. However, gender differences in co-offending by young people are in fact rather less pronounced than is commonly believed, and there are recent indications that young women who offend are slightly *more* likely than males to engage in co-offending (van Mastrigt, 2008[11]). Moffitt and colleagues (2001) go as far as to suggest that, due to the relative absence of biological factors predisposing girls to offending, as well as the subsequent rarity of girls, compared with boys, among life-course-persistent offenders,[12] 'the bulk of antisocial behaviour, *especially by females*, is best understood as a social phenomenon originating in the context of social relationships' (ibid.: xvi, my emphasis).[13]

Despite professionals' common conviction that friends and associates play a much more central role in boys' offending than in that of girls, a minority (*n* = 6) emphasised the (usually negative) effects of tightly knit female-only friendship groups in relation to 'bitch fights' or relational bullying, and the detrimental effects such altercations can have on girls' self-esteem:

> I'm a great believer in young women are their own worst enemies. [... T]hey're a lot more bitchy and emotionally abusive towards each other than young boys. [...] Young girls: you're either in, or you're out. And it must be quite soul-destroying, really.
>
> (Community Psychiatric Nurse, female, Midshire YOT)

Several practitioners,[14] who were usually referring to incidents of interpersonal violence between girls – emphasised the 'nasty', 'catty', 'bitchy' or 'poisonous' nature of young women's offending:

> Where it comes to girls and assaults ... I think girls ... tend to be far more, I'd say *poisonous*, if that's not too strong a word to use, is it? But do you know what I mean?
>
> (Police Officer, male, Castleshire YOT)

> I think when girls [fight], sometimes they do it rather well. [...] They're very nasty, you know? [...] I've always said that I'd rather fight with a bloke any day than a woman . . .because [with females] it's scratching, biting, spitting ... cat fighting stuff. [...] I think with lads, they can have a bit of a scrap, and then they drop it, and they can be best mates the next day. [...] Whereas with the girls ... they can sometimes carry it on, and be really, really nasty. [...] I think girls can be pretty malicious.
>
> (Police Officer, female, Midshire YOT)[15]

Female youth crime was understood to be very much a single sex affair, and there was little professional support for the 'bad boyfriend' hypothesis – girls offending due to coercion by males. One senior police manager contrasted what he perceived to be the current situation (of girls offending alone) with his experience earlier in his career:

> I think the majority of offences involving girls, in recent times, are committed either with other girls or on their own. [...] So they seem to stand very much on their own as a group, and don't appear to be overly influenced by boys. [...] I think it might have been true years ago that a girl ... may well have been influenced by the boy, who may have been boyfriend-girlfriend. Her offending may have been as a result of what *he* did. I don't think that's ... true now.
>
> (Police Youth Justice Process Marker, male, Midshire)[16]

One of the reasons why girls today are less influenced by boys than they used to be, according to the same police manager, is that they are behaving more like boys, as a result of broad social shifts which have led to gender role convergence:

> I think that when you look at society as a whole, you can't avoid it. Girls are seen, in many ways, very much like boys now. Or want to be, or act in the way that boys have acted, so there's more of an evening out of roles ... I'm not sure that's a good thing or not, but it's certainly how things seem to be.

I return to examine this point of view in more detail in the third part of this chapter, which analyses the opinions of professionals regarding the popular stereotype that female youthful behaviour is changing and that girls today are 'worse' than they used to be. In the meantime, the next section explores professionals' accounts of working with girls in the youth justice system.

Working with girls and young women

> Give me a boy rather than a girl to work with any day!
>
> (YOT Manager, female, Midshire)

Client–worker relationships: a female affair?

My arrival at Midshire YOT to begin fieldwork coincided with the introduction of a new 'casework allocation procedure', which included the mandate that:

> Female clients will be allocated, where practicable, to a female worker to ensure that their specific needs are met, unless there are positive grounds for not doing so.

While some YOT staff initially (and mistakenly) associated the policy with my presence in Midshire, a number of practitioners were keen to share their views on the 'gender allocation policy', as it was generally referred to. The directive met with strong and widespread discontent, much of which was directed at YOT 'management', who were thought to have imposed it without first consulting case-holding practitioners. It also provoked much debate about the 'special' status of female clients and the fact that no comparable statement was made about the needs of male or black and minority ethnic clients. The dissatisfaction of the 'restorative justice' team was the most vocal. The team consisted of one female and three male police officers, headed by a male manager, and their collective caseload included a higher proportion of female clients than most of the other YOT teams.[17] The restorative justice team had apparently resisted the policy on a number of occasions by allocating young women to male supervisors, even when the female team member had the capacity to supervise them. Objections advanced across the YOT to allocating female clients solely to female practitioners centred on two issues: first, the perception that girls will benefit from the influence of a positive male role model if their previous experience of adult males has been negative or abusive; and second, that male practitioners who do not have the opportunity to work with female clients will become deskilled and devalued. Indeed, several male staff commented that they felt that 'management' was now implying that they did not have the requisite abilities to supervise young women, despite regularly having done so before. As one police officer asserted:

> I think it's nonsense. I don't think a female necessarily could get any better from a good female worker than they could from a good male worker. [...] I'm personally very offended ... because it's an affront to my skills and abilities.
>
> (Police Officer, male, Midshire YOT)

Conversely, the protection of male staff from allegations of abuse by female clients (which I did not hear mentioned in relation to male clients) was put forward in support of the allocation of (some) young women to female practitioners. The anxiety and fear that girl clients can provoke in male workers, particularly in relation to the perceived threat of physical proximity, may result in them being subjected to a higher level of surveillance than boys (Alder and Baines, 1996; O'Neill, 2001).

Common (gendered) experiences

As I discuss in Chapter Eight, there was a widespread (though not universal) preference for female workers among the girls and young women I interviewed, either because they found women easier to talk to or because they felt uncomfortable being alone with men. By contrast, the views of professional interviewees rarely reflected these concerns; rather, practitioners and managers tended to focus primarily on their own professional development and their needs as practitioners.[18] However, a minority of professionals – and it is noteworthy that these individuals tended to be more experienced and usually female, and had backgrounds in probation and social work – did prioritise *young women's* need to feel safe and at ease, particularly in relation to disclosing information of a personal or intimate nature:

> I think [men are] always coming from a disadvantage as male supervisors, because ... in terms of ... anything sort of sexual – you know, adolescent issues – I appreciate are going to be more difficult to discuss with a male officer than with a female officer.
>
> (Probation Officer, male, Castleshire YOT)

> [Girls'] health needs, sexual needs, emotional needs, psychological needs, physical needs ... are different to those of a boy. And I think it's more likely that a woman, having experienced that herself, is likely to: (a) empathise; (b) understand; and (c) advocate for it.
>
> (Team Leader, female, Midshire YOT)

A different female team leader in Midshire suggested, conversely, that male staff would be 'let off the hook', in terms of addressing sexism, if they were not required to supervise girls, in the same way that white workers should not abdicate responsibility for addressing racism to black workers. Another senior manager unpicked some of the complexities of client–worker allocation through analogies with ethnicity and class:

> There's a number of narratives, aren't there? There's black workers who would say, just because I'm black doesn't mean that ... you can't, as a white worker, begin to appreciate some of the issues that black young people have. [...] And if you put all the black workers with black young people, then you're creating ghettoes within the Youth Offending Team. Another narrative might be black young people saying, well, this black worker actually understands my experience, so I *do* want a black worker, actually. [...] The other narrative is, he's a middle-class worker and I'm working-class, so he doesn't know anything about my experience at all. He's never lived on a council estate.
>
> (Operational manager, male, Midshire YOT)

A blanket policy of allocating girls to female workers – or indeed any other 'minority' client group to workers of a particular class, ethnic or religious background – is perhaps unwise and may, as this manager suggested, create 'ghettoes'. Moreover, many of the young women I interviewed insisted that the individual qualities of their YOT officer and the support they provided were just as important as their gender (see Chapter Eight). One might, however, question whether a girl of 14, for example, is likely (whether or not she has previously been abused) to feel comfortable on her own with a man who is socially, and most probably physically, much more powerful than she is. Clearly some young women do feel uncomfortable with male workers and, if allocated to one, the development of a productive client–worker relationship will in all likelihood be significantly compromised.[19] A growing body of empirical research attests to the importance of client–worker relationships in desistance-focused probation and youth justice practice (Batchelor and McNeill, 2005; Burnett and McNeill, 2005; Robinson, 2005; McNeill, 2006), and recent evidence regarding one-to-one supervision suggests that many women offenders prefer female supervisors (McIvor, 2007; Trotter, 2007).

While working with girls has been found to cause anxiety, particularly among female staff (A. Hudson, 1989; Worrall, 1999), women supervisors may be able to establish strong working relationships with girls on the basis of shared gendered experiences (Alder and Baines, 1996) and due to their superior understanding of 'girl stuff' (Seng and Lurigio, 2005), as a number of more experienced female practitioners emphasised:

> I think it's easier to talk to [girls]. [*Laughs*] It's much easier to go for a coffee and, with all of them, *every single one*, go and have a conversation. Whereas teenage boys are ... Anyway, all they're interested in is music that I don't know anything about [*laughs*] ... Even the chatty ones, it's harder to find a common interest.
>
> (Social Worker, female, Midshire YOT)

> Recently I did a report for a young woman [...] and ... she wanted to tell me that she wanted to go to prison. And she wanted to go to prison because she really couldn't cope. But what came out of the *What do YOU think?*[20] was, she wanted to tell me that she had tried to take her life. [...] So ... that's different sometimes, with girls. [...] I don't know whether they feel more at ease? [...] Because she felt able to talk to me. 'Because you're a woman. Because you'll know', is what she said.
>
> (Team Leader, female, Midshire YOT)

Young women were also felt to be better conversationalists than young men, and to place more emphasis on interpersonal relationships:

> I would say [girls] form relationships differently, and they place different importance on relationships than young men. And therefore a relationship with a worker is, in my view, a lot more significant for young women than it is for young men. [...] They are more open in terms of discussing and processing information. They talk, rather than ... grunt!
>
> (Operational Manager, female, Midshire YOT)

However, while young women's greater engagement in conversation, compared with their stereotypically monosyllabic brothers, has been linked with greater disclosure of problems to probation and youth justice officers, assumptions that girls and women *will* or *must* talk may mean that reluctance to do so is perceived as a failure to respond to supervision (Worrall, 1990: 125). One study found that the majority of probation officers admitted that they 'talked to girls more', but many felt uncomfortable 'acting like counsellors' (Gaarder *et al.*, 2004: 568). In England and Wales, in an increasingly managerialist youth justice climate with the attendant pressures of expanding caseloads, YOT workers may be ambivalent about how much time they wish to spend 'just' talking. Furthermore, while client–worker relationships are undoubtedly important, they are not everything. As one practitioner put it, 'we work with [girls] for ever, and don't achieve an awful lot, but we have good relationships'.

More difficult to work with?

Many professionals, consistent with previous studies,[21] considered girls to be more difficult to work with than boys, and some found girls particularly demanding of their time and energy. Paradoxically, it was almost always female practitioners – including those who also stated that they *liked* working with girls – who found girls more taxing, as this drug and alcohol worker, who ran a Girls' Group in Midshire YOT, described:

> [Girls] are a lot more demanding, and remember all the things you say. [They] can become too dependent as well. So you have to really be careful when you're working with them about how much you see them and about how much you're gonna call them, because otherwise they end up ringing you up and [asking] 'have you done this for me yet?'

Conversely, several other interviewees had positive recollections of young women who had telephoned them after their court order had ended to seek advice, or simply to let them know how they were getting on.

As discussed in greater detail later in this chapter, several practitioners drew attention to young women's emotional articulacy which, some believed, means that girls' needs and problems are more likely to be expressed and come to light. This might create the illusion that girls are more needy, and thus that YOT practitioners have to work harder to meet their needs. The perception that one 'has to do more' with girls created significant anxiety for some which, again, may have been exacerbated by an increase in the quantity of external audit and inspection in contemporary youth justice practice which, many interviewees felt, had significantly reduced the amount of time they were able to spend doing face-to-face work with young people.[22] A female YOT officer [YO] in Midshire highlighted this predicament and the consequent ambivalence she felt about working with young women:

YO: I always think, another female, help! It's going to be more work! [...] And I think the females with behavioural problems, in particular, seem to be ... Oh, I just dread it, because ... That's awful, isn't it? Because I know it's very difficult, then, to break down barriers with them, even as a female [...].

GS: What you were saying about dreading it, it seems to be connected in a way to the National Standards, volume of work, lack of staff thing as well.

YO: Yes, it is … It's definitely connected with that, yeah. 'Cause actually, I enjoy working with females as much, really'.

Female practitioners sometimes indicated that they found young women more interesting to work with than young men due to their superior self-awareness and communication skills:

I like [girls] because you can get into their head. And if you can get them talking, they have a deeper understanding of how they operate than a boy would. [… With] a girl, you can actually get in and talk … very much quicker than you can with a boy. They let you in a lot quicker. [Girls] do have a greater innate understanding. […] And there is a distinct way of communicating which is different.

(YOT Officer, female, Castleshire)

However, the line between interesting and emotionally demanding was a fine one, as one practitioner highlighted:

[Girls are] more verbal. They're more emotionally unstable, I would say. And practitioners find that quite difficult to deal with. [*Later in interview*] I've become much more … personally, individually, emotionally involved with the girls' cases than I have with the boys. 'Cause it's harder [. . .]. The cases are so involved. It's more damaging to the individual practitioner, working with girls [*laughs*]. Yeah, without a doubt … More emotionally demanding!

(Education Officer, female, Castleshire YOT)

Young women's needs and emotions appeared to be more transparent to female workers, due both to girls' greater verbal expressiveness as well as to some practitioners' superior ability – on account of their shared gendered experiences – to recognise girls' needs and problems. Paradoxically, though, this could result in censoriousness. Midshire YOT's only female police officer [PC], while stating that she found some girls 'demanding and dependent', acknowledged her heightened awareness, as a woman, of female clients' vulnerability to sexual exploitation, something which many male workers would perhaps not have noticed in the first place. This sometimes translated into her behaving more 'firmly' towards female clients, despite a benevolent intention to protect them. Not only could this have a detrimental effect on her working relationships with girls but it also presented her with a (gendered) dilemma, since she recognised the paradox of harsher treatment in the name of protection:

PC: I think sometimes females … can be harder on female kids, and whether that's because you're trying to protect them, and you know that ultimately, yes, they're probably more vulnerable than the lads. So you can be a bit firmer on them, and the girls react quite badly to that.

GS: What do you mean by 'firm'? Do you just mean, like, talking to them in a firm way?

PC: Yeah, talking to them in a firm way, and maybe giving them a bit of a bollocking, basically.

Anxieties about girls' particular vulnerabilities also led to concerns that practitioners themselves would be seen as failing if they were unable to prevent negative outcomes:

> There's this protective factor. And I think if you mess up with a girl ... then it's more obvious ... It's double standards, isn't it?
>
> (Operational Manager, female, Castleshire YOT)

Nasty and manipulative: decontextualising resistance

A further issue identified by practitioners was young women's propensity to deal with certain negative situations by being 'vile with their words'[23] instead of, or in addition to, using physical violence. Girls' 'slyness' and 'manipulativeness' meant that their behaviour was considered by some to be less straightforward, and hence more difficult to address. Very rarely did workers consider girls' apparently 'manipulative' behaviour in context. One exception was a community psychiatric nurse in Midshire YOT who, while conceding that she found girls 'more manipulative than boys', reflected that girls may learn to manipulate others as a tactic to get what they want or need while trying to survive in a male-dominated world.

Gaarder *et al.*'s recent American study of professionals involved in juvenile court decision-making similarly found that officers 'ascrib[ed] a personality trait' to undesirable behaviours: probation officers who described girls as manipulative, for example, failed to recognise manipulative behaviours as situationally contingent, but rather constructed 'the girl herself, and [...] all girls by extension, as manipulative by nature and therefore difficult to work with' (2004: 560). While delinquent boys have frequently been depicted as straightforwardly 'open' and 'honest', girls have tended to be described as 'devious', 'full of bullshit' and 'dramatic' (Baines and Alder, 1996: 481). Such perceptions have proved to be remarkably enduring.

Young women's resistance to governance within the youth justice system was rarely contextualised either. However, on the few occasions when it was, the purpose, and even the potential benefits, of girls' 'challenging' behaviour became apparent:

> [Girls a]re not more difficult, but perhaps more spirited, in that they're perhaps more honest, and they tell you when it's a load of rubbish and they challenge you. And perhaps they're more vocal. [...] Perhaps it means

they're just being more honest and more challenging, and I think if we had boys doing that as well, that would be a good thing.

(Team Leader, female, Castleshire YOT)

Given the lack of power and status enjoyed by teenage girls in general, and the lack of social capital among working-class and criminalised girls in particular, young women's apparently 'manipulative' behaviour might sometimes be best understood as resistance to control and constraint, and as a means of exercising agency by individuals whose rights and opportunities are restricted by virtue of their age, gender, class and 'race'.

(In)visible troubles and emotional articulacy

In the first part of this chapter, I argued that youth justice practitioners tend to consider offending girls and young women (and their families) to be both more emotionally troubled than their male counterparts and to have more 'welfare' needs. A number of practitioners believed, however, that the *perception* that young women have more 'baggage' is due, at least in part, to girls' superior self-awareness (compared with that of boys) and their consequent ability to identify and articulate their emotions and needs:

[Boys] don't express their emotions in the same way. They don't express their feelings, and they can't verbalise [them]. So they're not telling you ... because they can't identify what the problems are. [...] But with a girl, quite often, they will have identified it. And they will express it.

(Education Officer, female, Castleshire YOT)

One of the most significant implications of both young women's superior capacity for emotional expression, as well as certain (usually female) workers' apparently intuitive ability to recognise girls' needs, is that girls may appear to be complex and complicated, and hence practitioners may perceive them to be time-consuming and difficult to work with. Moreover, the apparent 'neediness' of female clients may translate into a perceived necessity to do more, or 'over-intervene', with girls, in an attempt to meet their complex needs:

We find it very much easier to tune into *need* in relation to the girls. [...] The girls arguably get more because arguably the girls need more. But actually, I might want to argue that the boys have equivalent – not *same*, but *equivalent* – needs, that don't get met. [...] If we are misperceiving level of need ... yes, girls are more time-consuming. [...] Because we are perceiving their needs and trying to meet them. And we're not doing that for the boys, arguably.

(Team Leader, female, Midshire YOT)

[Girls' ability to verbalise their needs] poses a risk for over-intervention with girls. And I think that practitioners – and I'm as guilty of it as anyone else – get drawn in by the very complex nature of the presentation of a young girl that you're working with.

(Education Officer, female, Castleshire YOT)

One possible reason why young women's welfare needs are often not addressed before they come to the attention of the youth justice system might be because their needs go unnoticed earlier, and thus remain invisible, due to girls' ability to contain or manage their problems until they reach crisis point. Some practitioners felt that many girls had 'exploded' into the youth justice system, their problems only having become visible after they had been arrested. This apparent paradox may be related to externalising behaviours being less common among pre-adolescent girls (Rutter *et al.*, 1998; Moffitt *et al.*, 2001), who are more likely to exhibit psychological problems or to 'bottle things up' in the face of distress, not least due to prevailing social expectations that girls should manage their difficulties without complaint. What is more, girls' 'difficult' behaviour at school may be less visible than that of boys (McLaughlin, 1991). For these reasons, some professionals felt that girls were often in crisis by the time they came to the attention of the youth justice system:

[When] we do pick the girls up … in terms of their … emotional state … how dysfunctional their families are, and how much disintegration … and family strife there is … they'd be far further down the road … than when we pick the boys up. [… I]n my experience, girls will manage a situation for a lot longer, and be emotionally strong, and be able to hold on with the situation for a lot longer. And then, when it does crash, and it does snap, it tends to explode.

(Education Officer, female, Castleshire YOT)

Young girls' behaviour isn't always visible to everybody … If they're sexually promiscuous, they're drunk, they're using drugs … that might be a night-time thing. And then … when they get to thirteen, fourteen, it then affects their school work. […] So you do think, well, why haven't they come to notice beforehand? […] But whereas boys might be aggressive in the playground, and shout out, and hit other people, with girls it's quieter … and then all of a sudden …!

(YISP worker, female, Castleshire)

It is important to note that professionals did not relate these 'explosions' to girls' *offending* behaviour, but to their problems or welfare needs more broadly conceived. They were thus often believed to have entered the criminal justice system, as discussed earlier, by default, since their needs had not been met (and perhaps not even recognised) by either mainstream or specialist education and social welfare agencies. I interviewed two senior managers in a voluntary organisation that provided services mainly to persistent and/or serious young offenders on behalf of Midshire YOT. Describing many of the young women they had worked with over the years as particularly 'difficult' and 'extreme', the managers highlighted girls' mental health problems, their 'rebellious' behaviour, abuse and self-harm as common themes. However, they also stressed that many of their female clients were 'not really offenders', but that inappropriate criminal justice responses to their 'naughty' or 'nuisance' behaviour had led to it escalating to the point where it had been criminalised. Whether young women are more criminally inclined today, rather than simply a nuisance, or whether 'naughty' girls are subjected to more formalised forms of social, or criminal, control than previously is the subject of the next section.

Are girls getting 'worse'?

In Chapter One, I discussed the substantial moral panic that was generated in Britain, as well as further afield, during the first decade of the twenty-first century, fuelled by apparent statistical 'evidence' that young women's offending, and particularly their violence, had increased dramatically. Although the 'girls are getting worse' thesis has been subjected to rigorous analysis elsewhere and found wanting (Steffensmeier *et al.*, 2005; Carrington, 2006; Sprott and Doob, 2009; see Chapter Three), little attention has been paid to whether media-promulgated moral panics about 'ladettes' and girl violence have infiltrated professional youth justice discourse. To this end, I asked professionals whether they believed the number of girls referred to them by the police and appearing before their local youth courts was increasing and, if so, how they accounted for this rise. Their views were complex and sometimes contradictory: interviewees frequently voiced uncertainty as to whether the visible increase in female bodies in the youth justice system was a result of widespread behavioural decline, or a social construct driven (partly or entirely) by changes in legislation and in the processing of youthful misbehaviour.

The trouble with girls today: more criminal ...?

Of the (20) practitioners who discussed the possibility that a genuine, rather than artefactual, increase in female youthful lawbreaking had occurred in recent years, more than half believed that this was the case, while one-fifth believed that it was not. The remaining six interviewees were either unsure or expressed ambivalent or contradictory opinions. Professionals with fewer years' experience of youth justice, as well as male interviewees, were more likely to be of the opinion that girls are 'getting worse'. Those who felt that girls today are more violent than their older sisters – and again, proportionately more male than female practitioners were of this opinion – strongly supported the 'masculinisation' hypothesis: namely, that girls' (offending) behaviour is increasingly resembling that of boys.[24]

Some interviewees expressed the view that increases in alcohol consumption by young women have been the driving force behind what media reports and some politicians have portrayed as a 'rising tide' of female youth violence. Conversely, a minority, most of whom were more experienced female professionals, felt that alcohol plays no greater role in female offending now than hitherto; instead, they blamed the attention conferred upon female binge drinking by the media, as well as the aggressive marketing of alcohol to young women. As one health professional explained:

> At the end of the day, I don't think anybody did any research ten years ago to the extent of binge drinking. [... T]he other way to look at it is it's being encouraged by society. Happy Hours and ... advertising women drinking and, you know, it's the sex appeal. [...] I mean, it probably is more socially acceptable, or it's, you know, frowned upon, depending on what article you're reading, really.
>
> (Community Psychiatric Nurse, female, Midshire YOT)

Scottish research by Jamieson and colleagues similarly found that criminal justice professionals believed that young women were becoming increasingly involved in offending – due both to increases in their drug use and to 'contemporary cultural influences which encouraged girls' identification with attitudes and behaviour traditionally associated with boys' (1999: 48). In the current study, professionals who supported the notion of a general increase in offending by adolescent females (that is, a rise in *all* types of lawbreaking, and not just acts of violence) tended to implicate girls' greater visibility in the public arena, which they believed was the outcome of a concordance of female and male social roles:

> Over the years, girls have become more ... equal to men, inasmuch that opportunity has become more equal. Girls aren't expected to stay at home and be housewives now. They are expected to go out and get careers. [...] And if there's not ... those same differentials between males and females in society, then it would follow that there's not going to be those differentials between crime rates between males and females as well. At a guess. I don't know. It must be a factor, you know?
>
> (Police Officer, male, Midshire YOT)

This police officer's concluding acknowledgement that his views were based on guesswork, rather than evidence, is instructive. Indeed, staff frequently stated or implied that they *did not know for sure* whether, and to what extent, real changes in girls' behaviour have occurred. The accounts of many professionals revealed that they had nonetheless been influenced by media and cultural stereotypes that gender role convergence, or 'equal opportunities', *must be a factor* in the widely publicised 'rise' in young women's offending.

... or subjected to more intensive social control?

Conversely, a smaller group of practitioners, all of whom had many years' professional experience in the field, believed that the net-widening effects of an 'arbitrary target' (Bateman, 2008b) to increase sanction detections (see Chapter Three), as well as a shift away from diversion to early intervention (and concomitant criminalisation), were entirely responsible for the increase in officially recorded female youth crime. These professionals highlighted the necessity that all incidents encountered by the police, however trivial, must 'hit paper' (in the words of one police officer). In addition, the criminalisation of playground fights and 'kicking off' in children's homes were emphasised as being particularly relevant, as another police officer explained:

> The classic is playground fights … which are coming in more and more and more and more. The police's hands are tied because obviously, in terms of sanction detections, and all the rest of it … when somebody says, I want to make a complaint about this … there has to be an end result to it. But two days later, the same young people that have made the complaint – or, you know, committed the assault – are best buddies again.
>
> (Police Officer, male, Castleshire YOT)

Moreover, several YOT professionals highlighted how, over a very short period, legislative changes resulting in greater interventionism, or 'mesh-thinning' (Cohen, 1985), had swollen the number of young people coming through the courts. One manager who had previously been a youth justice practitioner in the Diversion Unit, a precursor to Midshire YOT,[25] explained how just a few years earlier, a young person who might have received two or more cautions or even an informal warning would now be charged rather sooner than was previously the case:

> The system that we've got is actually so tight at the lower end that it just pushes young people into the criminal justice system much quicker than ever it did before. And that was something that I found, certainly, when I came into the YOT. […] A fortnight before, I would have been writing a report to the police suggesting that this young person be dealt with informally, that I'd been out to see the victim, that there'd been a resolution in terms of the offence. And a fortnight later – for the same offence, possibly – I would be writing a PSR report, and that young person would be in the court system.
>
> (Education Manager, female, Midshire YOT)

Several practitioners criticised what they considered to be increasing systemic intolerance towards juvenile misdemeanours – as evidenced particularly in the erosion of police discretion in arrest decision-making – which had, they believed, resulted in young women being arrested for 'silly offences', where perhaps they might previously have been given a 'second chance':

> There'll be a vast amount of kids – especially girls – who just won't be able to go into teaching, even … If you've got a bright young girl who's going to stay on and do her GCSEs and her 'A' levels, and she's committed a silly offence, or gone off the rails slightly … got drunk on a Saturday night, and she's had a final warning or a referral order, then that's it. She can kiss goodbye to that sort of work. […] We all make mistakes, but they'll be labelled as a criminal.
>
> (Police Officer, male, Midshire YOT)

Looking back further, Midshire YOT's manager acknowledged how, historically, police chivalry had sometimes meant that girls' crimes, and particularly offences typically associated with males, had been overlooked:

> In the past what we've seen is that the police were more inclined to divert young women than they were young men. [...] I could give examples ... where four youngsters have been involved in a TWOC[26] – one female or two females in that group. The lads are done for the TWOC, and the girls are done for allowing to be carried ... That was even the case on one occasion that I can remember when one of the girls was driving the car!

Several interviewees – notably senior practitioners and managers in Midshire, where, historically, there had been a strong ideological commitment to diverting young offenders away from court – felt that the pendulum had swung too far in the opposite direction. Midshire YOT's Manager, for example, suggested that police training in 'equal opportunities', misconstrued as a need to treat everybody the same, has ultimately led to the criminalisation of greater numbers of young women. Another manager with several decades' experience noted how the channels through which girls are processed had changed over time:

> If you ... looked at a court list twenty years ago and saw some of the offences that females were before the courts for, and then looked at them now ... [girls] may well not be charged with offences in the same way that they were twenty years ago. They may have been put through the welfare system or the mental health system in a slightly different way than they are now.
>
> (Operational Manager, male, Midshire YOT)

As noted above, there was considerable confusion among professionals as to whether national statistics signalling a sharp rise in girls' offending – the effects of which they saw reflected in their expanding weekly court lists – indicated a deterioration in girls' behaviour, or were rather the result of decreased tolerance towards young women, and towards female violence in particular. One manager oscillated between these contrasting explanations:

> I think there *is* an issue about girls' behaviour changing. [...] I think girls are drinking more. [...] Where you'd see a group of boys on the street corner with alcopops you'll now see a group of girls. [...] And this whole sort of ladette ... I mean, I don't know. I just don't know how much of it is media. [...] I don't know whether it's always been happening, or whether, you know, suddenly there's this concentration on it, this ladette culture ... and girls in gangs.
>
> (Team Leader, female, Midshire YOT)

While some professionals were sceptical about habitual media headlines declaring that increasing numbers of girls are turning into binge-drinking, violent 'ladettes', others had clearly accepted such moral panics relatively uncritically, assuming that there can be no smoke without fire. Real and dramatic rises in the number of young women appearing before the courts, due to decreases in diversion and increases in prosecution for minor offences, and the consequently heightened visibility of young female defendants, appeared to have encouraged the belief among some practitioners that girls today are more delinquent than their mothers or grandmothers ever were. At the same time, others struggled to reconcile their day-to-day experiences of working with needy and vulnerable girls with these popular stereotypes.

Professionals' perspectives on girls' pathways out of crime

Girls' and women's pathways out of crime has received little theoretical attention, and empirical research on desistance has tended to focus only on women who have previously been incarcerated (Eaton, 1993; Giordano *et al.*, 2002). Offending is restricted to the adolescent years for the majority of female offenders, and more so than for their male counterparts (Moffitt *et al.*, 2001). Girls and young women may also have a particular investment in consigning their 'criminal' selves to the past: the stigma of a criminal record at a transitional stage in their lives may be particularly strongly felt by young women, for whom an offending identity may be negatively associated with social recognition, particularly as they grow older (Barry, 2007).

Several professionals believed that girls have an attitudinal head start, as far as desistance is concerned, since they are more likely than boys to experience guilt and express remorse:

> I would say more of the girls want to move on, and maybe have a career, than the guys. [*Later in interview*] I think women – and probably girls as well – probably feel more guilty and do have morals. Whereas I think with the lads they basically, a lot of them, have a I-don't-give-a-shit attitude.
>
> (Police Officer, female, Midshire YOT)

> [Girls] are harder on themselves than boys. [...] The offending bit ... it horrifies them. Whereas for boys it's like, 'Yeah, well, I nicked a car, or I did this'. Boys are a bit more blasé about it. [...] The girls ... they don't brag about it in the same way as the boys do ... It's like, 'Why did I do that?' You know? 'I'm so ashamed'. And they're ... crucifying themselves, really, whereas the boys are, 'So what'?
>
> (Community Psychiatric Nurse, female, Midshire YOT)

Boys' boasting about their illegal exploits may, of course, reflect cultural expectations about working-class expressions of masculinity, rather than necessarily being indicative of a lack of shame or remorse. Many professionals also believed that girls, in contrast to their male peers, do not generally commit offences in order to gain recognition or kudos from their friends. Consequently, some practitioners thought that young women have a stronger desire to consign their offending to the past:

> For boys [offending is] kudos, I suppose. It's acceptance, being part of the peer group. With girls, it's more like something that happened. And girls tend to look at it as a one-off episode, rather than leading to other episodes. So they're more positive about stopping offending.
>
> (YOT officer, male, Castleshire)

The accounts of many of the girls I interviewed (see Chapter Six) contradicted this view. However, most resisted self-identifying as 'criminal' and did not see themselves as 'real' offenders. Importantly, interventionist and zero tolerance youth justice policies, which, as discussed in Chapter Three, have drawn girls disproportionately into the formal youth justice system in England and Wales, may well impede young women's ability to see their offending as just 'something that happened'.

Several practitioners believed that criminalised young women generally want to improve their situation and plan a better, brighter future for themselves and their (future) children:

> Boys, on the whole, seem to think that they will be OK ... So what if they ain't got a job, you know? 'My old man didn't have a job. Grandad hadn't got a job. So what?' [...] Whereas girls seem to get quite despondent in those situations. They'll actually ... want to get out of the crap that they see themselves in. They ... want to be in a position where ... they can have a family and they can provide for the family, and they can care for the family. [... I]f they've had a rough upbringing they want things to be better for their kids. And so they're ... thinking ahead. Whereas boys are, 'Well, I've got a fiver in my pocket now. So what?' You know, not thinking about tomorrow.
>
> (YOT Manager, female, Midshire)[27]

This YOT manager's point about (working-class) girls' frequent desire to have a family whose members they can care for echoes Monica Barry's contention that generativity – passing on care, attention or support to others, including by bringing up one's own children – is a significant channel through which young women, in particular, are able to desist from further offending (Barry, 2007: 34–7; see also Rumgay, 2004b).

Pregnancy and childbirth: an ambiguous inclusionary strategy

Many professionals – particularly those in Midshire, where I also interviewed a number of pregnant young women – highlighted the significance of pregnancy in some girls' decisions to stop offending. Practitioners saw young women's motivations for (planned) pregnancy as, variously, someone to love them unconditionally, a way of attracting attention in the context of low self-esteem, a means of getting housed[28] and, above all, facilitating the acquisition of social recognition or 'a sense of standing':

> A baby is the answer to everything, 'cause it's theirs. It's gonna love them unconditionally ... And then there's other factors, like it'll help them get a house. [...] A lot of them [have] been in care and just want out, and it's a way out for them. And it's a big attention thing. When you're pregnant you get so much attention. [...] It becomes the talk of the town ... And we all like to be talked about.
>
> (Drug and Alcohol Worker, female, Midshire YOT)

> ... that whole thing about girls wanting children isn't just about ... I want to reproduce. I think it is about having a stake, because then I have status. I am a mother. [...] I share that with other women in society as a kind of rite of passage, and there's so few rites of passage for kids these days. [...] The passage into adulthood is quite fractured.
>
> (Operational Manager, male, Midshire YOT)

Importantly, and as some of the girls' accounts confirmed (see Chapter Five), pregnancy and motherhood could signal an abrupt end to offending, as this YOT worker's recollection of one particular young woman illustrates:

> I had one [girl who] was one of the most prolific, out of control ... drinking [...] drugs, burgling her family ... Mum wouldn't let her in the house unless she was there. Chaos! She'd been raped. Her ex-boyfriend was a vile guy. He was in prison. Her dad wanted nothing to do with her ... She got pregnant, and she just sorted herself out, totally. It was unbelievable! [...] She ended up back at home, sorted. She hadn't re-offended. She was off the drink. [...] You almost *wish* your kids were getting pregnant!
>
> (YOT Officer, female, Castleshire)

Despite its association with desistance from crime (Graham and Bowling, 1995; Jamieson *et al.*, 1999; Barry, 2007) – and several other practitioners joked about the potential benefits of encouraging pregnancy among their female clients – the reality that teenage pregnancy may well further constrain young women's future prospects was also recognised:

> One of the reasons that a lot of young girls get pregnant is they have no other aim in life. They've been failed, often, by the education system. [...] So they've got no focus. They've got no ambition to get out there and get an education or get a good job. And this is their way out. This is their way of getting the income and accommodation and independence. And someone that will love them. [...] Children who have got an ambition, that's the last thing *they* want, because they know they'll never realise their ambition with that commitment.
>
> (Probation Officer, female, Midshire YOT)

Walkerdine and colleagues have similarly noted that teenage motherhood is largely confined to the working classes principally because 'no middle-class girl serious about her academic attainment would be allowed or would allow herself to get pregnant' (2001: 188). For young working-class female (ex-)offenders, getting pregnant is an ambiguous inclusionary strategy. There is a real risk that, while becoming a mother may allow young women (ex-)lawbreakers to relinquish the stigma associated with being a female offender, very young uncoupled mothers are exposed to a different, but no less stigmatising, form of scrutiny associated with dominant discourses that construct teenage single mothers as feckless, promiscuous, welfare scroungers.[29] Moreover, the material poverty that frequently accompanies lone motherhood may propel some young women into (further) acquisitive offending, when the statutory supports that teenage mothers are entitled to cease to be available.[30] While there may be widespread cultural support for young women, whether or not they have children, to stop offending – or, more accurately, perhaps, lawbreaking by females attracts sufficient social opprobrium to strongly discourage them from *continuing to offend* – the structural prerequisites of both desistance and social inclusion are not always in place for young mothers.

Conclusion

In this chapter, I have examined the perspectives of practitioners and managers employed in youth justice and related fields regarding the aetiology of young women's offending, their reflections on working with young female lawbreakers and their beliefs about whether or not girls' behaviour has been getting 'worse' in recent years.

The professionals' explanations of the causes of girls' offending tended to prioritise family pathology and individualised 'risk factors' – in particular, the 'baggage' that offending girls and young women were thought to be carrying – over and above the social–structural factors that, as Chapter Five demonstrated, constrain the life chances of youth justice system-involved young women. Moreover, many practitioners and managers personalised girls' 'problems' – manifested as low self-esteem, (sexual) vulnerability and drug and alcohol misuse – and discursively reconstructed the social–structural disadvantages that criminalised young women face as individualised deficits, thereby disconnecting girls' needs and problems from the contexts in which they originate. Practitioners' common belief that girls, more so than boys, are emotionally articulate and proficient at expressing their needs often meant that they found young women more demanding and more difficult to work with. Managerialist imperatives associated with the 'new' youth justice system – inspection and audit requirements and a concomitant increase in the volume of administrative tasks they were required to undertake – seemed to exacerbate the anxieties that many associated with working with girls.

I presented evidence that moral panics purporting that 'girls are getting worse' have, to some extent, entered the professional youth justice imagination. While practitioners tended to privilege family and individual factors in their explanations of young women's offending, and also to highlight what they believed to be the greater salience of such factors in girls' than in boys' offending, many were also of the opinion that girls' behaviour has changed for the worse and that today's young women are more criminally inclined than their older sisters were. However, a minority of more experienced practitioners blamed an increasingly interventionist and punitive youth justice system and the net-widening effects of changes in policing for artefactually elevating recorded female youth crime.

Many practitioners believed that girls who offend express more guilt and remorse than males and that they are consequently better able to desist from further offending. However, the interventionist thrust of contemporary youth justice in England and Wales may hamper young women's ability to grow out of crime. Although a number of YOT professionals highlighted the role of policing practices in criminalising 'naughty' girls, very few acknowledged that they themselves might play a part in accelerating female lawbreakers through the youth justice system. I return to this topic in the following chapter.

Note

* This chapter is an extended version of the following article: 'The Trouble with Girls Today: Professional Perspectives on Young Women's Offending', *Youth Justice* (vol 9(3), pp. 255–270), published by Sage Publications Ltd.

8 Youth justice for girls in the twenty-first century?

The criminalising consequences for girls of the contemporary youth justice system were highlighted in Chapter Three, where I argued that the new institutional focus on risk and prevention through youth justice intervention (as opposed to via welfare or diversionary mechanisms), in combination with managerialist imperatives to 'get tough' on crime, has served to artificially inflate the population of 'criminal' young women in England and Wales. Most important here during the 2000s was the formal policing and 'upcriming' of youthful misdemeanours which would previously have been either ignored or resolved informally, partly in response to targets to increase the number of 'offences brought to justice' (OBTJ). I also drew attention to the ways in which the antisocial behaviour agenda, with its preoccupation with governing the street life of marginalised young people, has accelerated the criminalisation of girls.

Chapter Seven showed how popular claims that a 'new' criminal girl has emerged in recent years, combined with the increased visibility of young women in the courts, have together encouraged the belief among many youth justice professionals that girls *must* be worse than they used to be. At the same time, practitioners highlighted the significant vulnerabilities of their female clients and the fact that their needs had often been invisible, and thus unmet, prior to their entry into the youth justice system.

In this chapter, I examine the workings of the 'new', prevention-focused youth justice system 'on the ground' from the contrasting perspectives of two key 'stakeholder' groups: criminalised young women and youth justice practitioners. In the first part of the chapter, I return to the 52 girls and young women who were the subjects of Chapters Five and Six, and examine their experiences both of policing and regulation on the streets and of youth justice supervision, including their views about 'what works', and what does not, in terms of the services they had received from youth justice and other agencies. The second part of the chapter focuses on the contrasting beliefs of the youth justice practitioners in the study, which differed from those of the girls in many important respects. I explore the possibility that an unintended consequence of the 'benevolent' and protectionist intentions of youth justice professionals – both those who deliver traditional 'post-crime' supervision and those responsible for 'pre-crime' intervention in the name of preventing future offending – is that their actions may contribute directly to the criminalisation of their female clients.

Youth justice? The young women's perspectives

As I noted in Chapter Six, the young women in the study generally referred to their lawbreaking as 'getting into trouble'. Running through their accounts was a common assertion that the unwanted attention of the police, as well as scrutiny by community members, was at least as problematic as their own behaviour. Consequently, many felt a 'sense of injustice' (Matza, 1964) about what they perceived to be unnecessary adult interference in their social lives.[1] Disengagement and exclusion from school were common features in the girls' backgrounds, as were family adversities of various kinds. Together, these factors led some young women to spend their considerable amounts of free time on the streets, where they believed that their activities were subject to heavy-handed policing and surveillance.

Perceptions of policing and adult interference

A recurrent feature in the young women's accounts of their brushes with the law was that police officers, teachers and adult neighbours or members of the public 'bothered' them and paid closer attention to their movements than to those of others on account of their own or family members' 'reputation', or simply because of their age and use of public space.[2] Kayleigh, for example, was convinced that certain police officers 'had it in for' her, and that they were 'always tr[ying] to get me done for stuff that I haven't even done'. Others complained similarly that adult officials, in particular the police, regularly criminalised their attempts to carve out some kind of social life for themselves – a social life that was particularly hard to achieve given the social, education, spatial and economic exclusions they faced, and above all because of their status as minors. Those who had committed relatively non-serious offences in public space were most likely to claim that the police expended a disproportionate amount of time and energy 'bothering' or 'bugging' them when there were bigger fish – 'real' criminals – to fry: such girls considered themselves particularly 'unlucky' to have been arrested and labelled criminal. These laments must of course also be understood in the context of their frequently having 'got away with' offending, particularly shoplifting, and their knowledge that their peers usually got away with it too.[3]

Young women who saw themselves as 'unlucky' had often been involved in fights with other girls – situations which they considered to be 'six of one and half a dozen of the other'. Dionne (18), who had been convicted of affray jointly with another young woman, believed that she had acted in self-defence and that the 'victim' who, according to Dionne, had 'started' the small group fight, had 'got lucky in court'. Erin (16) also considered herself unlucky to have been charged with assault for pulling the hair of a girl who was fighting with Erin's friend over a boy. Demonstrating a level of insight not untypical among the girls interviewed, Erin commented that many more young people get into trouble today than previously because people are quicker to involve the police in interpersonal disputes. She believed that in the past, the mothers of girls caught fighting with each other would have resolved such disputes themselves.

It was clear that popular stereotypes and demonising discourses constructing working-class teenagers as 'undisciplined' and 'lawless' (Goldson, 1997; Pearson, 1983) tainted the girls' opinions of adults in authority, and meant that they experienced their treatment by criminal justice professionals, and sometimes adults in general, as an abuse of power and lacking legitimacy. Anna (15) explained that if adults in her village saw her and her friends in the street, they would call the police and report that 'there's a bunch of yobs outside our house. Can you come and get them?' Charlie's indignation, too, was fairly typical: she conceptualised her own and her friends' behaviour as a normal, youthful response to boredom, which was unfairly policed and criminalised. Charlie believed that local residents complained excessively about their behaviour and that they would 'always' call the police 'for some silly reason. [...] We get done for just shouting, being noisy, sitting in flats. [...] Wherever we are, the police are usually there'. Charlie, who was standing trial for an Anti-Social Behaviour Order, stated: 'I ain't that bad. They've said I'm a persistent young offender, but I ain't that bad'.

Crawford (2009a, 2009b) has drawn attention to the governance of British young people through antisocial behaviour legislation and to new, predominantly civil, powers that have resulted in the widespread criminalisation of youthful socialisation, at the same time as eroding 'established criminal justice principles ... of due process, proportionality and special protections traditionally afforded to young people' (Crawford, 2009a: 810). The girls' views of policing, in particular, also echoed findings from the Edinburgh Study of Youth Transitions, which indicate that young person–police contact is predicted most strongly by a child's previous 'form': in other words, police officers tend to target the 'usual suspects', who are typically lower-class children from 'broken' families living in socially deprived areas. According to the Edinburgh research, a young person, once labelled a troublemaker, becomes 'part of the permanent suspect population', which 'serves to stigmatize certain groups of youngsters ... and importantly appears to have damaging consequences for young people's behaviour' (McAra and McVie, 2005: 26–7) in terms of deviancy amplification (Lemert, 1972). McAra and McVie found that gender was more or less irrelevant in predicting whether a young person had adversarial contact with the police. Nevertheless, boys constituted a majority of the suspect population in Edinburgh on account of their previous collective 'form'. The current study suggests that the 'usual suspects' are likely to be female as well as male.

Some girls felt that the police did not take them seriously, simply on account of their age. Jordan (15) had kicked the wing mirror off the car of a drunken man who had repeatedly hit her friend, also a teenage girl. Jordan was subsequently charged with criminal damage, but the car owner was not apprehended. When I asked her why she and her friend did not report him to the police, Jordan stated, 'I think they wouldn't listen to us. They'd rather believe a grown person, I think'. It is important to remember that a significant proportion of the girls had been victims of abuse and violence at the hands of adults (see Chapter Five) and, in most cases, the perpetrators of such violence had not been brought to justice. In the school context, the majority of the young women had been formally excluded from school, or else had opted out of education either because they felt that school had little to offer them or because school was not a safe place for them, emotionally and/or physically. Together, these experiences may well have contributed to a belief that official tolerance thresholds are significantly lower for children than for adults: young people who misbehave are not tolerated or treated with respect, yet abusive adults can mistreat children with impunity.

Subjective assessments of interactions with the police are of particular significance for working-class young people who, due to their frequent occupation of public space, experience high levels of police contact. Young people who report previous negative contact with the police – interactions which they view as harsh and unfair – have, unsurprisingly, been found to consider police officers to have less legitimacy (Fagan and Tyler, 2005; Hinds, 2007). Moreover, individuals' perceptions of legitimacy play an important role in their compliance with rules (Tyler, 1990), and there is evidence of a relationship between poor evaluations of the legitimacy of the police and the courts by young people and higher rates of self-reported offending (Fagan and Tyler, 2005).

Many of the girls made 'spontaneous downward social comparisons' (Taylor, 1989) between themselves and 'real' criminals, who were commonly perceived to be dangerous men who commit serious violent and premeditated crimes in cold blood. Reliance on such cultural stereotypes enabled them to minimise their own misdeeds by favourable comparison:

> I wouldn't call myself an offender. I just think of myself as stupid, really ... unlucky. [...] I don't go out of my way to cause people harm. And, to be fair, that's what most offenders do. (April, 16)

> The real criminals have done murder and everything. We're doing petty crimes.
>
> (Emily, 15)

The fact that none of the girls had been convicted of murder, and very few had 'gone out of their way' to cause harm to others, enabled most of the young women to resist identifying as 'criminal'. Indeed, in their accounts of their law-breaking, they frequently excused, neutralised or otherwise downplayed the criminality of their deeds, as illustrated by their habitual use of the relatively innocuous term, 'trouble'. Rather than indicating a failure to take responsibility for one's actions, such cognitive 'tricks' may serve a useful self-protective function: by resisting the stigma of the '*real* offender', individuals in trouble with the law are 'able to use this cultural belief as a way of protecting themselves against shame' (Maruna, 2001: 138). Importantly, such comparisons must also be understood against the backdrop of the increasing criminalisation of British young women in the early twenty-first century (see Chapter Three).

Perspectives on youth justice supervision

The young women in the study frequently complained that the impact of Youth Offending Team (YOT) interventions on their everyday lives was minimal and insignificant, and that they had received too little help, too late. Most maintained that the supervision requirements imposed upon them were not constructive or relevant to their lives; many wanted more advice and help, but resented the fact that support had only become available after they had entered the criminal justice system. Consistent with their complaints about boredom (see Chapter Six), they also wanted more (free) leisure and recreational activities: although very few girls had been involved in structured activity projects while subject to YOT supervision, those who had, rated them highly. Positive evaluations of YOT interventions usually related to practical, and sometimes material, assistance, such as help with finding independent accommodation (a particular strength in Midshire YOT) or with claiming state financial assistance. The personal qualities of individual workers were also frequently emphasised and half of the girls expressed a preference for a female supervisor.

Too little, too late

The majority of the young women I interviewed felt that the YOT interventions they were receiving or had received, although well intentioned, were unrelated to their social and welfare needs: specifically, they did not provide opportunities for leisure and social participation, housing advice and support or help with coming to terms with experiences of victimisation. However, despite their frequent reservations about youth justice services, most of the girls had many more positive things to say about their YOT officers than they did about social workers, who they tended to refer to as interfering 'shit stirrers', who 'twisted things'.[4] Moreover, several girls described social workers who they believed had simply given up on, or abandoned, them:

> She just didn't want nothing to do with us no more.
>
> (Rowan, 13, whose social worker
> had apparently 'disappeared' without explanation)

> [She] can't be bothered coming round mine every week.
>
> (Emily, 15, who had moved back home to live
> with her mother several months earlier, following a number
> of foster placement breakdowns, and had not seen her social worker –
> whose name she could not remember – since she had returned home)

> They said they're doing all they can for us, and then closed the case.
>
> (Charlie, 15, of a previous social worker)

These views must be understood in the context of an erosion of preventative and family support services within social services departments, whose increasingly rationed resources are narrowly concentrated on child protection and crisis intervention. Some young women acknowledged that they had rejected the support – or regulation, as many understood it – that social workers had offered them, because of their own 'bad attitude' when they were younger. However, many recalled having received little or no professional support prior to their involvement in the youth justice system, and those who had been offered help complained that welfare agencies, in particular social services, had let them down, even when they themselves had requested help. Feeling that one has been 'given up on', in view of the girls' frequent experiences of loss and disconnection, may have far-reaching emotional consequences. Few of the young women had access to mechanisms of support outside the YOT, and their own families – if they were still living with them – were not always able or willing to provide much in the way of emotional or material assistance. This left them resentful that their social and developmental needs had only been taken seriously when (and sometimes not even when) the focus of attention had shifted to their criminality and to behaviour which many considered to be relatively innocuous.

April had needed help with claiming state benefits and finding accommodation when her mother evicted her from the family home, but did not receive any support until she was convicted. She declared, 'until I became a youth offender I didn't know who to ask for help'. Isabelle had learning difficulties and mental health problems, and her relationship with her mother had been tempestuous when she was a younger teenager, which had resulted in periodic spells of homelessness for Isabelle. She described how she withdrew from school at 14 feeling that her teachers had done nothing to address the bullying she endured on account of her learning difficulties. Apparently she was offered no alternative education provision after this. Isabelle attributed the vandalism and drunk and disorderly behaviour she had engaged in when she was younger to wanting attention and 'someone to talk to … anyone' – police officers, YOT workers, even doctors in police cells – as she felt bereft of adult support.

Nineteen-year-old Kate had become homeless at 14, following a breakdown in her relationship with her mother when they moved in with her mother's new boyfriend, whom Kate disliked. She had also developed a heroin addiction. Although she had been 'sofa-surfing' at friends' (usually other addicts') homes or sleeping in stairwells, Kate had not received any official support until she was 16.[5] Kate had a mentor at school, but this relationship ceased when Kate dropped out of school due to her escalating drug use and chaotic lifestyle.

The support they were receiving from the YOT would, for almost every young woman in the sample, terminate abruptly at the end of their court order or period of statutory supervision. They often felt – unsurprisingly, perhaps, given the short duration of youth justice services most of them were receiving or had received (half of the girls were being supervised in the community for six months or less) – that YOT supervision had not effected change in their everyday circumstances:

> You only see them, like, once a week for half an hour, but when you leave you forget all about it.
>
> (Zoë, 18)

When you come off your licence you don't get anything.

(Rhiannon, 17)

They don't want you to get into trouble, but as soon as your referral order ends, you've still got nothing to do, and you're in the same situation. So you're still gonna keep on getting in trouble.

(Holly, 16)

Too easy?

In contrast to, and in spite of, recurrent avowals by the professionals I interviewed that their principal role is to help and support young offenders, as discussed later in this chapter, the girls tended to understand the purpose of the youth justice system principally as control and punishment (cf. Foucault, 1977). Tegan's confused exclamation following her meeting with the 'nice people' who made up her youth offender panel[6] illustrated these conflicting perspectives well: 'why everyone says they're trying to help you, I don't know!' The views of the young women in prison also reflected a fundamental confusion about the aims of (child) incarceration, wherein punishment is sometimes presented as 'care', and imprisonment as 'training' (see Carlen, 2002a).[7] Six of the twelve young women with current or previous experience of penal custody expressed positive opinions about it: these related to their educational achievements, the provision of counselling and staff 'trying to help' them. Seventeen-year-old Toni, together with several other young women, had harboured a stereotypical image of draconian Victorian prisons and been relieved to find that the STC was less 'scary' than she had expected. Toni had been homeless for the previous two years and was now serving her second custodial sentence. She commented that 'people could get themselves locked up just to get somewhere to sleep'.

Several girls considered YOT supervision 'too easy' and not a 'real' punishment. Zoë had found her previous community orders with the YOT 'just easy, really. It's not a punishment. They [YOT workers] were even picking me up and bringing me home' when she was required to go to her local library to make 'posters and stupid things like that', which she 'just didn't see the point of'. Rosie suggested that removing graffiti or working with old people – tasks she believed would embarrass and shame offenders – might be a more effective deterrent from further offending, while April thought that 'harsher' community service should be given to young people who had done something 'really bad'. Although April herself had been convicted of robbery, she evidently did not consider this to be a 'really bad' offence. Thus it seemed that while notions of 'populist punitiveness' (Bottoms, 1995) had infiltrated April's (and others') general views about punishment, she considered *herself* to be different from the 'really bad' people, and believed that humiliating treatment was inappropriate for her.

Relationships with workers

Despite having much to say about the shortcomings – and occasionally the benefits – of the activity requirements of their court orders and final warnings, the principal determinant of a young woman's evaluation of the quality of YOT interventions was her relationship with individual workers.[8] Highly rated worker attributes included trustworthiness, 'being there' to talk to and the ability to understand girls' own lives and experiences – 'knowing where we come from', as Letitia put it. Workers' personal characteristics and qualities in these areas appeared to be much more important than their professional background or role.

'Just talking' and completing worksheets were unpopular, although they perhaps reflected the pressures of work on staff with large caseloads. Some girls attributed their non-compliance with community orders to them being a 'waste of time'. Sharelle (16), who was in custody when I met her, had been breached and sentenced to custody for not attending appointments on an intensive (community) supervision and surveillance programme (ISSP). She complained that:

All [the ISSP team] ever did was just sit there in a little box room talking about nothing. So I didn't bother going.

Case worker gender was important for half of the girls I asked (cf. practitioners' views in Chapter Seven), and almost all of these preferred female workers on the grounds that women are easier to talk to, 'understand where you're coming from', and because 'girls don't talk to blokes'. Chloë (15) was glad that her YOT worker was not a man. She elucidated:

I definitely couldn't talk to a man. I prefer talking to a lady. I feel more confident talking to [female YOT officer]. I don't think the girls would really let their feelings out to a man.

Previous experience of abuse by men, as well as a generalised fear and distrust of males, was also an important consideration for young women like Jessica, who did not want a male worker because 'if you're on your own in a room, you don't know what they're gonna do'. Some girls gave specific examples of 'good' male workers, however, and there was no universal support for a blanket policy of female-only case allocation.[9] Nevertheless, it was clear that female workers were 'better' for a significant number of the young women, which indicates that same-gender caseworker allocation merits serious consideration for female youth justice clients, at the very least to ensure that girls feel safe.

Several young women who were reluctant to trust or engage with professionals, or who resented what they perceived to be the officialdom of YOT workers, spoke very positively about lay mentors or befrienders with whom they had become involved via their school or YOT.[10] Melissa (16) heaped praise on her resettlement and aftercare provision[11] worker, who she believed 'understood' her because he too had spent time in prison. This contrasted with her experience of YOT workers:

Some workers are just, like, posh, and they don't know what it's like. [...] They just think that they can tell you what to do [. . . and] they stereotype people.

Laura was generally unimpressed with the YOT supervision she had received in the past and characterised it as 'interference': she suspected that YOT workers disclose information to the police if young people discuss their offending with them. However, she talked at length about how much she had gained from her long-standing involvement with the female boxing coach who ran Midshire's Girls' (boxing and fitness) Group. The coach had initially been Laura's mentor – organised by her YOT worker – when Laura was on conditional bail several years earlier. Laura did not associate the boxing coach with the YOT, despite the fact that she had effectively supervised Laura throughout several court orders. Although she had not been subject to a court order for almost two years, Laura continued to be involved with her coach, and she was now training to be a fitness instructor.

Reparation

Reparation has been accorded significant prominence within contemporary youth justice policy and practice in England and Wales, and is now explicitly stated to be one of the purposes of youth sentencing,[12] and a 'fundamental part of any community sentence for a young offender' (Her Majesty's Government, 2008: 51). In practice, reparation is most often indirect, to the 'community at large', rather than to the direct victim of the offence. In such cases, the underlying principle might best be described as 'coerced restitution' (Bottoms and Dignan, 2004: 162), rather than offence resolution or restoration.

Indirect reparation or 'community payback', which was a supervision requirement for the majority of the young women subject to community penalties, was almost universally disliked. Several girls had even refused to complete the reparation element of their court order despite otherwise being compliant, and found the reparation tasks they were required to do demeaning and 'slave labour'; some also felt that they had been treated 'like little kids'. Several girls in Midshire were required to manicure the nails of the female residents of an elderly people's home. While jokingly acknowledging that the project reinforced gender stereotypes as well as being of dubious value to its recipients, YOT practitioners highlighted the relational benefits of the work, as well as the fact that the girls were learning a vocational skill in the process. Ellen, however, explained that the prospect of manicuring elderly women's nails made her 'feel sick'.

Rarely did the young women consider reparation to be relevant either to their own offending or to the victims of their crimes, and few understood its relevance even as a punishment.[13] Sixteen-year-old April, for example, had been made to undertake conservation work in a wood, which involved a 35-mile round trip from her home. She reflected, 'I don't think digging holes is going to stop me getting into trouble!' Such views contrasted starkly with the intended benefits of reparation as set out in official policy documentation: good practice guidance for YOTs states that the most effective reparative activities are, inter alia, 'restorative ... contribute to repairing harm ... fully "owned" by the young person, and build the young person's skills and learning' (Youth Justice Board, 2008: 4).

Community involvement

The handful of girls who had become engaged in leisure and activity projects via a referral from the YOT or another agency spoke extremely positively about them. Several young women were involved, variously, in a youth project led by the fire service, army cadets and a girls' boxing and fitness group. Their accounts of these activities revealed a positive impact on their feelings of self-worth, most notably when their achievements had been recognised by certificates and positive feedback from staff – forms of recognition that few had received via the education system.[14]

Participation in projects not specifically targeted at offenders has several potential benefits. The normalising effect of integrating offenders with non-offenders – in particular, through voluntary sector provision – seems to be especially beneficial for female offenders (Gelsthorpe *et al.*, 2007; Roberts, 2002), not least because this reduces the stigma associated with projects for offenders only, thus bolstering offenders' non-criminal identities. Mainstream services have the further advantage of avoiding some of the problems associated with including very small numbers of females in group programmes for offenders, which are overwhelmingly male-orientated – including a reluctance to attend on the part of girls and women, due to previous experiences of victimisation by men (Gelsthorpe *et al.*, 2007). Perhaps of greatest importance is the voluntary, non-coercive nature of involvement and the fact that, in contrast to statutory criminal justice programmes, participation tends not to be contingent either on prior lawbreaking or on any assessed risk of future offending and may, where needed, extend beyond the rigid time limits of court-ordered supervision. Third sector involvement may also lead to opportunities to adopt a prosocial 'identity script' (Rumgay, 2004b) by becoming a volunteer oneself.

Practitioners' perspectives on youth justice

I argued in Chapter Two that if young people's welfare needs are identified within the context of a criminal justice agency, they are easily transformed into intervenable risk factors (Hannah-Moffat, 2005; Maurutto and Hannah-Moffat, 2007). In light of the statutory principal aim of the youth justice system to prevent offending by children and young persons (Crime and Disorder Act 1998, s.37), and given the ascendancy of the risk paradigm in contemporary youth justice and the attendant focus on assessing 'criminogenic needs' or risk factors, I asked practitioners what they understood to be the differences between the 'criminogenic' and 'welfare' needs of their young clients.

Youth offending, crime prevention and compensatory intervention

The vast majority of the professionals believed strongly that there is no meaningful distinction between 'criminogenic' and 'non-criminogenic' needs, or needs and risk factors; in fact, practitioners rarely employed the language of risk at all when describing the young people with whom they worked, except in relation to – and, importantly, interchangeably with – preventing offending, as one team leader explained:

> I think [welfare needs and criminogenic needs a]re hugely intertwined ... Because arguably, if you look at the Asset, all of those things lead to risk of re-offending. Anything that proves to be a problem that is linked to risk of re-offending is also probably a welfare need.
>
> (Team Leader, female, Midshire YOT)

Indeed, YOT practitioners asserted that, in view of their statutory duty to prevent offending, and since the presence of *any* welfare need could potentially make it more likely that an individual will re-offend, it is the YOT's responsibility to address *all* the unmet needs of their young clients.

Crime prevention imperatives were not the only justification voiced by practitioners for delivering welfare from within a youth justice framework. Perhaps of even greater importance was the view that child welfare services are spread so thin, and/or that their eligibility thresholds are so high, that they are no longer able to meet the welfare needs of young people who are not subject to statutory court (care) orders, even if they are in significant crisis, the reality of their very limited resources being that child protection cases involving small children and infants have to be prioritised over the support of teenagers and their families. Some practitioners believed that the erosion and rationing of statutory child and family welfare services, which have severely restricted non-criminal justice avenues of support for young people in difficulty, were partly responsible for 'defining up' young people's misbehaviour. Professionals frequently and repeatedly complained that when young people who *are* receiving social work or related services commit an offence, mainstream child welfare services, and especially social services, are very quick to 'pass the buck' or 'drop' them 'like hot potatoes' as soon as they see any evidence of YOT involvement. The police officers I interviewed were, understandably, particularly vocal in their complaints about social services departments 'passing the buck'. One police officer in Midshire told me that he had recently received a very thick social work file on a young person who had received a final warning, and been told by the social worker that they were 'transferring the case' to him, since the young person was now an offender. The team leader quoted earlier questioned the legitimacy of this imbalance between the state's response to young people as children in need and as young offenders:

> Even if they offend once a week, the offence might only take half an hour – out of a week. So that's a week minus half an hour ... So the need – if you look at [a] fourteen year old that's about to become homeless – *is* linked to the ... risk of re-offending. But it's also linked to everything else ... So I can't say there isn't a link, but I *can* say this is also a child in need who, for the most part, *isn't* offending, actually. And why are these people not

entitled to these allegedly universal services, suddenly, because they've committed an offence?

A number of professionals further noted that the asymmetry between the help provided by mainstream child and youth welfare agencies and the greater level of support accessible through the contemporary youth justice system risked creating a perverse incentive to offend, since young offenders (at least in the two areas I studied) were able to access accommodation, health, education and accommodation services – and even financial support – more rapidly in the YOT than outside it.[15] An operational manager in Midshire YOT outlined this predicament:

> I mean we're ... we're not an income support agency, but, I mean, we do provide an awful lot of money here and there for people who are waiting for their benefits, who have lost their jobs ... . and you know that if you don't do that, then they're not going to be getting any money for two or three weeks, so you have to do it to fill that gap, and it's not how it should be. [...] What you worry about is there's a perverse incentive to offend. Because, you know, we've had a number of young people saying, well, if you're going to make me homeless, then, if I commit an offence can I come back on your books? Because then I'll have somewhere to live. This is mad. This is mad. But that's how it is.

While acknowledging that the YOT was effectively doing the work of education and social work services, as well as the benefits agency, in ways that it should not be, the same manager explained that he and other senior colleagues had become tired that their repeated complaints about mainstream agencies' neglect of their statutory responsibilities to protect, house and educate young people fell on deaf ears. Consequently, Midshire's YOT management had resigned themselves to the necessity of delivering such services themselves:

> I think that we've had to, again, think about ways that we can avoid just saying over and over again, it's the education department's responsibility to look after and educate these children and young people, because it became a bit of a mantra. I mean, it is their responsibility, at the end of the day, but they're not doing it, so, you know, can we live with this situation any longer? Can we just sit back and not do anything about it other than have a go at the education department for not providing, or do we have to try and do something about it? Try and build bridges, try and build some sort of linkage with staff here to them, so that we can say we are offering something. Say with accommodation, if we didn't have tenancy support workers who support young people in that accommodation, then we'd never get the kind of relationships with the borough councils. So we've got to give them something to actually get something back, and I think we've got a similar kind of relationship that we need to exploit in future with the education department. If we've got teachers and tutors, then we can say, well we're doing this, but you need

to do that. If we're just saying, it's your responsibility, the defences come down. And that's not how it should be, but that's how it is, really. And I'm sure there's alternative viewpoints to that, but it seems to me that that's really the only way forward now.

It was sometimes difficult to discern in practice whether the study YOTs' delivery of education and other 'welfare' services was simply reactive (to plug the gaps left by a lack of mainstream provision) or whether their benevolent intentions also had the effect of drawing young people (further) into the youth justice system. Both YOTs had invested significant resources and energy into strengthening their in-house health, accommodation and education provision, which was a clear manifestation of both teams' commitment to holistic working and to addressing young people's welfare needs. Building work was underway adjacent to Midshire YOT's offices to construct several classrooms – for the use of, and funded by, the YOT, rather than the education authority – during the course of my fieldwork, and Castleshire YOT, already proud of its excellent and unusually large team of health professionals, was in the process of recruiting a new team of parenting support workers.[16] Certainly these resources, and rapid access to them, must have been attractive to magistrates sentencing homeless young people or children who had not been attending school for some time. But YOT-based services generally only continue as long as the court order a young person is subject to which, as highlighted earlier, is often just a few months.

In addition to acknowledging the limited resources of front line social care workers, in particular, there was recognition of institutionalised intolerance (Muncie, 1999) towards young people known to be offenders, even from professionals who one might expect to be more sympathetic. Castleshire YOT's manager described how the language of some senior managers within the local authority reflected popular discourses demonising young people who offend:

I mean, I think the tone now of ... well just ... the media influence, the whole sense of young people just being a nuisance. It's horribly depressing, you know, it really is. Because it's very difficult to cut through. [...] And even within the local criminal justice board as an example. You know, language is used about young people that you wouldn't really ... I mean, I challenge it from time to time, but sometimes, you know ...? [...] And sometimes you have to go along with it politically because, you know, it's not always helpful, actually, to be overly sensitive about it. But it's just too easy for people to, you know . ...? And I think that the sentencers are not impervious to that.

Sentencing young women

Acknowledgement of how sentencing played a role in how girls came to be supervised by them was evident from many YOT practitioners' observations of local youth court proceedings. A significant proportion of the professionals ($n = 15$) were of the opinion that magistrates sentence girls more harshly than boys, in particular for violent offences. Female magistrates were believed to be especially disapproving of girl defendants,[17] but to commonly accept that 'boys will be boys', of whom offending is 'half expected'. Several practitioners thought that violent girls are perceived to be deviant on account of their sex:

> I think that we, as a system, we don't like girls that offend. We tend to see them as more deviant. My experience of that would be a … young person … that committed a very serious violent offence, a very nasty violent offence. She was pregnant at the time … And the judge called her 'perverted' … I guess that's probably stayed with me … It's like the social understanding of what a woman, or what a girl, does … is so much worse if they do something that is violent.
>
> (Team Leader, female, Castleshire YOT)[18]

Consequently, a greater degree of reproachful 'moral lecturing' from magistrates was almost to be expected, some believed. Several professionals recounted comments made by magistrates, which had given the impression that a girl's very presence in the courtroom requires more explanation than that of a boy. One YOT officer recalled how, in his experience as a court officer, magistrates gave girls more opportunity (or, one might argue, put them under more pressure) to speak in court:

> Maybe the magistrates felt that, excuse me, why is a young female up in court? What are you doing here? You shouldn't be here!
>
> (YOT Officer, male, Castleshire)

Equally, and somewhat paradoxically, the irregularity of a girl's presence in the courtroom could elicit a particularly lenient response from magistrates, females' very incongruity (Worrall, 1990) in court signalling that something must be seriously wrong, warranting particular tolerance and understanding. This apparent inconsistency was well illustrated by one team leader:

> Magistrates will make comments like, you're a young girl, you should be doing this and doing that, when that's not, generally, the message that the boys are getting. […] Perhaps … the sort of moral lecturing doesn't go on as much in the court [with boys] as it sometimes does with girls. But then, on the other hand, when young girls are … in court and they're not being respectful to the magistrates, then the court will tolerate it a little bit more. […] I've had some young girls who've had outbursts in court and swore at the magistrates … whereas if that was a boy of the same age, they probably would have taken him down to the cells for an hour or so for … contempt of court.
>
> (Team Leader, female, Castleshire YOT)

Another YOT officer in Castleshire drew attention to the fact that girls can (and do) exploit courtroom stereotypes by presenting their offending as out of character and inconsistent with their usual 'sweet and innocent' selves:

Sometimes [girls] get away with absolute murder. We had [*refers to a young woman who had committed four distraction burglaries, including stealing elderly women's wallets*] ... Nasty piece of work. She got a three-month order for it, right? She did another two [*burglaries*] ... they gave her a one-month extension. That's absolutely unheard of, to give someone a one-month extension! [...] And it's 'cause she ... fluttered her eyelashes, and was sweet and innocent ... If it was a boy, they could even have sent him to custody. [...] It really varies. I've seen both extremes. I've seen them ... get off really lightly, cause they've put their hair down, put a school uniform on ... and looked like a little girl, and convinced them all that butter wouldn't melt.

(YOT Officer, female, Castleshire)

These apparently contradictory observations are consistent with research by Gelsthorpe and Loucks (1997), whose interviews with magistrates revealed that extra-legal factors such as appearance and demeanour are disproportionately likely to affect female defendants' credibility among sentencers. Conversely, though, the rarity of an 'outburst' by a young woman in court may engender confusion or panic, leaving magistrates (as well as practitioners) at a loss as to how to respond.

There was also recognition of the actual or potential role of sentencing in drawing girls into the formal youth justice system on account of their complex (and previously unmet) welfare needs, rather than the severity of their offending or their danger to the public. The apparently widely held perception among magistrates and judges that there is a 'need to do something with women'[19] may translate into them imposing needs- or welfare-based disposals (which typically involve lengthy periods of community supervision), rather than deeds-based or proportionate ones. The outcome of this, intentional or otherwise, may well be a lengthier and more restrictive and punitive response – what Carlen (2002a) has referred to as 'therapunitive' sentencing objectives. Of course, welfare-based sentencing has a long and ambiguous history in respect of girls and women. However, in recent years, the reduced likelihood of girls (and boys) receiving support from statutory 'helping' agencies given both the retrenchment of the welfare state and a shift from universal to rationed or targeted services available only to children deemed to be 'at risk of offending' has probably further intensified youth court interventionism – and, by implication, sentencing severity – in part as a 'benevolent' compensatory measure. As one practitioner commented, 'I was talking to a magistrate the other day, and she was saying that she was getting really fed up of having to sentence people to welfare'.

Pre-crime intervention and risk/need confusion

I argued in Chapter Two that the history of young women and youth justice reveals a long-standing preoccupation with regulating the sexuality of (predominantly working-class) girls presumed to be in 'moral danger'. While 'moral danger' has not been deemed a sufficient criterion to legitimate criminal justice intervention for over 20 years, I found that in practice, the policing of girls' sexuality through the youth justice system was still very much in evidence. In the twenty-first century, it appears that 'pre-crime' risk assessment and referral practices are drawing young women into the youth justice system on account not of the risks they present to others but because of their own vulnerability or 'at-riskness'. This was most clear in the activities of Castleshire's Youth Inclusion and Support Panel (YISP).

The authors of the national evaluation of YISPs offer the following commentary on the genesis of the panels, which were introduced by the Youth Justice Board in 2002:

> The new panels were designed to identify and support young people aged 8–13 who are at high risk of offending and antisocial behaviour before they enter the youth justice system [. . .]. YISPs were described as multi-agency planning groups which seek to prevent offending and antisocial behaviour by offering *voluntary* support services and other complementary interventions for *high risk* children and their families'.
>
> (Walker *et al.*, 2007: ix, emphasis added)

Several years ago, Lucia Zedner contended that we were 'on the cusp of a shift from a post- to a pre-crime society, a society in which the possibility of forestalling risks competes with and even takes precedence over responding to wrongs done' (2007: 262). While YISPs can be described as 'pre-crime' intervention strategies, their emphasis on forestalling risks is fused – indeed *confused* – with benevolent intentions to 'support' young people on a 'voluntary' basis. I interviewed five professionals – one male manager and four female caseworkers – in Castleshire YISP. According to one caseworker, the local police[20] referred girls to the YISP:

> [M]ainly because they're at risk from the people around them, and from the families that they come from, rather than the children have done anything particular themselves. The older ones have been shoplifting, but the younger ones are at risk because of their surroundings and the people that they're mixing with.

Each caseworker provided me with a list of individuals on their respective caseloads which, at the time,[21] totalled 102 boys and 19 girls, a male-to-female ratio of just over five to one. Detailed data regarding the reason for each child's referral were available for just two of the five areas of Castleshire covered by the YISP, which together included 44 boys and 11 girls. Examination of the team's referral records revealed that of these 11 girls, seven had been referred because they were 'sexually promiscuous' or 'sexually active'. By contrast, none of the 44 boys had been referred on these grounds.[22] The vast majority of the boys had been referred because of aggressive or violent behaviour or, less often, because they had engaged in vandalism. There was evidence of lawbreaking (excluding drug use) by just three of the eleven girls: in two cases 'stealing' was recorded, and a third was said to be 'involved in crime'. A fourth girl was subject to an acceptable behaviour contract (ABC).[23] One caseworker was supporting a six-year-old girl – two years younger than the eligibility threshold for the programme – whose referral form stated that she was '[q]uiet and withdrawn at home. Family in crisis. Witnessed domestic violence'.

The ethical and practical implications of early identification and intervention in the name of preventing offending have been subjected to detailed critical analysis elsewhere (Case, 2007; Case and Haines, 2009; see also Burnett, 2007; Kemshall, 2008). However, gender has been overlooked. Three decades ago, Annie Hudson cautioned that

> the use of such an ambiguous and shifting category [as being 'at risk of offending'] means that girls identified as having the characteristics of becoming a 'problem' can be drawn into a net of increasingly intense contact with welfare and criminal justice agencies.
>
> (1989: 202)[24]

For the majority of girls referred to Castleshire YISP, the reasons for their referral constituted clear and sufficient grounds for the local social services department to provide them with support under Section 17 of the Children Act 1989, which confers a duty upon local authorities to safeguard and promote the welfare of children in need. By contrast, the eligibility criterion for intervention by YISPs – that a child should be at *high risk* of (future) offending and antisocial behaviour – had not been met in the majority (if any) of the referrals of girls they had accepted. The YISP staff I interviewed emphasised, as did the YOT practitioners, that in cases where social services were working with a child and his or her family with whom the YISP subsequently became involved, the social worker would more often than not close the case, given their capacity to engage only in crisis management. However, Castleshire YISP readily accepted referrals of children with welfare needs who had not offended from social workers, thereby providing them with a suitable channel through which to 'offload' children and families whom they have insufficient resources to support.

Conclusion: youth crime prevention, compensatory intervention and repressive welfarism

I have suggested in earlier chapters that families, and particularly mothers, might be using the police as an agency of last resort when they are unable to access help from any other source, and because a police response may now be more reliable, and certainly more speedy, than welfare support in responding to families of teenagers in crisis. My interviews with YOT practitioners further revealed that, for those young people who they supervise, they consider it necessary (albeit not ideal) to play a compensatory role by providing education, health, housing and similar services for their young clients, since mainstream services either have inadequate resources to cater for them, and/or because they do not deem young offenders to be deserving of welfare support.

However, very few YOT professionals acknowledged that they themselves might play a role – however unintentional – in the criminalisation of young women, by proactively proposing to the courts that YOTs might be well placed, and indeed well-resourced, to fill the void left by the erosion of (or individual girls' exclusion from) state education and welfare services. The dilemmas of YOTs filling these gaps as well as the sentiment, expressed by so many interviewees, that mainstream agencies effectively compelled them to do so by abdicating responsibility for all children in need who have committed an offence, were illustrated very well by one education practitioner:

> You are expected to provide the whole service, and be social services for offenders, education for offenders ... The whole idea of setting up a YOT was a multi-agency team ... so that you're all working together. And so we take people out of education, we put them in YOT; we take them out of social services, we put them in YOT. [...] What those home agencies have decided, therefore ... if a youngster is an offender, they've got their own team to deal with them. And [they], as mainstream services, no longer have responsibility for them. [...] They just see us as a team that ... OK, well, they're with YOT, so we can close [the case]. It's ... absolute nightmare!
>
> (Education Officer, female, Castleshire YOT)

Indeed, the much-celebrated post-1998 multi-agency YOT model, incorporating as it does professionals from social services, probation, the police, education, health and often numerous other agencies in the interests of efficient, holistic and 'joined-up' working, seems to be part of this problem. A review of the 'reformed' youth justice system by the Audit Commission in 2004 found that young people on supervision orders received, on average, 1.1 weekly contact hours with youth justice workers in 2003, compared with one hour in 1996. This stability is somewhat surprising given the substantial expansion of personnel when youth justice teams, which were funded and managed predominantly by social services departments and staffed by social workers, were superseded by multi-agency YOTs following the Crime and Disorder Act 1998. The lack of increase in direct contact with individual young people is likely to be a result of two factors. The first of these is the rise in the number of first-time entrants into the youth justice system from 2002 (Department for Children, Schools and Families, 2008) the same year that the Government implemented a national target to increase the number of OBTJ (see Chapter Three), until 2007, which undoubtedly increased individual YOT practitioners' workloads. The second is the increase in auditing, assessment and output targets and other performance indicators within the significantly more managerialist 'new' youth justice system (McLaughlin *et al.*, 2001).[25] However, the perception of mainstream social work and adolescent services may be somewhat different, and unsurprisingly so: unprecedented government funding for youth offending services from the late 1990s onwards has contrasted sharply with a contraction of resources dedicated to child and adolescent welfare services, leading one recent report to claim that 'mainstream services often mistakenly assume YOTs are capable of carrying out specialist and continuing casework' (Independent Commission on Youth Crime and Antisocial Behaviour, 2010).

While it might seem somewhat perverse to criticise youth justice workers for addressing the obvious needs of their clients, thereby demonstrating a welcome retention of social work values within an increasingly risk- and surveillance-dominated environment, an unintended consequence of delivering 'welfare' from within this same risk-focused and correctionalist framework may be that young people, and particularly girls and young women, may experience repressive welfarism (see also Phoenix, 2009). As Chapter Three showed, the number of community penalties imposed on girls rose substantially during the 2000s and, very importantly, breach rates for non-compliance by young women rocketed by 134 per cent in just five years between 2002/03 and 2007/08; many young women were incarcerated not for committing (further) offences but for non-compliance with the requirements of a community penalty. Non-compliance is arguably more likely if young women's assessments of their needs, and of what effective interventions might look like, do not concur with those of youth justice professionals which, as the evidence presented earlier in this chapter indicates, is likely to be the case.[26] The young women in the sample generally conceptualised YOT interventions as punitive and regulatory, rather than benevolent; in fact, many stated that YOT supervision had little or no discernible impact on the material circumstances of their lives, and numerous girls resented the fact that they had only been offered support *after* becoming involved in the youth justice system.[27] Moreover, the short duration of YOT interventions and frequent changes of workers (or worker 'overload' – some young women had different specialist YOT workers to address their mental health, education and housing needs, as well as a case-managing 'YOT officer', for example) – mirrored the disruptions that many had faced elsewhere in their lives.

Slightly different net-widening consequences were evident at the preventative, or 'pre-crime', end of the spectrum, as a result of what were above all the protectionist, and also compensatory, motivations of Castleshire's YISP, who worked with (sometimes very young) girls deemed to be 'at risk of offending'. Evidence of 'risk' was understood rather broadly to incorporate individual vulnerability as well as – and in practice more frequently than – a likelihood of future offending. The YISP's work with girls 'at risk', while undoubtedly prompted by benevolent intentions, ultimately resulted in girls being 'supported' within a crime control, rather than a child welfare, framework.

It appears that relatively well-resourced youth justice services – both 'post-crime' YOTs and 'pre-crime' YISPs – are blurring the boundaries between welfare and crime prevention services by filling the gaps left by the erosion of statutory social welfare provision. As a consequence, they may be criminalising girls' welfare needs (Sharpe, 2009). When the protectionist and compensatory motivations of youth justice professionals coincide with more straightforwardly punitive (and also compensatory) sentencing imperatives, young women may find themselves deeply embroiled in the youth justice system without having committed a serious offence and without posing a significant risk to the public.

9 Conclusions and recommendations

I set out in this book to examine the 'new' offending girl and to scrutinise, through an empirical study of youth women in the contemporary youth justice system, whether there is indeed a 'new breed' of girl criminal, as the media have claimed. A further aim was to examine responses to female youthful lawbreaking in England and Wales – nationally in the twenty-first century, in recent historical context, and in more detail, in three fieldwork sites in England.

The world that young women inhabit today has undergone considerable social shifts since earlier research about girls and youth justice was conducted a generation ago. In many ways, girls and young women today enjoy unprecedented freedoms and opportunities; they are more visible than ever before in the public arena, in tertiary education, in the professional employment sector and in the night-time economy. Their successes at school and in the workplace, in particular, are widely celebrated. However, as Chapter Five showed, the material conditions of working-class criminalised young women appear to have changed very little in the course of a generation. Indeed, offending girls' life chances continue to be constrained by multiple disadvantages and their backgrounds are frequently characterised by experiences of disconnection, disruption and exclusion within the family and at school.

This lack of change in girls' pathways into crime during a period of substantial social and cultural change clearly requires some explanation. The dominant popular message is that girls today are doing very well. Indeed, many of them are. One consequence of this is that expectations of *all* young women as female subjects have increased. Growing up girl today means not only keeping up with the boys at school and at work (and occasionally attracting criticism for outdoing them), but young women also experience significant cultural pressure to demonstrate that they are enjoying a glamorous feminine lifestyle (while not drinking too much or appearing uncouth). At the same time, 'old' expectations regarding reproduction and (heterosexual) femininity remain more or less intact, despite having been reconfigured in some important respects. For example, as the average age at childbirth has increased, teenage mothers have become vilified as irresponsible and unacceptably dependent on state welfare; in addition, while normative Western expectations regarding female sexual activity have, to some extent, been relaxed, girls continue to be condemned if they appear too 'easy', too 'cheap' or too 'masculine'. And while increased social, educational and employment opportunities are undoubtedly available to (some) young women, there are now more avenues through which their behaviour is scrutinised and judged and more ways in which girls can be constructed as failures. In particular, young women who do not attain the successful and glamorous lifestyles that are often believed to result from personal merit and hard work alone are perhaps more readily and harshly condemned as failures and 'bad' girls than they used to be. Indeed, new markers of female class differentiation seem today to be in evidence, characterised by widespread vilification of the (presumed-to-be-personal) moral delinquency of offending girls, at the same time as public celebration of the achievements and 'classiness' of their more advantaged female peers. This has enabled new, more public and more pernicious forms of stigmatisation of the white working-class offending girl to emerge.

An important question relating to the study girls' backgrounds (see Chapter Five) is what is the salience of gender in young women's pathways into crime, and how does gender intersect with class, generation and 'race'?[1] While 'mainstream' theorists have tended to ignore gender, feminist theories – in particular, those which focus on what Daly (1994) has termed the 'leading feminist scenario' of 'harmed-and-harming women' – have been accused of essentialising female offending and ignoring the social–structural, historical, racialised and generational contexts in which female lawbreakers live and act, thus at once over-determining girls' and women's criminality and failing to engage with the complexity and dynamism of their (offending and law-abiding) lives.[2] An exclusive focus on gender has sometimes also meant that theoretical debate has tended to ignore the fact that female crime, like that of males, is predominantly a youthful phenomenon, thus sustaining the myth that female criminality is individualistic, pathological and essentially non-social (Jamieson *et al.*, 1999). Young women's offending 'careers' are, generally speaking, significantly shorter than those of their male counterparts, and there are indications that girls and women are better able to effect a transition from offending to a (relatively) crime-free adulthood than boys and men are.[3] The effect of recent increases in criminalisation on British young women's pathways out of crime is worthy of future study.

Although many of the same class-driven and generational adversities and circumstances affect both girls' and boys' pathways into crime to differing degrees, young women's relationships with the family and school, and with consumption and reproduction, are somewhat different from those of young men. Perhaps most importantly, perceptions of appropriate youthful conduct, judgements about what constitutes 'good' and 'bad' behaviour and the ways in which young people are regulated vary considerably by gender. It is, however, important that we recognise the diversity of girls' pathways into crime. Each of the 52 criminalised young women who feature in this book had a unique life history, and I have tried to avoid essentialising or homogenising either their pathways into crime or their accounts of their lawbreaking. However, various common and gendered features emerged from the girls' case histories: many had been forced to live independently from an early age, sometimes as a consequence of family violence; experiences of familial abuse and victimisation were commonplace, as were troubled relationships between young women and their mothers; a significant proportion had self-harmed, and several were pregnant or mothers themselves. Gender is perhaps a less salient feature in relation to experiences of bereavement and loss, although the reconfiguration of family responsibilities and care arrangements following a significant bereavement may well be gendered.

Amidst the public panic about girls' violence, real social and cultural changes in the area of consumption have been overlooked. I argued in Chapter Six that cultural pressure to consume, and to be glamorous and sexually attractive, may well have criminogenic consequences, especially for working-class young women with limited or no legitimate income. The issue of how consumption plays out in young women's lives according to gender, age and class, and its impact on female lawbreaking and criminalisation deserves further theoretical and empirical attention. Although most girls, including shoplifters, grow out of crime, I wondered how many of the young women in the current study might, once they were old enough to have access to credit, replace their shoplifting habits with debts to credit card companies or loan sharks.

Young women may also be vulnerable to sexual exploitation as a consequence of their involvement in the youth justice system. At the same time as being increasingly imagined as consuming *subjects*, young women (and they must always be young) are seen as *objects* of consumption, as evidenced, for example, in the mainstreaming of the pornography and 'glamour' industries and the recent proliferation of sexual encounter venues in the night-time economy. While none of the young women in the current study told me that they were employed in the sex or glamour industries, the involvement of criminalised young women in such work, and their vulnerability to exploitation by adult males, is a fruitful area for future research, as one recent case illustrates. In August 2009, a male former Youth Offending Team (YOT) manager from Yorkshire was struck off the register of social workers. Posing as a modelling agency representative, he had anonymously approached four YOT-involved young women, the youngest of whom was 15, inviting them to pose topless or naked for money.[4]

Increases in alcohol and drug use and shifts in normative cultural expectations relating to drug and alcohol consumption among British young people have clearly had an impact on young women's behaviour in public space. The young women in the study sample were not, however, drinking in glamorous pubs and nightclubs, but in parks or on the streets, where they were subject to intensive policing and surveillance. Their accounts of their alcohol and drug use complicated popular representations of hedonistic binge-drinking 'ladettes': the creation of excitement and a daily routine against the backdrop of poverty and boredom was a common feature in many of the young women's stories; in addition, for others, the emotional consequences of family conflict, victimisation, loss and exclusion had apparently led them to self-medicate with alcohol and other substances.

Popular representations of girls' offending in recent years have focused almost exclusively on female violence, and on assumptions that violent so-called 'ladettes' are simply acting like boys. However, as Chapter Three demonstrated, increases in girlhood violence during the 2000s were largely, if not entirely, a statistical artefact resulting from the criminalisation of minor misdemeanours within a target-driven framework premised on crime prevention through formal youth justice intervention combined, deeper into the system, with an emphasis on progressive interventionism and tougher enforcement. In the youth justice arena, the primacy of offending prevention has meant that the likelihood of criminalisation and punishment increased substantially for young women in the early twenty-first century; girls were drawn into the youth justice system in increasing numbers, in the absence of any robust evidence that their lawbreaking had increased. I have also argued that girls are being transferred from the welfare to the justice spheres for matters relating to family disputes and on account of their vulnerability, or 'at-riskness'. This seems to be occurring for two reasons: first, because the police are being called upon in the absence of (timely) social work support because they are perhaps perceived as a reliable source of disciplinary backup for families in distress. In practice, this appears to have led to increasing numbers of girls being arrested as violent offenders, where previously they may have been dealt with under the auspices of family support services. Second, youth justice services – both 'pre-crime' 'preventative' services and YOTs, who deal with young people charged with offences – are in some instances doing the work of mainstream welfare services, by providing accommodation and mental health support, and even classroom teaching, to young offenders in order to compensate for the abrogation of their rights by education, health and social services and the unwillingness and/ or inability of the state to meet the needs of young people who offend.

Recent developments signal some grounds for optimism, however. Since the fieldwork for this study took place, the number of 'first time entrants' into the youth justice system has decreased – by almost 22 per cent between 2007/08 and 2008/09 alone (Ministry of Justice, 2011; see also Nacro, 2010). The number of offences resulting in a disposal among girls has also fallen very recently. According to the Ministry of Justice, these decreases 'appear to broadly reflect the changes in police behaviour in response to the Offences Brought to Justice (OBTJ) target' (ibid.: 22[5]), which was changed in 2008: the target, which previously included all types of crime, now measures only more serious offences. There have also been larger decreases in the number of community and custodial sentences imposed on young women than on young men (but smaller decreases in pre-court disposals) since 2006/07 (Ministry of Justice, 2011). Interestingly, however, the dramatic decrease in recorded female youth crime that is apparent in the recent published statistics – as spurious as the increase reported throughout much of the 2000s as it may well be – has not attracted any media attention. There have been no claims that Britain is experiencing an unprecedented *drop* in crimes committed by teenage girls, nor that 'ladette binge-drinking' has *plummeted*.

A fresh start for offending girls?

I shall conclude with some brief critical reflections on the potential consequences for girls and young women of a recent proposal that a 'new response' to youth crime is required in England and Wales. In 2010, the Independent Commission on Youth Crime and Antisocial Behaviour published a major report, *Time for a Fresh Start*, which set out a 'blueprint' for reforming responses to children in trouble with the law in England and Wales.[6] The Commission proposed that responses to young offenders should be based on three guiding principals: prevention, restoration and integration. In addition, two further principles were put forward: first, that 'measures taken to prevent antisocial behaviour or in response to children and young people's criminal behaviour should do no harm' (p. 34) and second, that 'services and interventions in response to youth crime and antisocial behaviour should be based, wherever possible, on sound evidence concerning their effectiveness' (34).

Prevention

The principle of prevention does not in fact signal a break from current policy and practice as *Time for a Fresh Start* suggests, as discussed elsewhere in this book, the current statutory principle aim of the youth justice system is the prevention of offending. Crime prevention is an attractive principle which, at face value, appears commonsensical and uncontentious. However, as Chapter Eight showed, in practice, 'preventative' services may be rather ambiguous where young women are concerned. The assessment of girls' risk of future offending is particularly problematic (see Chapter Two), both practically and ethically, and risk prediction is a notoriously inexact science. In addition to universal issues of false positives and false negatives, the fact that many young women have passed the peak age of offending before they come to the notice of the police might mean that the best way of preventing further offending by them is non-intervention.

More importantly, the prevention agenda in the 'new' youth justice system in England and Wales has, as Chapters Three and Eight showed, had particularly criminalising consequences for young women in the first decade of the twenty-first century. Girls have been swept into the formal youth justice system both for minor misdemeanours which would be better dealt with via welfare mechanisms, and also due to vague notions of 'risk' and 'at-riskness' through which their vulnerabilities (as potential victims of abuse) are easily translated into risk factors which are deemed to warrant preventative youth justice or 'pre-crime' intervention. This practice has been exacerbated by the erosion of non-criminal justice avenues of support for young women in difficulty and their families.

The Commission does emphasise the need for a problem-solving approach that 'meet[s] the immediate needs of children and their families' (p. 41) and stresses the need to avoid the stigma that is likely to be associated with identifying needy children as 'potential criminals'. However, it is difficult to envisage – in the current climate of particularly aggressive cutbacks to universal child and family welfare services – how, and by which agencies, such needs-led services might be delivered. One might also question why 'needs-led' services need to be framed in the language of *crime prevention* and why they cannot be delivered from outside the youth justice framework altogether.

The role of schools is important here. As I highlighted in Chapter Five, neither the relationship between young women's behaviour within school and on the streets nor the parallel between the regulation of girls within the education and youth justice systems has received sufficient theoretical or policy attention. Disengagement or exclusion from school may well precipitate offending by young women (Graham and Bowling, 1995). Moreover, the disciplinary actions of teachers, which have become increasingly characterised by zero tolerance and a hardening of discipline (Simon, 2007; Stephenson, 2006), may construct girls as failures and troublemakers in ways which work against them in subsequent police or court decision-making.[7] Chapter Five documented substantial evidence that, despite popular stories championing young women's unprecedented successes at school, the education system is failing criminalised young women and pushing them off the path to success at an early age. There were also strong indications among the girls in the current study that school problems sometimes constituted an indirect pathway into crime.

Restoration

In the companion volume to *Time for a Fresh Start*, David Smith has suggested that one of the reasons why a youth justice system based on restorative justice principles 'could be at least as effective as the present system in controlling youth crime' is that 'it is a tougher way of holding young offenders to account' than most of the existing youth court disposals in England and Wales (2010: 387). Leaving aside the thorny issues of prioritising 'controlling youth crime' and 'toughness' as indicators of 'effectiveness' in youth justice, there are several additional dilemmas specific to delivering justice to young women – both as offenders and as victims – via restorative processes.

Although there is, to date, no evaluation of the 'effectiveness' of restorative justice as a response to young female offenders, and although the 'advocacy and critical literature on gender and restorative justice is strong on speculation and weak on evidence' (Daly, 2008: 112), a handful of commentators have drawn critical attention to the complexities of restorative justice where the perpetrators of crime are girls (Alder, 2000; Daly, 2008; Toor, 2009). Christine Alder (2000) has pointed to a number of challenges, including the appropriateness of encouraging offending girls to express shame and self-blame, the fact that girls are frequently considered to be recalcitrant and more difficult to work with than boys (see Chapter Seven), and the extent to which 'community reintegration' is realistic or desirable for offending girls. In relation to shame and self-blame, Alder argues that restorative conferences may feed into girls' existing self-blaming tendencies, and that there might be a fine line between demonstrating remorse and contrition, and sentiments of self-blame and guilt amongst young female participants. Importantly, the expression of shame or remorse may have little direct relationship with successful desistance from crime[8]; indeed, many of the girls in the current study employed various techniques of neutralisation which, while apparently serving to minimise responsibility for their lawbreaking, may have functioned as means of protecting themselves against shame and stigma. Explicitly encouraging girls to express feelings of self-blame may have a negative impact on their self-esteem and may even lead them to self-harm.[9]

Kathleen Daly's observations and analysis of Australian young women involved in restorative conferences following girl-on-girl 'punch-ups' – which, as national statistics in England and Wales, as well as evidence from the current study confirm, are particularly common among offending girls – are of particular interest from the point of view of the 'no harm' principle advocated by the Independent Commission. The majority of the girls involved in assaulting young female victims in Daly's (2008) study either contested the 'facts' of the case, or minimised their behaviour, to varying degrees. This set up an adversarial encounter, which is contrary to the aims of the restorative process, leading Daly to conclude that 'the gap between the aspiration and reality of restorative justice may be even higher for offending girls than boys' (2008: 114).[10] Moreover, many young female 'violent' offenders see themselves as 'victims' as much as, if not more than, 'offenders' (see Chapter Six) and, according to Daly's observations, they may perhaps sometimes be justified in their perceptions, there often being a history of mutual conflict between 'offender' and 'victim' over time. Consequently, offending girls may not admit at conferences that their behaviour was wrong and they may not be interested in making amends or in discontinuing their behaviour, which in turn may 'produce a damaging dynamic that brings more suffering to those injured' (ibid.: 134). Furthermore, where the outcome of a restorative conference involves an agreement to undertake indirect reparation to the 'community at large', young women are unlikely to consider reparation to be relevant either to their crimes or to their victims; indeed, they may even refuse to undertake community reparation at all (see Chapter Eight), thereby calling into question its 'restorative' potential.

Integration

Chapters Five and Six illustrated how many of the study girls had been harmed and violated by, and felt disregarded or disrespected by, their 'communities' – the families, schools and neighbourhoods in which they had grown up. The reintegration of young female lawbreakers back into such toxic 'communities' – particularly if they are, or have been, excluded by and from them for prolonged periods – is problematic and perhaps undesirable.

Individual casework currently dominates youth justice practice with girls in England and Wales, and this was particularly the case in the two study YOTs.[11] However, individual and family-based interventions cannot address the broader structural inequalities that offending girls face on account of their age, class, race and gender. Youth justice supervision with girls is also typically very short-lived: half of the young women in the current study were subject to youth justice supervision in the community for six months or less, and many were more 'deeply' involved in the youth justice system than the average offending girl. Moreover, to only address the needs of girls who have been criminalised means that many other similarly marginalised young women will be overlooked. A better solution might, as I have argued elsewhere (Sharpe, 2011), be to increase – and, where it does not already exist, *create* – groupwork provision for young women within mainstream youth services, or within the voluntary sector, to which youth justice professionals can refer (and divert) their female clients but which is accessible to *all* girls in difficulty within a particular locality. Defining girls' needs in collective (but not criminogenic or 'deficit') terms has the potential both to acknowledge the experiences young women have in common and to empower them to actively provide support to one another (as well as perhaps encouraging group resistance and politicisation), rather than resigning them to be the passive recipients of what many experience as unreliable and stigmatising youth justice services. It is important also to note that 'getting tough' on girls' drinking and antisocial behaviour, but providing them with no legitimate avenues for self-expression, socialisation or involvement is unlikely to reduce their lawbreaking. There is a growing body of evidence that any contact with the formal youth justice system may impede desistance, since labelling processes within youth justice agency cultures repeatedly 'recycle' certain categories of young people – 'the usual suspects' – through the youth justice system (McAra and McVie, 2005, 2007). Conversely, the mainstreaming of young women's services outside the formal youth justice system is more likely to adhere to the 'no harm' principle advocated by the Commission. Such an approach would also go some way towards taking seriously the citizenship rights of marginalised and criminalised young women, and take some of the attention away from their offending.

Appendix 1

Appendix 1 Study participants: girls and young women (*n* = 52)

Name	Age	Ethnicity	Current disposal	YOT/STC area
Rhiannon	17	White	12-month detention and training order	Midshire
Isabelle	19	White	12-month supervision order	Midshire
Aimee	14	White	6-month supervision order	Midshire
Danielle	16	White	18-month community rehabilitation order	Midshire
Kate	19	White	36-month supervision order	Midshire
Sophie	15	White	4-month referral order	Midshire
Dionne	18	White/African Caribbean	12-month supervision order	Midshire
Vicky	18	White	18-month supervision order; community punishment order	Midshire
Jenny	15	White	Final warning	Midshire
Lisa	16	White	3-month action plan order	Midshire
Naomi	16	White	6-month referral order + 4-month extension	Midshire
Natasha	15	White	9-month supervision order	Midshire
Chloë	15	White	6-month referral order	Midshire
Laura	19	White	4-month detention and training order	Midshire
Amber	16	White	Final warning	Midshire
Tegan	13	White	3-month referral order	Midshire
April	16	White	6-month referral order	Midshire
Holly	16	White	3-month referral order	Midshire
Hannah	16	White	Final warning	Midshire
Ellen	17	White	4-month referral order + 8-month extension	Midshire
Jodie	15	White	3-month action plan order	Midshire
Rowan	13	White	6-month referral order	Midshire
Bethan	13	White	Final warning	Midshire
Courtney	15	White	24-month supervision order	Midshire
Eloise	14	White	7-month referral order	Castleshire
Rosie	14	White	3-month referral order	Castleshire

(Continued)

Appendix 1 (Continued)

Name	Age	Ethnicity	Current disposal	YOT/STC area
Anna	15	White	12-month supervision order	Castleshire
Abby	16	White	12-month supervision order	Castleshire
Aisha	15	Asian	12-month referral order	Castleshire
Zoë	18	White	6-month supervision order + community punishment order	Castleshire
Emily	15	White	9-month referral order	Castleshire
Gemma	15	White	5-month referral order	Castleshire
Jordan	15	White	3-month referral order	Castleshire
Maddison	16	White	18-month supervision order	Castleshire
Amy	17	White	6-month referral order	Castleshire
Lauren	16	White	Detention and training order, length unknown	Castleshire
Kayleigh	14	White/African Caribbean	12-month supervision order	Castleshire
Natasha	15	White	12-month supervision order	Castleshire
Jessica	16	White	9-month referral order	Castleshire
Alex	17	White	6-month community rehabilitation order	Castleshire
Rachel	17	White	18-month detention and training order	Castleshire
Kelly	15	White	3-month referral order + 3-month extension	Castleshire
Grace	16	White	3-month referral order	Castleshire
Erin	16	White	6-month referral order	Castleshire
Elizabeth	16	Black African	5-year custodial sentence	STC
Sharelle	16	Black African/ Caribbean	24-month detention and training order	STC
Melissa	16	White	18-month detention and training order	STC
Alice	16	White	6-month detention and training order	STC
Sam	16	White	18-month detention and training order	STC
Letitia	15	White/Black Caribbean	3-year custodial sentence	STC
Jennifer	17	White	18-month detention and training order	STC
Toni	17	White/Black Caribbean	4-month detention and training order	STC

Appendix 2

Appendix 2 Self-reported offending by the sample young women (*n* = 51[a])

Offence	Girls reporting ever having committed	
	N	%
Dropping litter	46	90.2
Shoplifting	44	86.3
Common assault	44	86.3
Criminal damage	43	84.3
Drinking alcohol in a public place	42	82.4
Drunk and disorderly	37	72.5
Possession Class C drug	35	68.6
Being carried	34	66.7
Handling/receiving stolen goods	34	66.7
Buying alcohol under 18	34	66.7
Breach of the peace	33	64.7
Carrying drugs for someone else	32	62.7
ABH	31	60.8
Fare evasion	29	56.9
Trespass	27	52.9
Possession of an offensive weapon	26	51.0
Resisting arrest	26	51.0
Possession of Class A drug	24	47.1
Breach of bail	24	47.1
Harassment	23	45.1
Theft from a person	23	45.1
Affray	22	43.1
Public Order Act offence	22	43.1
Interfering with a motor vehicle	21	41.2
Theft from a motor vehicle	20	39.2
Possession of Class B drug	20	39.2
Robbery	18	35.3
Supply Class C drug	18	35.3
Breach of court order	17	33.3
Fraud/deception	17	33.3
(Attempted) dwelling burglary	17	33.3

(Continued)

Appendix 2 (Continued)

Offence	Girls reporting ever having committed	
	N	%
Arson	17	33.3
TWOC	16	31.4
GBH	15	29.4
Assault on a police constable	15	29.4
Driving without insurance	15	29.4
Theft of a bicycle	15	29.4
Dangerous driving	13	25.5
Supply Class A drug	13	25.5
(Attempted) non-dwelling burglary	12	23.5
Breach of conditional discharge	11	21.6
Theft from a meter or machine	9	17.6
Drunk driving	8	15.7
Supply Class B drugs	8	15.7
Forgery	7	13.7
Blackmail	6	11.8
Begging	6	11.8
Driving while disqualified	2	3.9
Indecent assault	1	2.0

Note
a   One of the 52 young women refused to complete the self-report exercise.

Notes

1 New offending girls?

1 I use the terms 'girls' and 'young women' interchangeably throughout this book, to avoid repetition. Unless otherwise stated, I am generally referring to young females aged from 10 and up to 18 years, as this age group falls within the remit of the youth justice system in England and Wales. I acknowledge that the categories 'girl' and (young) 'woman' are socially, historically and legally constructed, and thus unstable.

2 The word 'ladette' seems to have first appeared in the press in 1995. Coverage rose from two articles during that year to 403 in 2003 to 2,216 by the middle of March 2005 (Jackson and Tinkler, 2007: 252). The word entered the *Concise Oxford Dictionary* in 2001 and is defined as 'a young woman who behaves in a boisterously assertive or crude manner and engages in heavy drinking'. Jackson and Tinkler, following Skeggs (1997, 2004), have pointed to the loaded and derogatory nature of the word in classed terms:

> whilst ladette behaviours are represented as spanning social class groups, this does not eradicate their working-class associations; the excessive (drinking, smoking, sex), disruptive (social order), crude (swearing, rudeness), aggressive (verbal and physical), 'open' (sexual) behaviours attributed to ladettes remain associated with the 'least desirable', 'unrespectable' elements of working-class lifestyles.
>
> (2007: 255)

3 Aapola, Gonick and Harris have proposed that there are two competing dominant discourses – which they call 'girlpower' and 'reviving Ophelia' or 'girlhood as crisis' – which give shape to a dual conception of girls and girlhood in late modern Western societies. *Reviving Ophelia: Saving the Selves of Adolescent Girls* is the title of a 1994 *New York Times* bestselling book by Mary Pipher, which 'railed against girls' plummeting self-esteem during adolescence' (Chesney-Lind and Irwin, 2008: 1) and focused on teenage girls' supposedly 'new' vulnerabilities.

4 See Heidensohn (1996: 154–60) for further discussion.

5 Unfortunately, Box and Hale did not investigate young women and girls separately from adult females.

6 The invention of the contraceptive pill was important here. There are, of course, religious and cultural differences in expectations governing girls' (abstinence from) sexual behaviour.

7 This is not to say that marriage and motherhood are not still expected of women, who are frequently criticised (or criticise themselves) for 'leaving it too late'.

8 Gill's interpretation of this shift towards the sexual re-commodification of the female body is that it constitutes, essentially, a new and more pernicious form of female

objectification. She further argues – persuasively, to this reader – that the 'figure of the autonomous, active, desiring subject has become ... the dominant figure for representing young women, part of the construction of the neo-liberal feminine subject' in recent times (2003: 105).

9 I am not suggesting here that the shift away from criminalising girls' sexuality is anything but a good thing. However, I question whether the shift towards violence as the new central site of sanction and moral outrage *vis-à-vis* young women signals any real improvement on earlier discourses and criminal justice practices problematising young women's sexuality.

10 There is, however, little evidence of any abatement of sexual insults directed towards young women who are 'up for it'. Indeed, the perception that young women are desiring sexual subjects can work against them if they are constructed as willing and culpable participants in their own 'victimisation' (see Miller, 2008, xvi).

11 An award-winning weblog, *Working with the Underclass*, by residential supported housing worker Winston Smith (not his real name) describes young women in care in very similar terms. Examples include Kirsty, 'a slightly obese, uncouth 21-year-old female member of the underclass', Rachel, 17, and Sammie, 'her partner in obesity and coarseness'. See 'Children in care: Where the she-louts rule', *The Guardian*, Wednesday 14 April 2010, and http://winstonsmith33.blogspot.com/, accessed 10 February 2011.

12 The *Daily Mail*, which has always featured articles focused specifically at women, is the only British newspaper whose readership is more than 50 per cent female.

13 For organisational analyses of youth justice in England and Wales, see Burnett and Appleton (2004), Field (2007), Holdaway *et al.* (2001), Newburn *et al.* (2002), Phoenix (2006) and Souhami (2007). Bateman's (2008a) review of provision for girls in custody, Batchelor and Burman's (2004) review of working with girls who offend and Ofsted and Her Majesty's Inspectorate of Prison's (2004) joint report on girls and young women serving detention and training orders are rare contemporary British analyses of youth justice policy and practice with young women. However, none of these includes any empirical research.

14 See Batchelor (2007a), Batchelor *et al.* (2001), Burman (2004), Pearce (2004) and Phillips (2003) in the United Kingdom. A large body of North American and Canadian work has also focused on violent girls: see Artz (1998) in Canada and Ness (2010) in the United States on girls' violence, Miller (2001) on girls in gangs in the United States, as well as edited collections by Alder and Worrall (2004) and Chesney-Lind and Jones (2010). Schaffner's (2006) work on girls in trouble with the law in the United States is a rare example of an empirical study which examines *both* girls' law-breaking (violent and otherwise) *and* official responses to it.

2 Historical perspectives on offending girls

1 The first of these institutions, for boys only, was in Borstal in Kent, its purpose being the training of delinquent children. Borstals catered for young people aged 16–23 prior to 1948 and aged 16–21 thereafter, until the Criminal Justice Act 1982 replaced them with youth custody centres. Borstals operated outside the youth justice system, although many children sent to reformatories and later to approved schools were sent to borstals for misbehaviour either while at the schools or when out on licence (Cox, 2003). Home Office open institutions aimed at reforming delinquent and criminal young people comprised industrial schools (for children in need of 'rescue' as well as those under 14 who had committed offences) and reformatories (for adolescent criminals up to the age of 16) – together known as certified schools.

2 The relevance of biology to female offending continues to be debated. On the one hand, the ubiquity of the sex difference makes it likely that some forms of biological

influence are relevant (Rutter *et al.*, 1998: 276), which has led some scholars to call for a re-evaluation of the implications of biological, and particularly evolutionary psychological, theories (Rafter, 2006). On the other hand, as some sociological theorists maintain, '[i]f the gender gap ha[s] a biological basis, it would not vary, as it does, across time and space' (Steffensmeier and Allan, 1996: 467). Early puberty, long believed to be causally associated with girls' offending – both in terms of sexual delinquency specifically and as a risk factor for female offending more broadly – has recently been revisited theoretically, and the claim made that 'early pubertal timing [...] is an important aetiological factor in the development of girls' adjustment problems' (Moffitt *et al.*, 2001: 50). A less deterministic view is that the effects of early puberty on girls' offending, rather than being biologically fixed, may inhere in the social repercussions of early maturity, such as the fact the (some) girls associate with people, especially males, who are older than they are (Caspi *et al.*, 1993; Giordano, 1978; Haynie, 2003). Caspi and colleagues (1993) found that early puberty was associated with delinquency in girls, but only if they associated with boys at mixed sex schools; those in single sex schools did not encounter similar risks. They theorised that the increase in delinquency was attributable to a disjuncture between girls' biologically mature physical appearance and their relative cognitive immaturity, as well as the girls' access to delinquent (male) role models. It is interesting, therefore, that early puberty has been conceptualised elsewhere as a risk factor or an 'adjustment problem' for *individual* girls, rather than as a social consequence of associating with offending peers or 'bad boyfriends'.

3 Cowie, Cowie and Slater's sample comprised 318 girls admitted to an approved school during 1958.

4 Indeed, none of the detention centres admitted girls except for a brief period between 1962–8 (Cox, 2003: 105).

5 Its full title was the *Report of the Committee on Children and Young Persons*.

6 Cowie *et al.* inferred a causal relationship between girls' physical attractiveness, or lack thereof, and their offending, observing that delinquent girls 'are noticed to be oversized, lumpish, uncouth and graceless' (1968: 166). Helen Richardson remarked that 40 per cent of the girls in her approved school sample were 'sturdy', 'stocky', or 'tubby', while 12 per cent were 'stalwart' or 'obese' (1969: 67). As Smart (1976) has highlighted, these authors failed to acknowledge that institutionalised girls would be given stodgy food to fill them up at minimal cost, and that they would have few opportunities to exercise and little reason to make themselves look attractive.

7 Shacklady Smith examined the case records of girls aged 14–16 referred to Bristol juvenile court in 1969.

8 IT was originally conceived to be used either as a requirement of a supervision order, or on a voluntary basis – that is, needs-based rather than justice-based. In practice, however, a range of philosophies and models coexisted within IT schemes, from schemes that restricted the use of IT to young people otherwise likely either to receive a custodial sentence or be committed to care ('alternative to custody' and 'care pure' schemes) to 'broad-based' schemes combining 'preventive' work with non-offenders or those 'at risk' of offending with alternatives to custody or care to those at high risk of committal to a penal or care institution (see Bottoms *et al.*, 1990).

9 Gelsthorpe and Morris also note that paradoxically, diversion was repeatedly affirmed by Government throughout the 1980s.

10 Barbara Hudson further maintained that welfare-oriented juvenile justice interventions were experienced by young people – and particularly young women – as punitive and pathologising.

11 I am not, however, suggesting that girls' and boys' needs are *always* different. Indeed, generation as well as class and race – and the intersections between gender and these other factors – have often been sidelined by feminist criminologists. As Jody Miller (2001: 9–11) has noted, while many theorists are guilty of overlooking the

significance of gender in explaining female crime, some feminist criminologists can equally be accused of overemphasising gender differences.

12 See also Belknap (2007), Belknap and Holsinger (1998, 2006), Bloom *et al.* (2003), Chesney-Lind and Pasko (2004), Gilfus (1992) and Holsinger (2000). The phenomenon of 'criminalising girls' survival strategies' is closely linked to status offences in the United States: troublesome or antisocial behaviour declared criminal or quasi-criminal purely due to the age of the perpetrator, where similar behaviour by an adult would not be considered unlawful. Although the 1974 Juvenile Justice and Delinquency Prevention Act officially decriminalised status offending, ample empirical evidence attests to the continued criminalisation of 'delinquent' responses to victimisation, particularly among girls (Acoca, 1998; Davis, 2007). Status offending (with the exception of activities such as driving or buying alcohol underage) does not explicitly exist in England and Wales. However, the use of the Anti-Social Behaviour Order (ASBO) has been disproportionately used against children and young people in response to troublesome behaviour in public space (see Chapter Three). Secure accommodation via the welfare route for teenage runaways and prostitutes too, while not a criminal sanction, may be experienced as such by young people (see O'Neill, 2001).

13 The operational definition of sexual harassment in the Edinburgh study included a man touching or attempting to touch the young person, trying to get him/her to go somewhere with him, indecently exposing himself and asking the young person to touch him.

14 A number of studies of adult female offenders have found similarly high levels of childhood and adulthood sexual abuse. See, for example, Baskin and Sommers (1998), Daly (1994), Gilfus (1992), Morris *et al.* (1995) and Siegel and Williams (2003).

15 Interestingly, sexual and physical abuse victimisation did not predict adolescent delinquency in Cernkovich and colleagues' longitudinal study, the reasons for which were unclear. The authors point to a need for more qualitative research examining the possible role of girls' and women's agency and adjustment in mediating the effects of their victimisation experiences.

16 Fagan (2001: 457) notes that whilst retrospective studies of child abuse tend to find that a majority of offenders report childhood maltreatment, most prospective studies suggest that only between one-third and a half of victims become offenders. Graham and Bowling (1995: 40) found that attachment to school was significantly associated with offending for females, but not for males. See Chapter Five for further discussion of the significance of both victimisation and experiences of schooling in girls' pathways into crime.

17 The current Conservative/Liberal Democrat coalition government announced in October 2010 its intention to abolish the YJB within 12–18 months, after which its functions would be transferred to the Ministry of Justice. However, on 29th March 2011, the House of Lords voted against the abolition of the Board. In June 2011 Secretary of State for Justice, Kenneth Clarke, announced that the YJB will indeed be abolished, and its main functions brought into a newly created Youth Justice Division within the Ministry of Justice.

18 See Chapter Three for a detailed discussion of the net-widening consequences of the Crime and Disorder Act.

19 Section 37 of the Crime and Disorder Act established that the principal aim of the youth justice system is to prevent offending by children and young people.

20 The National Offender Management Service (NOMS) was created in 2004, in order to distinguish between purchasers and providers of services for offenders, as well as to encourage criminal justice agencies, most notably prisons and probation, to work together more closely to provide a seamless service combining public protection and the reduction of reoffending.

21 See Armstrong (2004), Case (2007) and Case and Haines (2009) for a detailed critique of the risk factors approach.

22 Asset, which was introduced in 2000, is a structured risk/need assessment tool for use with all young offenders at various stages of youth justice system involvement.

23 Baker (2004) has suggested that it might be possible in the future to introduce weightings into the Asset assessment, in order to adjust the significance of risk factors according to gender, age and ethnicity. While this is well intended, it is difficult to envisage exactly how the complexities of social-structural, contextual and relational 'risk factors', which research has consistently highlighted are particularly salient for female offenders, might be incorporated into 'weightings' within a single actuarial assessment tool. Perhaps, as Kemshall has proposed, it might be preferable to abandon the pursuit of the 'inappropriate amendment of [male-centred actuarial tools] to risk prediction with women', and instead focus our efforts on 'extending our understanding of the specific conditions, circumstances and characteristics of female violent and sexual offending, so that we can better identify and respond to those risk circumstances that indicate likely dangerous behaviour' (2004: 222).

24 See http://www.yjb.gov.uk/en-gb/practitioners/youthjusticethescaledapproach/, accessed 10th March 2011. The Scaled Approach coincides with the introduction in 2009 of a single generic youth penalty, the Youth Rehabilitation Order, by the Criminal Justice and Immigration Act 2008.

25 The reality 'on the ground' is in fact rather more complex than this, as I argue in Chapter Eight. In contemporary youth justice practice, there appears to be an interest in addressing children's welfare needs in the youth justice context both for instrumental ends (i.e. to reduce (re)offending) but also for normative reasons; in fact, the two YOTs in my study were strongly welfare-focused and most managers and practitioners believed that an important part of their role is to provide welfare services in order to compensate for the neglect of mainstream services to meet young offenders' welfare needs.

3 The construction of a girlhood crime wave

1 'Serious' offences included assault with injury, theft from a person, theft of a vehicle, burglary, selling Class A drugs and robbery. Overall, 12 per cent of males aged between 10 and 25 years reported having committed a serious offence, 8 per cent were classified as frequent offenders and 5 per cent as both serious and frequent. Comparable figures for females were 8 per cent, 3 per cent and 3 per cent, respectively.

2 'Broad' delinquency as defined in the Edinburgh Study of Youth Transitions and Crime included fare dodging, shoplifting, theft at school, writing graffiti, assault and truancy, while 'serious' delinquency included joyriding, carrying a weapon, damaging property, housebreaking, robbery, fire-raising and breaking into cars.

3 The peak age for male self-reported offending in England and Wales was around 18 years for many years, although the latest OCJS data put the peak for both males and females in the mid-teenage years (Roe and Ashe, 2008).

4 It is important to note that the Ministry of Justice's annual *Criminal Statistics* and *Youth Justice Annual Workload Data* publications (the latter having been published by the Youth Justice Board until 2009 and by the Ministry of Justice thereafter) are not directly comparable. *Criminal Statistics* covers 'offenders found guilty or cautioned by type of offence' and records only the key index offence leading to a disposal. By contrast, *Youth Justice Annual Workload Data* details all offences resulting in a disposal, but does not record the number of individual offenders receiving disposals.

5 The number of pre-court disposals imposed on young people in England and Wales, which was growing rapidly at the time the fieldwork for this study was undertaken (June 2005 to June 2006), almost trebled between 2003/04 and 2007/08. The use of pre-court disposals has fallen since then, however (see Ministry of Justice, 2011).

6 There have been recent developments to extend the two existing pre-court disposals with a third, the youth conditional caution (YCC) (see note 20, below).

7 A conditional discharge is not a conviction, but has been described as 'a useful provision designed to operate as a deterrent against future offending, while minimizing the consequences of criminalization' (Bandalli, 2008: 84). A 'discharge' period of between six months and three years is set and, provided that the young person does not commit further offences during this time, no punishment will be imposed. However, if the young person commits another offence during the discharge period, they can be brought back to court and re-sentenced, in which case the conditional discharge will appear on the young person's criminal record. Section 66(4) of the Crime and Disorder Act 1998 stipulates that if a young person has already received a final warning in the two years preceding the commission of the current offence(s), the court must not impose a conditional discharge 'unless it is of the opinion that there are exceptional circumstances relating to the offence or the offender which justify its doing so'. The absolute discharge may still be used in such circumstances, however.

8 The referral order requires the young person to attend a youth offender panel, which includes a member of the local Youth Offending Team, two lay panel members (volunteers from the local community), the young person and usually his or her parent(s) or guardian(s). Any victim of the offence is also invited to attend, although this is relatively uncommon in practice (Earle, 2005). Panel attendees must draw up a 'contract' requiring the young offender to undertake a 'programme of behaviour', which must include reparation either directly to the victim or indirectly to the wider community, as well as activities which adhere to the principal aim of preventing re-offending. The length of the order, which is decided by the court, is between 3 and 12 months. In contrast to a community sentence, a referral order is 'spent' as soon as it comes to an end and does not normally have to be disclosed when applying for work.

9 There is also provision to extend a referral order if fresh offences which pre-date the imposition of the original order come to light and, at the court's discretion, for minor offences committed subsequent to the imposition of an existing referral order (Youth Justice and Criminal Evidence Act 1999, Schedule 1, Part 2, paras. 11 and 12). The Criminal Justice and Immigration Act 2008, section 35(3), further modified the criteria governing the imposition of a referral order by giving the court the power to make a second referral order, on the recommendation of the local Youth Offending Team, although only in 'exceptional circumstances'.

10 As Table 3.3 shows, the number of custodial sentences imposed on both girls and boys decreased substantially in the year 2009/10. However, it is too early to say whether or not this is the beginning of a downward trend.

11 Research spanning several decades confirms that females appearing in court are less likely to be fined and more likely to be placed on a restrictive community penalty than similarly placed males (Feilzer and Hood, 2004; Hedderman and Gelsthorpe, 1997; May, 1977), suggestive of a general belief that 'something must be done' about female offending.

12 Initially only a civil order, the ASBO was extended by the Police Reform Act 2002 to include a criminal version, colloquially known as the CrASBO, which can be made on conviction.

13 Crime and Disorder Act 1998, section 1(1)(a).

14 During the same period 7,228 males and 1,412 females aged over 18 years received an ASBO.

15 The comparable rate for young males of cases where breach resulted in a custodial sentence was 42 per cent. All ASBO data reported here were obtained from http://webarchive.nationalarchives.gov.uk/20100418065544/crimereduction.homeoffice.gov.uk/asbos/asbos2.htm, accessed 1 October 2010.

16 The UK Conservative/Liberal Democrat coalition government indicated in July 2010 that they were considering abolishing ASBOs, and in February 2011 announced plans to create new Criminal Behaviour Orders and Crime Prevention Injunctions, among other measures, to replace them. ASBOs were still in place at the time of writing.

17 Despite overall stability in offences committed by boys attracting a formal disposal, their detected violent offending rose by a slightly less dramatic but nonetheless considerable 49 per cent during the same three-year period.

18 See Burman and Batchelor (2009) on Scotland, Carrington and Pereira (2009) on Australia, Steffensmeier and Schwartz (2009) on the United States and Sprott and Doob (2009) on Canada.

19 See Maguire (2007) for further discussion of the impact of the NCRS on recorded crime rates.

20 Out-of-court sanctions applicable to youths include penalty notices for disorder (PNDs or 'on the spot fines'), 3,682 of which were imposed on 16- or 17-year-old females in 2008, falling to 3,132 in 2009 (Ministry of Justice, 2010d, 2010e), fixed penalty notices (FPNs, which are generally imposed for offences such as dropping litter and writing graffiti), reprimands, final warnings and Youth Conditional Cautions (YCCs). The YCC effectively introduces a third tier (after the reprimand and final warning) into pre-court sanctions and conditions may include provisions to support rehabilitation, carry out reparation or punishment, a fine or attendance at specified activities for a maximum of 20 hours. The YCC was piloted from January 2010 in five regions of England, initially for 16- and 17-year-olds only, although legislation makes the YCC available for 10- to 17-year-olds (Criminal Justice and Immigration Act 2008, Schedule 9). See Morgan (2008) for a full description of summary justice powers relating to juveniles in England and Wales.

21 The sanction detection target was not renewed after 2007/08. However, the Youth Justice Board established a different and apparently contradictory target to reduce the number of children entering the youth justice system for the first time (Bateman, 2010). This new indicator inevitably encouraged the police to respond more informally towards first-time child offenders committing less serious crimes, thereby removing a higher proportion of minor offenders from the youth justice system altogether. The result – the exact opposite of the earlier sanction detection target – was a steep drop in the level of detected youth crime during 2008, which decreased most markedly for girls (Nacro, 2010) and has continued to decrease subsequently (Ministry of Justice, 2011).

22 Steffensmeier and colleagues examined four major sources of US longitudinal data, including arrest statistics from the Uniform Crime Reports, victimisation data from the National Crime Victimization Survey (where the victim identifies the sex of the offender) and self-reported violent behaviour from 'Monitoring the Future' and the National Youth Risk Behavior Survey.

23 See, for example, *The Telegraph* (2008).

24 Ministry of Justice figures indicate that the average monthly under 18 secure population of both sexes has dropped sharply, and most notably in the case of young women, since the end of 2008 (see http://www.justice.gov.uk/publications/youth-custody-data.htm). Girls and young women were sentenced to 416 custodial disposals in the year 2008/09 (Ministry of Justice, 2011), which accounted for 8 per cent of all youth custodial sentences. After a sustained rise in male youth imprisonment throughout most of the 2000s, the number of custodial sentences imposed on male juveniles in England and Wales also fell towards the end of the decade, from a peak of 6,476 in 2006/07 to 6,099 in 2008/09 to 4,714 in 2009/10 (Youth Justice Board, 2008; Ministry of Justice, 2010f, 2011). Nacro have directly attributed this recent decline in the youth custodial population to the simultaneous decrease in the number of young people entering the youth justice system for the first time, which is in turn a consequence of the abandonment of the sanction detection target, discussed earlier. Nacro's persuasive conclusion on the relationship between young people entering the system at the 'front' end and those sentenced to custody at the 'deep' end is that 'the number of children coming into the system has a considerably greater influence on the use of custody than many

commentators have allowed' (2010: 7). It is important also to note that the Ministry of Justice no longer publishes data detailing the length of youth custodial sentences imposed.

25 The number of girls sentenced for breach of a statutory order increased from 1,171 in 2002/03 to 2,741 in 2007/08. Comparable numbers for boys were 7,085 and 14,101, representing a 98 per cent rise (Youth Justice Board, 2004a, 2009). Breach rates have fallen sharply since 2008, in tandem with all other offences resulting in a youth disposal. In the year 2008/09, 2,103 girls and 10,441 boys were sentenced for breach of a statutory order (Ministry of Justice, 2011).

26 Jacobson *et al.* (2010) report that breach of a statutory order, bail or a discharge was the primary offence of 27 per cent of girls in custody, compared with 21 per cent of boys, in the second half of 2008.

27 There was a 26 per cent rise in the number of boys imprisoned for 'delinquency' during the same period.

28 In Canada, by removing status offences from the jurisdiction of the youth court, and in the United States, by legislating to reduce the use of custodial sentences for status offences. See Sprott and Doob (2009; chs 5 and 6) for further discussion.

4 Researching new offending girls

1 Young women's intersubjective accounts of their lawbreaking have been the focus of a number of recent British studies. However, as I noted in Chapter One, this body of work has concentrated almost exclusively on girls' violence.

2 Twentieth century British empirical studies of delinquent girls include Ackland, 1982; Cowie *et al.*, 1968; Gelsthorpe, 1989; Gibbens, 1959; Hoghughi, 1978; Petrie, 1986 and Richardson, 1969. Ackland's work is rare in its focus on both professionals' and girls' perceptions of residential 'care'. O'Neill's (2001) more recent gendered exploration of children in secure accommodation also compared the views of young women and professionals; however, just three of the 18 girls in her sample were offenders, the remainder having been secured on welfare grounds.

3 Perceptions of sex differences in offending are, however, included in my analysis of professional perspectives in Chapter Seven, since practitioners often talked at length about offending by boys.

4 Maguire points out that 'appreciative' (Matza, 1969) fieldwork methods are an important counterpoint to criminologists who might otherwise 'lose their sense of reality and begin to perceive offenders not as people, but merely as "problems" or "numbers"' (Maguire, 2008: 285).

5 For example, the work of Pat Carlen (Carlen, 1988, 1996; Carlen *et al.*, 1985) and Anne Worrall (1990) on criminalised women, as well as Ann Campbell's (1981) study of 'girl delinquents' and Jody Miller's more recent North American work on gang-involved girls (2001). The *View from the Girls* study of Scottish young women's views about violence (Batchelor *et al.*, 2001; Burman *et al.*, 2001; Burman, 2004) constitutes an important recent contribution to the (scant) British literature on young women's offending.

6 Harding (1987b) further emphasises the plurality of (different) women's experiences, which are mediated by class, 'race' and culture.

7 See Oakley (2000: 72) for further discussion of 'objective' and 'subjective' methodologies in research on women.

8 Blumer outlined three central premises of symbolic interactionism: first, that people act towards things – including physical objects, other people, activities, institutions, ideals and so on – according to the meanings that these things have for them; second, that the meanings of things arise out of social interactions with other people; and third,

that these meanings are modified through 'an interpretative process used by the person in dealing with the things he [*sic*] encounters' (1969: 2).

9 One young woman whom I interviewed in custody did not consent to me reading her case file. Case files varied considerably in thickness, since the young women had been involved in the youth justice system for differing lengths of time; the data therein (which included YOT and STC assessments, court and (rarely) psychiatric reports, referral forms, letters and case diaries) also varied considerably in quality and completeness. I photocopied case file documents at the YOT offices and took them away with me. I read the case files of the girls in custody in situ, taking notes on my laptop computer. These files tended to be fairly short, as historical documentation had not always been forwarded to the STC by YOT workers.

10 Case file documents are not, of course, unmediated by interpretation, but are social constructs with subjective meanings and thus cannot be accepted uncritically as 'factual' (see Scott, 1990). Court reports in particular may be more accurately described as documents of persuasion.

11 One YOT did respond to my letter and, following a meeting to discuss the research in more detail, the designated manager agreed that the YOT would be involved. However, she later informed me that her superiors had changed their minds, on workload grounds.

12 There are four YOI 'units' for young women attached to, but separate from, adult women's prisons in England. Each unit holds between 16 and 24 17-year-old prisoners. They are the Josephine Butler Unit at HMP Downview in Surrey, the Mary Carpenter Unit at HMP Eastwood Park in Gloucestershire, the Rivendell Unit at HMP New Hall in West Yorkshire and the Toscana Unit at HMP Foston Hall in Derbyshire. Ten mixed sex local authority-run (public) secure children's homes each accommodate between 6 and 36 children, including girls aged 12–16. Staff-to-prisoner ratios and levels of staff qualifications are highest in secure children's homes and lowest in YOIs. In the year 2005/06, when I conducted the fieldwork for this study, 623 custodial disposals were given to girls and young women in England and Wales (Youth Justice Board, 2007). Remand figures for this group are not published. Snapshot data for May 2006 indicate that 207 young women under 18 were held in penal custody at that time (see http://www.yjb.gov.uk/en-gb/yjs/Custody/Custodyfigures/, accessed 5th January 2010).

13 Several YOT workers maintained sporadic telephone contact with young women with whom they had previously worked. Former female clients often appeared to stick in practitioners' minds, sometimes for a very long time. This may be because they remembered them as being different from the (male) norm, or as more difficult (or interesting) to work with (see Chapter Seven), or because some practitioners had established stronger relationships with their female clients.

14 Written consent was obtained from the girls themselves, and from their parent(s) or guardian(s). Further written consent was obtained from the girls at the STC and from their respective YOT officers to read their case files.

15 Young defendants appearing in court for the first time and pleading guilty in England and Wales are ordinarily eligible only for a referral order or a custodial sentence (see Chapter Three).

16 The ethnic background of the female under-18 custodial population, based on monthly averages, was 74 per cent white, 8 per cent black, 8 per cent mixed and 1 per cent Asian. Data were missing in 8 per cent of cases.

17 Eighty-nine per cent reported having started offending by the age of 14.

18 The case files of some of the girls in the STC were incomplete. Consequently, these figures underrepresent their collective recorded offending.

19 Reprimands and final warnings, respectively, constituted 44 per cent and 17 per cent of female youth disposals in England and Wales in the year 2005/06 (Youth Justice Board, 2007).

20 This was particularly the case in Castleshire YOT during the fieldwork period, due to police officer vacancies. From 1st April 2006, YOTs have had a target to provide interventions for 100 per cent of young people receiving a final warning if any of the following apply: (1) they score 12 or more on the Asset (risk assessment) tool (each of 12 sections of the assessment must be scored between 0–4, where 0 means that the particular factor or area (e.g. 'thinking and behaviour' or 'neighbourhood') is not associated with the young person's risk of reoffending and a score of 4 denotes a high associated risk); (2) there are concerns about risk of harm to others; or (3) the total Asset score is less than 12 *but* any single section of Asset scores 4 (see Bateman, 2006). Compliance with final warnings is not legally enforceable.

21 There is no legal requirement to do so, however (see McCarry, 2005).

22 In several cases, I met girls in person when I was at the YOT office or, in Midshire, at a girls' group, run by the YOT, that I attended several times.

23 Interviews with girls at the STC all lasted just less than one hour. A strict requirement written into STCs' contracts with the Youth Justice Board stipulates minimum education and training contact hours for young people in custody; the time I was allowed to spend with each girl was thus restricted so as not to interfere with the curriculum.

24 Nobody requested payment in cash and most thanked me, sometimes profusely, for taking them out for something to eat. One young woman even offered to pay half the bill.

25 However, I sometimes avoided asking certain questions in the presence of these friends or relatives, to avoid embarrassing the young woman or compromising confidentiality.

26 Four young women who initially agreed to be involved did not keep their appointments. A fifth girl's mother decided that I could not interview her daughter, and I did not pursue a sixth girl, who had missed two appointments, on discovering that her sister had very recently been murdered. Since many of the girls had chaotic lifestyles and regularly forgot appointments, it was difficult to discern whether a girl's failure to be at home when I had arranged to meet her indicated forgetfulness or unwillingness to be interviewed. I made up to three appointments with each individual; if she did not keep the third one, I did not contact her again.

27 I was also aware of the girls' vulnerability while conducting interviews in public places with others present (for example, at nearby tables in a café or restaurant), where there was the potential for eavesdropping. If this situation did arise, I changed the topic of conversation or indicated to the young woman that we could be overheard.

28 I asked each young woman to report whether she had ever committed a range of common offences, the names of which were typed on 'flash' cards that I brought to each interview.

29 These included four case workers and one manager in Castleshire's Youth Inclusion and Support Panel (YISP; see Table 4.4, note a), two workers from a national voluntary agency providing bail supervision and support, emergency accommodation, and Intensive Supervision and Surveillance Programmes (ISSPs) on behalf of Midshire YOT, a police 'youth justice process marker' who was responsible for decision-making in relation to whether to divert (by way of a reprimand or final warning) or prosecute young offenders in Midshire, a unit manager in the STC, and a female boxing and fitness coach who led a girls' group funded by Midshire YOT.

30 I interviewed all YOT police officers (with the exception of one who joined the YOT at the end of the fieldwork period) and most YISP staff, on the basis that young female offenders are disproportionately represented at the lower end of the disposal tariff. Consequently, police officers (who tend to carry out final warning assessments and interventions within YOTs) and YISP workers (who work with younger children who have not generally been charged with offences) deal with the lion's share of youth justice system-involved young women. My selection of professionals who work with female clients contributed to the female bias of the sample since most of the young

women offenders in Midshire and Castleshire were allocated to female practitioners. Moreover, female practitioners and managers were in the majority in both YOTs among staff at all levels, including senior management.

31 I did not tape-record four interviews because they took place in open or public spaces. The fifth was impromptu and I did not have my tape recorder with me that day.

32 At least, in middle-class circles.

33 According to Scott and Lyman, accounts containing socially approved vocabularies can take the form of *justifications* (where one accepts responsibility for one's actions but denies the pejorative quality associated with them) or *excuses* (where one admits that the act is wrong but denies full responsibility for it), both of which function to protect the account-giver's self-esteem and social status (1968: 47).

34 I began my analysis by coding each transcript and summarising the key themes from each interview. A number of themes and concepts identified in individual interviews with the young women amassed. I then mapped out the identified themes visually on a large chart to help me to group them conceptually and identify connections between them. I transcribed all staff interviews in full (where they had been tape-recorded) and coded them using NVivo7. Using a software package helped with the consistent coding of data, and with systematically comparing, and checking the frequency of, identified conceptual themes. However, I later returned to paper, reading and re-reading the staff interview transcripts and comparing these with printouts of the 'nodes' (codes) collated in NVivo7. Throughout these various processes, I made extensive use of the 'constant comparative method' (Glaser and Strauss, 1967), reading and re-reading my notes, testing out provisional hypotheses on different cases, and systematically comparing data and themes emerging from the transcripts with similar phenomena in other cases or in the existing literature.

5 Pathways into crime and criminalisation

1 Pseudonyms are used throughout when individuals are referred to by name.

2 A large body of empirical research examining the lives of young women offenders has documented frequent histories of familial distress, abuse and victimisation (e.g. Batchelor, 2005; Belknap and Holsinger, 2006; Chesney-Lind and Pasko, 2004; Douglas and Plugge, 2006; Howard League, 1997, 2004; Miller, 2001; Ofsted/Her Majesty's Inspectorate of Prisons, 2004; Schaffner, 2006; Wilkinson and Morris, 2002; Williams, 2008) and 'placement' in state care (Carlen, 1987; Douglas and Plugge, 2006; Howard League, 1997, 2004; Tye, 2009, Worsley, 2006).

3 Residential instability was more common among girls in Midshire and the STC than among girls in Castleshire.

4 'Homelessness' as defined here included sleeping rough, staying in homeless hostels or temporary bed and breakfast accommodation, 'sofa-surfing' at friends' houses and sleeping in cars. Recent British research examining the accommodation needs of young offenders reported that a significantly greater proportion of females than males had experienced homelessness: 60 per cent cf. 36 per cent (Arnull *et al.*, 2007). However, the number of girls in Arnull and colleagues' sample was small – 25, compared with 127 boys.

5 However, middle-class (and indeed working-class) girls may become psychologically distressed, develop eating disorders or inflict deliberate self-harm.

6 I discuss feminine consumption and the sexualisation of contemporary consumer culture in Chapter Six.

7 The national incidence of childhood bereavement is difficult to ascertain. Estimates of the proportion of young people under 16 who experience parental death vary from 3.9 per cent to 7.4 per cent, and bereavement of a grandparent is rather more common. Importantly, the likelihood of a young person experiencing family

bereavement varies significantly according to social class and locality (see Ribbens McCarthy, 2006: 16–17).

8 In Gwyneth Boswell's (1996) research on the backgrounds of children imprisoned for grave crimes, including murder, manslaughter, arson and rape, 10 per cent of a random sample of 200 such children, which included 12 girls, had experienced the death of a parent, and 39.5 per cent had experienced loss of contact with a parent. Fifty-seven per cent had experienced significant loss (experiences defined by professionals or the offenders themselves to have had a distinct impact upon them and their subsequent behaviour), either through bereavement or through the termination of contact with a parent, grandparent, other relative or carer, or close friend. Twenty-two per cent of the 41 young people (just two of whom were female) in Liddle and Solanki's (2002) study of persistent young offenders had suffered bereavement, details of which the authors do not describe. In a recent detailed profile of the backgrounds of 300 imprisoned children by the Prison Reform Trust (Jacobson *et al.*, 2010), 12 per cent of children in prison in England and Wales were known to have been bereaved of a parent or sibling.

9 Several of the girls had committed more than one such offence.

10 Parenting orders were first introduced in 1998 and can be issued to parents when their child is convicted of an offence or receives a child safety order, a sex offender order (Crime and Disorder Act 1998, ss.8–9) or an anti-social behaviour order (Anti-Social Behaviour Act 2003, s.26). They can also be imposed in education cases where a parent is successfully prosecuted by the local authority for failing to secure his/her child's regular attendance at school or where a pupil has seriously misbehaved (Education Act 1996, ss.443–4). Parenting orders have been criticised for creating a mechanism to expand disciplinary power (Foucault, 1977) simultaneously over both the parents of young offenders and young lawbreakers themselves, and because they are disproportionately issued to mothers, lone parents and parents living in deprived areas (Holt, 2008; see also Ghate and Ramella, 2002).

11 In England, a child may by law leave school on the last Friday in June of the school year in which s/he turns 16.

12 A further two girls were enrolled on what they referred to as a 'computer thing', aptly named 'notschool.net', which they both told me they did not do. However, they and others previously enrolled on the programme reported that they did use MSN Messenger and web surfing facilities on the computer they had been given.

13 One of the 19 had not, she told me, been excluded officially, but had been led to believe that she was permanently excluded. Elizabeth insightfully explained that her mother had not been formally notified of the 'exclusion' so that the school might keep her on their roll in order to retain the funding attached to her school place.

14 The GCSE is the standard academic qualification taken in a variety of subjects by school pupils in England and Wales at the age of 15 or 16. Universities and employers generally regard only grades A to C as a pass. CLAIT, NVQ and AQA stand, respectively, for Computer Literacy and Information Technology, National Vocational Qualification, and Assessment and Qualifications Alliance. STCs typically provide entry-level accreditation via the AQA Unit Award Scheme, which provides formal recognition for students who complete short units of work in subjects such as English, maths and art and design.

15 McLaughlin (2005) notes that many girls self-exclude from school as a result of distress and personal difficulties, which are frequently not recognised by teachers.

16 Jonathan Simon's recent thesis in the US context is very relevant here. Simon (2007) argues that a variety of state agencies, including schools, have increasingly become 'governed through crime', evidenced, for example, in the increased surveillance of pupils through the use of metal detectors. Chesney-Lind and Irwin (2008) have also pointed to the 'upcriming' of schoolyard fights involving girls in the United States. Claims have been made in England and Wales that the police are increasingly called

on to intervene in incidents involving young people 'in settings that used typically to consume their own smoke' (Morgan and Newburn, 2007: 1044). The Safer Schools Partnerships programme, which was mainstreamed in 2006, involves police officers being based in, or attached to, schools in order to reduce crime and victimisation among school children.

17 The Children and Young Persons Act 1969, s.1(2)(c) allowed a young person to be brought before a juvenile court for them to consider care proceedings on the grounds that 'he [sic] is exposed to moral danger'. This condition did not reappear in the Criminal Justice Act 1982, and seems to have been superseded when subsequent legislation overtook the 1969 Act. In 1989, the Children Act s.90 separated the care and control functions of the (now) youth and family proceedings courts – which respectively deal with criminal and care matters involving young people – by removing the offence condition from the criteria empowering courts to impose a care order.

18 This is of course not true for all British girls. When engaged in by Muslim young women, for example, unmarried sexual activity may not be culturally acceptable at all and may be severely punished.

19 Anti-social behaviour order.

20 There was no evidence either from our conversations or from their case files that any of the young women I interviewed in custody were mothers or mothers-to-be, although I did not specifically ask them about motherhood. By contrast, one survey found that 12 per cent of young women in custody in England and Wales were pregnant (Her Majesty's Prison Service and Youth Justice Board, 2003).

21 Tender loving care.

22 A report by the Conservative Party, *Labour's Two Nations*, published in February 2010, falsely claimed that more than half of teenage girls in poor areas become pregnant, the actual rate being 5.4 per cent (see Booth, 2010).

23 These figures are broadly in line with estimates of the prevalence of self-harm among the incarcerated female juvenile population, which range from 22 per cent of 15- to 17-year-olds (Howard League, 1997, lifetime prevalence), to 36 per cent of 17-year-olds (Douglas and Plugge, 2006, previous month prevalence), to 57 per cent of 16- to 24-year-olds (Batchelor, 2005, lifetime prevalence). Douglas and Plugge found that young women in prison self-harm at approximately twice the rate of adult female prisoners.

24 In one empirical study of 111 girls aged 15–18 in contact with an advice project in the juvenile wing of Bullwood Hall prison in Essex (Howard League, 2004), half of the girls had been referred to a drugs advisor for help with drug- or alcohol-related problems. Similar findings were reported in earlier research by the Howard League (1997) and in Lyon and colleagues' (2000) investigation of young people in prison. Wilkinson and Morris (2002) interviewed 15 girls aged 15–17, as well as older women, in custody and following their release. Many more of the girls than the adult women reported both sexual abuse histories and regular drug use. In Hammersley and colleagues' (2003) survey of a cohort of 14- to 17-year-old YOT clients about substance use, young women scored significantly lower on self-esteem measures than young men, and a greater number of female than males respondents injected drugs, despite the small proportion (20 per cent) of females in the sample.

6 Accounting for trouble

1 This was almost universal among the young women in the secure training centre.

2 The fact of Aisha's arrest and initial custodial sentence (against which she appealed, successfully) had far-reaching consequences for her subsequent reputation at home, at

school and in her local community. Toor (2009) has highlighted the shame (*sharam*) that criminalised British Asian girls bring upon themselves and their families which, in combination with criminal justice sanctions, constitutes a form of double punishment.

3 Barry (2006) makes the point that many young people offend because lawbreaking affords them a degree of social capital and recognition from their peers, which is often unavailable through other means to working-class young people during their teenage years.

4 Toni stated that around a quarter of the members of her branch of the gang were girls and young women, who were aged between 12 and 13 and around 20-years old.

5 Toni did not reveal what kind of 'jobs' she had undertaken to 'rep the higher ones'.

6 Female gang membership has received relatively little scholarly attention in the United Kingdom, not least due to its rarity (Batchelor, 2011; Young, 2009). North American gang research has consistently revealed that female gang members' backgrounds are characterised by domestic violence, sexual and physical abuse, unstable accommodation, and structural (especially racial) discrimination and constraint (Campbell, 1984; Chesney-Lind and Hagedorn, 1999; Joe and Chesney-Lind, 1995), and that gang-involved girls come from more troubled families than both their male gang counterparts and 'at-risk' girls who do not join gangs (Miller, 2001). In Jody Miller's (2001) study of predominantly African-American teenage female gang members, girls' decisions to join a gang were influenced by neighbourhood and peer contexts facilitating exposure to gangs, by serious family problems – which both contributed to weak supervision in the home and encouraged girls to attempt to meet their social and emotional needs elsewhere – and by having gang-involved family members.

7 While I was out with Holly, another young woman from Laura's home town and a drinking associate of hers, we bumped into Laura in a shopping centre. Holly was taken aback when I addressed Laura by name, since she only knew her as 'Mad Bird'.

8 Previous research has also highlighted the significance of (dis)respect and righteous indignation in female, as well as male, violence (see, e.g., Batchelor, 2005, 2007a; Miller and Mullins, 2006a; Miller and White, 2004; Ness, 2010; Pearce, 2004; Phillips, 2003). It is nonetheless relatively rare for girls to use physical violence on a regular basis. Artz (1998) has contended that some young women, having been victims of patriarchal violence, internalise violence as being morally right and hence legitimate. They thus go on to victimise each other, engaging in 'horizontal violence' in an attempt to gain power. According to Artz, girls who engage in serious violence make moral judgements about their (usually female) victims, 'because within their life-worlds, they still apply narrow notions of male-focused behavior as the standard for what is right and good for women' (1998: 201). Thus violence becomes justified when other girls transgress patriarchal 'rules' relating to dress, sexuality and propriety.

9 Sophie pointed out that her memory of this incident was patchy, since she had drunk 'two or three litres' of cider beforehand.

10 Burman and colleagues, examining teenage girls' beliefs about violence in Scotland (Batchelor *et al.*, 2001; Burman, 2004; Burman *et al.*, 2001), found that in spite of their frequently condemnatory attitudes towards *other people's* violent behaviour, many girls identified contexts in which they believed *their own* violence was justified, including 'victim precipitation', retaliation, 'sticking up' for themselves and the protection of personal reputation. These findings emphasise the importance of social context as well as cultural norms in understanding the apparent contradiction between girls holding other people accountable for their violent behaviour while rationalising their own violent acts as morally justified when they occur 'in particular social-situational and spatial contexts' (Burman, 2004: 90).

11 This was not the case for everyone, however. Several of the girls in the STC came from large inner-city neighbourhoods, while other young women in the sample lived in small villages.

12 The girls themselves did not blame poverty for their offending, nor would many of the others, I believe, have described themselves as 'poor', even though, objectively speaking, they were.

13 Giordano and colleagues' theory of cognitive transformation emphasises the importance of individual agency or 'fundamental shifts in identity and changes in the meaning and desirability of deviant/criminal behavior' (2002: 992) in women's desistance from crime.

14 Matza and Sykes discussed juvenile delinquency and subterranean values only in regard to male delinquency, however, conceptualising thrill-seeking and adventuresomeness as expressions of toughness and machismo, rather than a search for excitement by young people of either sex.

15 Griffin (1997) has argued that (certain) young women and young men have been singled out for attention as a result of adult anxiety and panic over their 'disordered' relationships to cycles of consumption (drugs, alcohol, food), reproduction (teenage pregnancy and motherhood) and production (education and employment), and that policy attention focuses on such young people primarily in an attempt to improve or correct their transitions to responsible and productive adulthood.

16 Data from four 'waves' of the European School Survey Project on Alcohol and Other Drugs (ESPAD) during the 1990s and 2000s indicate that 'binge' alcohol consumption levels are highest among teenagers in the United Kingdom, Denmark, Belgium, the Netherlands, Sweden, Norway, Poland and Ireland and rather lower in southern European counties (Hibell *et al.*, 2004, 2009).

17 In Pavis and colleagues' (1997) examination of the motivations underlying 'risky' drinking among 14- to 17-year-olds, young women were more than twice as likely as young men to report getting drunk for reasons of social facilitation.

18 Research by Coleman and Cater (2005) found that a greater proportion of young women than young men state that they drink as a form of escapism, in order to forget their problems.

19 Others accounted for their psychological absence in terms of anger, rage, distress and not taking prescribed medication.

20 Being 'looked after' may be a particular risk factor for female offending and criminalisation: one north American study found that being 'placed' by social services away from one's family of origin following frequent family moves increased females' risk of adult arrest by almost 200 per cent; however, a similar placement reduced the likelihood of subsequent arrest for males (McMahon and Clay-Warner, 2002).

21 Ritalin, the brand name for the drug methylphenidate, is commonly used to treat attention deficit disorder (ADD), ADHD and narcolepsy. Although both Vicky and Naomi implied that it was their *personal* choice to not take their prescribed medication, it is possible that medical professionals had instilled into them that their behaviour, and by extension their emotions, could only be controlled with medication. Naomi was pregnant when I interviewed her and had stopped using the Ritalin she was prescribed without experiencing any adverse behavioural symptoms.

22 The young women's perceptions of unfair treatment by authority figures are discussed in more detail in Chapter Eight.

23 Toni was not prepared to elaborate on this, and told me that she did not like to talk about her past 'because I don't think it would help'. I noted in Chapter Five that Toni, the only self-reported gang member in the sample, had been forced to move frequently between family members, and she had lived alone in hostels during the two years preceding our interview.

24 See Campbell (1981: 103). It is not clear whether Campbell meant that 66 per cent of *all* girls shoplifted in 1959 or whether 66 per cent of *girls who broke the law* were shoplifters.

25 Details of the sample young women's self-reported offending are provided in Appendix 2.

26 Aged 11 or 12.

27 Facial make-up.

28 Lisa (16), for example, told me that she had recently stolen hair dye, despite having resolved to give up shoplifting, because 'I *needed* to dye my hair'. Older women with some form of legitimate income might of course 'pay' for items such as clothes and make-up with credit cards, which are not available to the under-18s.

29 According to either their self-reports in interview and/or their official criminal records. It is probable that a larger proportion had stolen such items: exactly what they had stolen was not always apparent from the girls' case files and some – especially those with a history of more serious offending – may have not deemed their shoplifting worth discussing with me.

30 Penalty notices for disorder (PNDs) or 'on the spot fines' have, contrary to their title, frequently been used in respect of retail theft offences (Morgan, 2008), and in many cases imposed on young women aged 16 and above. The use of PNDs increased exponentially during the mid-to-late 2000s. See Chapter Three for further discussion.

7 The trouble with girls today

1 See Chapter Four for a description of the roles and professional backgrounds of the practitioners and managers in the sample.

2 I did not ask the professionals exclusively about the girls and young women who featured in Chapters Five and Six, although many practitioners and managers did talk about these same individuals.

3 A widespread belief that 'the family is functionally and normatively more important to girls than to boys' (Nye, 1958: 49) has led to assumptions that 'broken homes' have a greater negative impact on females than males (e.g. Morris, 1964; Datesman and Scarpitti, 1975). Cowie *et al.* (1968), for example, reported that the genesis of girls' psychological problems lay in their families' lack of moral discipline. The girls in their institutionalised sample were found to have worse backgrounds and/or more pathological personalities than boys, encompassing economic, 'moral', disciplinary and family and domestic relationship factors. Conversely, more recent research by Moffitt and colleagues (2001), testing the 'family pathology' hypothesis, found that most of the family risk factors that were analysed – including harsh and inconsistent discipline, family conflict, multiple caregivers and spending more time with a lone parent – had a slightly stronger effect on *boys* than on girls. The authors suggest that girls and boys might respond differentially to stressful family events – namely, that girls might display greater resilience or superior coping mechanisms – and also that male and female children might be treated differently by parents and carers.

4 As I noted in Chapter Five, the Crime and Disorder Act 1998 (s.8) created a new mechanism – the parenting order – for holding parents responsible for the actions of their children.

5 Self-esteem and female offending were said to be linked in 23 interviews (53 per cent).

6 Female offenders have been found to score lower than male offenders on measures of self-esteem (McMurran *et al.*, 1998), although this finding does not in itself provide evidence of causal direction. A raft of studies of incarcerated girls and young women in the United Kingdom (e.g. Howard League, 1997, 2004; Wilkinson and Morris, 2002; Douglas and Plugge, 2006; Batchelor, 2007a) has demonstrated that young

women in prison have significantly higher levels of mental health needs than both young men and adult women in custody.

7 This comment was made during a group interview with workers from Castleshire's Youth Inclusion and Support Panel (YISP). Referrals to the YISP are analysed in Chapter Eight; suffice to say here that the majority of girls YISP worked with had been referred because of concerns about sexual abuse and sexualised behaviour, and not because they had offended or behaved in an antisocial manner.

8 Homeless young women were identified as particularly vulnerable. Midshire YOT's accommodation manager reflected that there is 'always somebody willing to put a young lady up', but 'sometimes you wonder about the price that goes with that'.

9 Bereavement was mentioned in just six interviews (14 per cent).

10 Health professionals are represented among YOT personnel. Indeed, Castleshire YOT had an unusually large team of mental health professionals, including two qualified child psychiatrists who worked with young people on a voluntary basis: they did not breach young people who failed to keep appointments with them and they were willing and able to work with young people beyond the end of a statutory court order. However, several YOT practitioners in Castleshire told me that girls sometimes refused to see the nurse or psychiatrist for fear that this would constitute tacit consent to being labelled mentally ill or 'mad'.

11 Van Mastrigt analysed co-offending data in a sample of over 105,000 notifiable 'cleared' offences committed by 61,646 offenders in the North of England between 2002 and 2005.

12 Moffitt's (1993) typology of 'adolescence-limited' and 'life-course-persistent' offenders stipulates that for the majority of young people who offend (and girls in particular fall into this category), their lawbreaking is restricted to the adolescent years, while a minority begin offending earlier in childhood and persist well into adult life.

13 The relevance of peers to girls' offending was ignored or refuted even when sociological theories of offending focusing on gang culture and peer associations dominated the mainstream criminological literature. While group solidarity, excitement and status seeking were believed to form the basis of *boys'* offending, delinquent *girls* continued to be portrayed as socially isolated misfits well into the 1970s (Campbell, 1981). Empirical research by Campbell (1981, 1984) and Phillips (2003), among others, has demonstrated the significance of peers in girls' offending, and not only that of their brothers.

14 $n = 9$ (19 per cent), of whom all but one were female.

15 The protracted and vindictive nature of girls' 'nasty' behaviour, as the two police officers quoted here perceived things, was also reflected in professionals' accounts of their experiences of supervising female clients, discussed later in this chapter.

16 It might of course be argued that coercion of females by males has in the past been exaggerated in explanations of female offending, which have often negated or minimised the role of women's agency in their lawbreaking.

17 The role of members of the restorative justice team was primarily to assess and supervise young people subject to final warnings and referral orders, rather than to undertake restorative justice interventions specifically. The team had the highest throughput of female clients, as case-holding practitioners in other teams within the YOT tended mainly to supervise young offenders subject to community penalties and those in custody, where the proportion of female clients is lower.

18 I asked all the professionals I interviewed – and not just those employed in Midshire YOT, where the 'gender allocation' policy had been implemented – about their views on worker gender and client allocation.

19 While I was conducting fieldwork in Midshire, I attended a workshop about working with young women who offend. One participant, a male YOT practitioner, revealed that his YOT operated a policy that male workers supervising female clients must

always work in pairs. The policy the worker described did not apply to young male clients, despite the fact that, as a group, they present a significantly higher level of interpersonal risk than females. While false allegations of abuse can of course occur, they may also be levelled at female staff working with clients of either sex. Moreover, there is a need to create a safe working environment for girl clients, very many of whom have suffered abuse at the hands of adult males. Such pair-working policies not only reinforce stereotypes that girls are 'liars' and 'manipulators' (Gaarder *et al.*, 2004); they also raise issues about the efficient use of human resources and beg the question of whose needs such policies are designed to meet. Importantly, anti-sexism training for male and female professionals who work with *boys* may be beneficial to both girls and boys if it enables practitioners to challenge the sexist language which teenage boys so frequently direct at their female counterparts.

20 *What do YOU think?* is a standardised assessment form, used by all YOTs in England and Wales, which is completed by the young offender him- or herself. *What do YOU think?* accompanies the Asset assessment completed by YOT practitioners, although National Standards for Youth Justice indicate that its use, unlike that of Asset, is not compulsory.

21 See Alder (1998), Baines and Alder (1996), Gelsthorpe (1989), Kersten (1990) and Gaarder *et al.* (2004).

22 Midshire YOT was subject to an external inspection when I conducted fieldwork there. A number of YOT staff were off sick with stress, sometimes for prolonged periods, which had further increased the remaining practitioners' workloads.

23 In the words of one female YOT Officer in Castleshire. Notably, interviewees who talked in these terms tended to be female. One might cynically suggest that male staff do not realise when they are being manipulated.

24 Thirteen professionals believed that girls are becoming more violent, including six men (6/16 interviewed) and seven women (7/32 interviewed). Just five individuals believed that female youth violence was not increasing.

25 The Diversion Unit was an inter-agency partnership which worked with young offenders who had received a police caution. The multi-agency nature of the Diversion Unit was similar to that of its successor, the YOT; however, YOTs work with *all* young offenders and the bulk of their work involves young people subject to court orders.

26 Taking a vehicle without the owner's consent.

27 One interviewee noted that girls' mothers, too, were often adamant that their daughters 'would not end up like them'.

28 Contrary to popular stereotypes, getting housed was the least commonly identified motivation for teenage pregnancy among the professionals I interviewed.

29 See Chapter Five for further discussion of teenage pregnancy.

30 For example, the Sure Start initiative, which targets young children and their families living in disadvantaged neighbourhoods.

8 Youth justice for girls in the twenty-first century?

1 Sykes and Matza referred to this phenomenon as 'the condemnation of the condemners' (1957: 668).

2 Twenty-three interviewees (44 per cent of the sample) commented on the unfairness or injustice of their treatment by the police, teachers or other adults.

3 Comparison between self-reported and convicted criminal histories among all age groups demonstrates that the majority of criminal acts go undetected.

4 Just two young women, both aged 19 and both previously in the 'care' system, spoke positively about their respective social workers: Laura saw her social worker as someone she could trust (in contrast to YOT staff, who she associated with the police and

with being prosecuted), and Kate highlighted the considerable practical and moral support her social worker had given her.

5 Kate attributed this to her current social worker being unable to take on young people aged under 16, and no other professional being able or prepared to offer her support at an earlier age. I was not able to verify Kate's account.

6 A young person must attend a youth offender panel if s/he has been given a referral order by the court (see Chapter Three).

7 In an essay on 'carceral clawback' Pat Carlen argues that

the punitive function of the prison has been multiply veiled by governmental, professional or reforming claims that prisons – especially women's prisons – are, or could be, for something other than punishment: for psychological readjustment, training in parenting, drugs rehabilitation, general education or whatever else the 'programmers' of the day may deem to have been lacking in a prisoner's life.

(2002b: 116)

The name 'secure *training* centre' similarly serves to mask the fact that STCs are, in reality, *prisons* for children.

8 Other studies of both young people and women on probation and youth justice supervision have reported similar findings: see Batchelor and McNeill (2005) and McNeill (2006) on young offenders; Covington (2008) and Trotter (2007) on women offenders and Rumgay (2004b, 2007) on the role of professional relationships in encouraging women's desistance from crime.

9 As discussed in Chapter Seven, Midshire YOT had introduced what had become a highly controversial female-only 'casework allocation procedure' for female clients around the time I started the fieldwork for this study.

10 It is important to note that enthusiasm for youth mentoring is not matched by evidence of its effectiveness: evaluations of mentoring schemes targeted at disaffected young people have yielded equivocal evidence at best, in terms of impact on re-offending rates (Jolliffe and Farrington, 2007) with benefits being most apparent in relation to engagement in education, training and employment (Newburn *et al.*, 2005). Few studies have considered mentoring with women who offend, although there is some evidence of higher reported satisfaction with mentoring among female than male clients (Trotter, 2011), and mentoring may have particular benefits for women leaving prison (Brown and Ross, 2010).

11 Resettlement and aftercare provision is attached to YOTs and provides support to young people with substance misuse problems during the (latter) community part of a detention and training order.

12 Criminal Justice and Immigration Act, section 9(3)(d)

13 There was no evidence that any of the girls I interviewed had undertaken direct reparation to the victims of their crimes. Had they done so, their views might have been different.

14 Laura, for example, proudly showed me a box full of certificates that she had obtained after completing numerous boxing and fitness courses.

15 A good example of this in Castleshire YOT related to waiting lists for mental health screening and services. The YOT psychologist told me that his response time for YOT clients with identified mental health needs was no more than five working days for an acute need and 15 working days for a non-acute need. This compared with up to six months for an assessment and a wait of up to two years for an intervention from the (mainstream) child and adolescent mental health team.

16 Castleshire YOT also had a high number of qualified social work practitioners and managers from a social work background and several new YOT workers were undertaking a part-time social work qualification.

17 Previous research examining the sentencing of adult women lends some support to this view. Farrington and Morris (1983) reported a tendency for women offenders sentenced by a majority of female magistrates to be dealt with more severely than when men on a 'bench' of three outnumbered women.

18 Donzelot's contention that the juvenile court 'examines individuals' and upholds and promulgates social norms through its distribution of penal sanctions (1979: 110), is particularly pertinent to the sentencing of girls. Negative perceptions about women's and girls' morality – embodied in, and enacted through, their sexualised and violent behaviour – have been central considerations in the courtroom (Gelsthorpe and Loucks, 1997). Where direct sex comparisons have been made, gender bias in sentencing (although by no means always to females' disadvantage) has been demonstrated, and perceptions of neediness, dependency and vulnerability have underpinned interventionist sentencing practices in respect of females, who are less likely to be fined and more likely to be placed on a restrictive community penalty than similarly placed males (Feilzer and Hood, 2004; Hedderman and Gelsthorpe, 1997; May, 1977). By contrast, young single women who commit offences in company and thus pose a threat to conventional images of femininity may receive little sympathy from magistrates (Worrall, 1990). These themes have been evident for some time: Parker and colleagues, for example, observed more than three decades ago that girls charged with violent offences 'were regarded with a mixture of horror and amazement by many benches' (1981: 71).

19 According to the (female) education manager in Midshire YOT.

20 YISPs accept referrals from a variety of sources, including education, social care, the police, YOTs, the voluntary sector, health and housing agencies, as well as self-referrals.

21 The interview took place in June 2006.

22 A small number of the boys *had* been sexually abused, according to official documentation, but such reasons were not documented in connection with their referral.

23 An ABC is a written agreement between an 'anti-social behaviour perpetrator' and his/her landlord, the local authority, YISP or the police. Contracts, which usually last six months, but can be extended, can be imposed on anyone aged 10 or above. The ABC lists acts that the 'perpetrator' agrees to discontinue and outlines the consequences should s/he breach the contract. ABCs are not legally binding, but they can be cited in court as evidence in any subsequent Anti-Social Behaviour Order application.

24 The evaluation of Intermediate Treatment (IT) schemes in the 1980s found that girls were significantly more likely than boys to be involved in such schemes on a 'voluntary' basis and for reasons other than the commission of offences (Bottoms *et al.*, 1990).

25 A number of the practitioners I interviewed complained that they spent more time in front of a computer screen than they did conducting face-to-face work with young people.

26 The recent Government Green Paper, *Breaking the Cycle*, proposed that YOTs should establish 'compliance panels' in an attempt to reduce the use of youth custody for breach. Contradictorily, the paper also highlights a need for 'robust enforcement' in respect of breaching young offenders, as well as proposing that young people who breach the community supervision requirement of a Detention and Training Order should be returned to custody, even if their order has expired (Ministry of Justice, 2010g: 70–1).

27 I did not interview any girls subject to YISPs and thus cannot comment on the views of this group.

9 Conclusions and recommendations

1 My analysis of the racialised dimensions of lawbreaking and youth justice control in respect of black and minority young women has been limited throughout this book, as

it has elsewhere, and the experiences of criminalised black and minority ethnic (BME) young women warrant further study. My analysis was hampered significantly by the small number of BME young women in the interview sample, as well as the fact that the majority of these young women were interviewed in a secure training centre, where my interviews were subject to strict time limitations so as not to interfere with the centre's education curriculum.

2 See Maher (1997), Miller (2001) and Miller and Mullins (2006b).

3 See Barry (2006), Graham and Bowling (1995), McIvor *et al.* (2004) and Uggen and Kruttschnitt (1998).

4 No criminal charges were brought against this man. See Puffett (2009) and *Yorkshire Post* (2009).

5 See Chapter Three for further discussion of the OBTJ target.

6 The Independent Commission on Youth Crime and Antisocial Behaviour was established in 2008 under the auspices of the Police Foundation, with the purpose of providing 'a blueprint for an effective, humane and sustainable approach to youth crime and antisocial behaviour that is based on clear principles and on sound evidence' (Smith, 2010: xix). The *Time for a Fresh Start* report was accompanied by a book, *A New Response to Youth Crime* (Smith, 2010), which 'presents the more detailed analysis and evidence that forms the background to the Commission's proposals' (ibid.: xix).

7 Pre-sentence reports on young offenders must include information on young people's school performance and behaviour and head teachers are usually asked to supply individual reports for this purpose.

8 See Maruna (2001), ch. 7 for further discussion. Maruna further points out that 'if making an excuse (even if it is a "lie" of sorts) about one's past is required to explain one's present behavior, then this might be an important part of the desistance process' (2001: 145).

9 Sunita Toor has also highlighted that shame (*sharam*) functions as a particularly powerful tool of social control in the lives of Asian women and girls which, she argues, means that 'the moral imperative of restorative justice is not compatible with the cultural context within which Asian girls' lives are determined', since criminalised Asian girls 'are [already] stigmatized and vilified through a process of insular disintegrative shaming administered first and foremost by their families' (2009: 249).

10 Maxwell *et al.* (2004) found that girls involved in restorative conferences in New Zealand were less positive about them than boys were and the authors described girls as more challenging of, and less compliant with, the conference process than boys.

11 In a scoping exercise of provision for girls and young women in the youth justice system conducted by the Youth Justice Board in 2004, 40 per cent of YOTs claimed to provide female-specific programmes of some sort; however, evidence detailing the content of such programmes was provided by just 19 YOTs (Youth Justice Board, 2004b). Several new 'gender-specific' projects for young women offenders have been established recently, including the *Pink Project* in Nottinghamshire and a girls' programme in East Hertfordshire.

References

Aapola, S., Gonick, M. and Harris, A. (eds.) (2005) *Young Femininity: Girlhood, Power and Social Change*. Basingstoke: Palgrave Macmillan.

Ackland, J. (1982) *Girls in Care: A Case Study of Residential Treatment*. Aldershot: Gower.

Acoca, L. (1998) 'Outside/Inside: The Violation of American Girls at Home, On the Streets, and In the Juvenile Justice System', *Crime & Delinquency*, 44(4): 561–89.

Acoca, L. (1999) 'Investing in Girls: A 21st Century Challenge', *Juvenile Justice*, 6(1): 3–13.

Adler, F. (1975) *Sisters in Crime*. New York: McGraw-Hill.

Alder, C. (1998) '"Passionate and Wilful" Girls: Confronting Practices', *Women & Criminal Justice*, 9(4): 81–101.

Alder, C. (2000) 'Young Women Offenders and the Challenge for Restorative Justice', in H. Strang and J. Braithwaite (eds.) *Restorative Justice: Philosophy to Practice*. Aldershot: Ashgate.

Alder, C. and Baines, M. (eds.) (1996) *And When She Was Bad? Working with Young Women in Juvenile Justice and Related Areas*. Hobart, Tasmania: National Clearinghouse for Youth Studies.

Alder, C. and Worrall, A. (eds.) (2004) *Girls' Violence: Myths and Realities*. Albany: State University of New York Press.

Allen, H. (1987) *Justice Unbalanced: Gender, Psychiatry and Judicial Decisions*. Milton Keynes: Open University Press.

Anderson, B., Beinart, S., Farrington, D., Longman, J., Sturgis, P. and Utting, D. (2001) *Risk and Protective Factors Associated with Youth Crime and Effective Interventions to Prevent it*. London: Youth Justice Board.

Anderson, S., Kinsey, R., Loader, I. and Smith, C. (1994) *Cautionary Tales: Young People, Crime and Policing in Edinburgh*. Aldershot: Avebury.

Apter, T. (2004) *You Don't Really Know Me: Why Mothers and Daughters Fight and How Both Can Win*. New York: W.W. Norton & Co.

Armstrong, D. (2004) 'A Risky Business? Research, Policy, Governmentality and Youth Offending', *Youth Justice*, 4(2): 100–16.

Arnull, E. and Eagle, S. (2009) *Girls and Offending – Patterns, Perceptions and Interventions*. London: Youth Justice Board.

Arnull, E., Eagle, S., Gammampila, A., Patel, S., Sadler, J., Thomas, S. and Bateman, T. (2007) *Accommodation Needs and Experiences of Young People Who Offend*. London: Youth Justice Board.

Arthur, R. (2005) 'Punishing Parents for the Crimes of Their Children', *Howard Journal*, 44(3): 233–53.

Artz, S. (1998) *Sex, Power, and the Violent School Girl*. Toronto: Trifolium.

Ashworth, A., Gardner, J., Morgan, R., von Hirsch, A. and Wasik, M. (1998) 'Neighbouring on the Oppressive: The Government's Anti-Social Behaviour Order Proposals', *Criminal Justice*, 16(1): 7–14.

Audit Commission. (1996) *Misspent Youth: Young People and Crime*. London: Audit Commission.

Audit Commission. (2004) *Youth Justice 2004: A Review of the Reformed Youth Justice System*. London: Audit Commission.

Baines, M. and Alder, C. (1996) 'Are Girls More Difficult to Work With? Youth Workers' Perspectives in Juvenile Justice and Related Areas', *Crime & Delinquency*, 42(3): 467–85.

Baker, K. (2004) 'Is Asset Really an Asset? Assessment of Young Offenders in Practice', in R. Burnett and C. Roberts (eds.) *What Works in Probation and Youth Justice*. Cullompton: Willan.

Bandalli, S. (2008) 'Conditional Discharge', in B. Goldson (ed.) *Dictionary of Youth Justice*. Cullompton: Willan.

Barry, M. (2006) *Youth Offending in Transition: The Search for Social Recognition*. Abingdon: Routledge.

Barry, M. (2007) 'The Transitional Pathways of Young Female Offenders: Towards a Non-Offending Lifestyle', in R. Sheehan, G. McIvor and C. Trotter (eds.) *What Works with Women Offenders*. Cullompton: Willan.

Bartky, S.L. (1990) *Femininity and Domination: Studies in the Phenomenology of Oppression*. London: Routledge.

Baskin, D.R. and Sommers, I.B. (1998) *Casualties of Community Disorder: Women's Careers in Violent Crime*. Boulder, CO: Westview Press.

Batchelor, S. (2005) '"Prove Me the Bam!" Victimisation and Agency in the Lives of Young Women Who Commit Violent Offences', *Probation Journal*, 52(4): 358–75.

Batchelor, S. (2007a) *'Prove Me the Bam!' Victimisation and Agency in the Lives of Young Women Who Commit Violent Offences*. Unpublished Ph.D. thesis, University of Glasgow.

Batchelor, S. (2007b) '"Getting Mad Wi' it": Risk Seeking by Young Women', in K. Hannah-Moffat and P. O'Malley (eds.) *Gendered Risks*. Abingdon: Routledge-Cavendish.

Batchelor, S. (2011) 'Beyond Dichotomy: Towards an Explanation of Young Women's Involvement in Violent Street Gangs' in B. Goldson (ed.) *Youth in Crisis? 'Gangs', Territoriality and Violence*. Abingdon: Routledge.

Batchelor, S. and Burman, M. (2004) 'Working with Girls and Young Women', in G. McIvor (ed.) *Women Who Offend*. London: Jessica Kingsley.

Batchelor, S., Burman, M. and Brown, J. (2001) 'Discussing Violence: Let's Hear it from the Girls', *Probation Journal*, 48(2): 125–34.

Batchelor, S. and McNeill, F. (2005) 'The Young Person-Worker Relationship', in T. Bateman and J. Pitts (eds.) *The RHP Companion to Youth Justice*. Lyme Regis: Russell House Publishing.

Bateman, T. (2006) 'Changes to Final Warning Guidance', *Youth Justice*, 6(3): 219–28.

Bateman, T. (2008a) *Review of Provision for Girls in Custody to Reduce Offending*. Reading, MA: CfBT Education Trust.

Bateman, T. (2008b) '"Target Practice": Anction Detection and the Criminalisation of Children', *Criminal Justice Matters*, 73(1): 2–4.

Bateman, T. (2010) 'Reoffending as a Measure of Effectiveness of Youth Justice Intervention: A Critical Note', *Safer Communities*, 9(3): 28–35.

Beck, U. (1992) *Risk Society: Towards a New Modernity*. London: Sage.

Beck, U., Giddens, A. and Lash, S. (1994) *Reflexive Modernization: Politics, Tradition and Aesthetics in the Modern Social Order*. Cambridge: Policy Press.

Becker, H. (1967) 'Whose Side Are We On?', *Social Problems*, 14(3): 239–47.

Belknap, J. (2007) *The Invisible Woman: Gender, Crime and Justice* (3rd edition). Belmont, CA: Wadsworth.

Belknap, J. and Holsinger, K. (1998) 'An Overview of Delinquent Girls: How Theory and Practice Have Failed and the Need for Innovative Changes', in R. Zaplin (ed.) *Female*

Offenders: Critical Perspectives and Effective Interventions. Gaithersburg, MD: Aspen Publishers.

Belknap, J. and Holsinger, K. (2006) 'The Gendered Nature of Risk Factors for Delinquency', *Feminist Criminology*, 1(1): 48–71.

Biggart, A. (2002) 'Attainment, Gender and Minimum-Aged School Leavers' Early Routes in the Labour Market', *Journal of Education and Work*, 15: 145–62.

Black, D. (2002) 'The Family and Childhood Bereavement: An Overview', *Bereavement Care*, 21(2): 24–36.

Bloom, B., Owen, B., Rosenbaum, J. and Deschenes, E.P. (2003) 'Focusing on Girls and Young Women: A Gendered Perspective on Female Delinquency', *Women & Criminal Justice*, 14(2/3): 117–36.

Blos, P. (1969) 'Pre-oedipal Factors in the Aetiology of Female Delinquency', *Psychoanalytic Studies of the Child*, 12: 229–49.

Blumer, H. (1969) *Symbolic Interactionism: Perspective and Method.* Englewood Cliffs, NJ: Prentice-Hall.

Booth, J. (2010) 'Tories under attack over teen pregnancy blunder', *The Times*, 15th February.

Boswell, G. (1996) *Young and Dangerous: The Backgrounds and Careers of Section 53 Offenders.* Aldershot: Avebury.

Bottoms, A. (1974) 'On the Decriminalisation of English Juvenile Courts', in R. Hood (ed.) *Crime, Criminology and Public Policy.* London: Heinemann.

Bottoms, A. (1995) 'The Philosophy and Politics of Punishment and Sentencing', in C. Clarkson and R. Morgan (eds.) *The Politics of Sentencing Reform.* Oxford: Clarendon Press.

Bottoms, A. (2008) 'The Relationship Between Theory and Empirical Observations in Criminology', in R. King and E. Wincup (eds.) *Doing Research on Crime and Justice* (2nd edition). Oxford: Oxford University Press.

Bottoms, A. and Dignan, J. (2004) 'Youth Justice in Great Britain', in M. Tonry and A. Doob (eds.) *Youth Crime and Youth Justice: Comparative and Cross-National Perspectives.* Chicago, IL: University of Chicago Press.

Bottoms, A., Brown, P., McWilliams, B., McWilliams, W. and Nellis, M. (1990) *Intermediate Treatment and Juvenile Justice: Key Findings and Implications from a National Survey of Intermediate Treatment Policy and Practice.* London: HMSO.

Bottoms, A. and Pratt, J. (1989) 'Intermediate Treatment for Girls in England and Wales', in M. Cain (ed.) *Growing Up Good. Policing the Behaviour of Girls in Europe.* London: Sage.

Bowlby, J. (1973) *Attachment and Loss, Volume 2. Separation: Anxiety and Anger.* Harmondsworth: Penguin.

Box, S. and Hale, C. (1983) 'Liberation and Female Criminality in England and Wales', *British Journal of Criminology*, 23(1): 35–49.

Bracchi, P. (2008) 'The feral sex: The terrifying rise of violent girl gangs', *Daily Mail*, 16th May.

Brown, M. and Ross, S. (2010) 'Mentoring, Social Capital and Desistance: A Study of Women Released from Prison', *Australian & New Zealand Journal of Criminology*, 43(1): 31–50.

Budd, T., Sharp, C. and Mayhew, P. (2005) *Offending in England and Wales: First Results from the 2003 Crime and Justice Survey.* Home Office Research Study 275. London: HMSO.

Burman, M. (2004) 'Turbulent Talk: Girls' Making Sense of Violence', in C. Alder and A. Worrall (eds.) *Girls' Violence: Myths and Realities.* Albany, NY: State University of New York Press.

Burman, M. and Batchelor, S. (2009) 'Between Two Stools? Responding to Young Women Who Offend', *Youth Justice*, 9(3): 270–85.

Burman, M., Batchelor, S. and Brown, J. (2001) 'Researching Girls and Violence: Facing the Dilemmas of Fieldwork', *British Journal of Criminology*, 41(3): 443–59.

Burnett, R. (2007) 'Never Too Early? Reflections on Research and Interventions for Early Developmental Prevention of Serious Harm', in M. Blyth, E. Solomon and K. Baker (eds.) *Young People and 'Risk'*. Bristol: Policy Press.

Burnett, R. and Appleton, C. (2004) 'Joined-Up Services to Tackle Youth Crime: A Case-Study in England', *British Journal of Criminology*, 44(1): 34–54.

Burnett, R. and McNeill, F. (2005) 'The Place of the Officer–Offender Relationship in Assisting Offenders to Desist from Crime', *Probation Journal*, 52(3): 221–42.

Burney, E. and Gelsthorpe, L. (2008) 'Do We Need a "Naughty Step"? Rethinking the Parenting Order After Ten Years', *Howard Journal*, 47(5): 470–85.

Buzawa, E. and Hotaling, G. (2006) 'The Impact of Relationship Status, Gender, and Minor Status in the Police Response to Domestic Assaults', *Victims and Offenders*, 1: 1–38.

Cain, M. (1990) 'Towards Transgression: New Directions in Feminist Criminology', *International Journal of the Sociology of Law*, 18: 1–18.

Campbell, A. (1981) *Girl Delinquents*. Oxford: Basil Blackwell.

Campbell, A. (1984) *The Girls in the Gang*. Oxford and New York: Basil Blackwell.

Carlen, P. (1983) *Women's Imprisonment*. London: Routledge.

Carlen, P. (1987) 'Out of Care, into Custody', in P. Carlen and A. Worrall (eds.) *Gender, Crime and Justice*. Milton Keynes: Open University Press.

Carlen, P. (1988) *Women, Crime and Poverty*. Milton Keynes: Open University Press.

Carlen, P. (1996) *Jigsaw: A Political Criminology of Youth Homelessness*. Buckingham: Open University Press.

Carlen, P. (2002a) 'Introduction: Women and Punishment', in P. Carlen (ed.) *Women and Punishment: The Struggle for Justice*. Cullompton: Willan.

Carlen, P. (2002b) 'Carceral Clawback: The Case of Women's Imprisonment in Canada', *Punishment & Society*, 4(1): 115–21.

Carlen, P., Hicks, J., O'Dwyer, J., Christina, D. and Tchaikovsky, C. (1985) *Criminal Women: Autobiographical Accounts*. Cambridge: Polity Press.

Carrington, K. (1993) *Offending Girls: Sex, Youth and Justice*. St. Leonards, New South Wales: Allen and Unwin.

Carrington, K. (2006) 'Does Feminism Spoil Girls? Explanations for Official Rises in Female Delinquency', *Australian & New Zealand Journal of Criminology*, 39(1): 34–53.

Carrington, K. with Pereira, M. (2009) *Offending Youth: Sex, Crime and Justice*. Leichhardt, Australia: The Federation Press.

Case, S. (2007) 'Questioning the "Evidence" of Risk that Underpins Evidence-Led Youth Justice Interventions', *Youth Justice*, 7(2): 91–105.

Case, S. and Haines, K. (2009) *Understanding Youth Offending: Policy, Practice and Research*. Cullompton: Willan.

Caspi, A., Lynam, D., Moffitt, T.E. and Silva, P.A. (1993) 'Unraveling Girls' Delinquency: Biological, Dispositional, and Contextual Contributions to Adolescent Misbehavior', *Developmental Psychology*, 29: 19–30.

Cernkovich, S.A. and Giordano, P.C. (1987) 'Family Relationships and Delinquency', *Criminology*, 25(2): 295–319.

Cernkovich, S.A., Lanctôt, N. and Giordano, P.C. (2008) 'Predicting Adolescent and Adult Antisocial Behavior Among Adjudicated Delinquent Females', *Crime & Delinquency*, 54(1): 3–33.

Chesney-Lind, M. (1974) 'Juvenile Delinquency and the Sexualisation of Female Crime', *Psychology Today*, July: 4–7.

Chesney-Lind, M. (1986) 'Women and Crime: A Review of the Literature on the Female Offender', *Signs: Journal of Women in Culture and Society*, 12(1): 78–96.

Chesney-Lind, M. (1989) 'Girls' Crime and Woman's Place: Toward a Feminist Model of Female Delinquency', *Crime & Delinquency*, 35: 5–30.

Chesney-Lind, M. (2002) 'Criminalizing Victimization: The Unintended Consequences of Pro-Arrest Policies for Girls and Women', *Criminology & Public Policy*, 2(1): 81–90.

Chesney-Lind, M. and Eliason, M. (2006) 'From Invisible to Incorrigible: The Demonization of Marginalized Women and Girls', *Crime, Media, Culture*, 2: 29–47.

Chesney-Lind, M. and Hagedorn, J. (1999) *Female Gangs in America: Essays on Girls, Gangs, and Gender*. Chicago, IL: Lakeview Press.

Chesney-Lind, M. and Irwin, K. (2008) *Beyond Bad Girls: Gender, Violence and Hype*. New York: Routledge.

Chesney-Lind, M. and Jones, H. (eds.) (2010) *Fighting for Girls: New Perspectives on Gender and Violence*. Albany, NY: State University of New York Press.

Chesney-Lind, M. and Pasko, L. (2004) *The Female Offender: Girls, Women, and Crime* (2nd edition). Thousand Oaks, CA: Sage.

Chesney-Lind, M. and Shelden, R.G. (2004) *Girls, Delinquency and Juvenile Justice* (3rd edition). Belmont, CA: Wadsworth.

Chigwada-Bailey, R. (2004) 'Black Women and the Criminal Justice System', in G. McIvor (ed.) *Women Who Offend*. London: Jessica Kingsley.

Cohen, S. (1985) *Visions of Social Control*. Cambridge: Polity Press.

Coleman, L. and Cater, S. (2005) *Underage 'Risky' Drinking: Motivations and Outcomes*. York: Joseph Rowntree Foundation.

Conservative Party. (2010) *Labour's Two Nations*. London: The Conservative Party.

Covington, S. (2008) 'The Relational Theory of Women's Psychological Development: Implications for the Criminal Justice System', in R. Zaplin (ed.) *Female Offenders: Critical Perspectives and Effective Interventions* (2nd edition). Sudbury, MA: Jones and Bartlett Publishers.

Cowie, J., Cowie, V. and Slater, E. (1968) *Delinquency in Girls*. London: Heinemann.

Cox, P. (2003) *Gender, Justice and Welfare: Bad Girls in Britain, 1900–1950*. Basingstoke: Palgrave Macmillan.

Crawford, A. (2009a) 'Governing Through Anti-Social Behaviour: Regulatory Challenges to Criminal Justice', *British Journal of Criminology*, 49(6): 810–31.

Crawford, A. (2009b) 'Criminalizing Sociability Through Anti-Social Behaviour Legislation: Dispersal Powers, Young People and the Police', *Youth Justice*, 9(1): 5–26.

Crick, N. and Dodge, K. (1996) 'Social Information-Processing Mechanisms in Reactive and Proactive Aggression', *Child Development*, 67: 993–1002.

Crozier, J. and Anstiss, J. (1995) 'Out of the Spotlight: Girls' Experience of Disruption', in M. Lloyd-Smith and J. Dwyfor Davies (eds.) *On the Margins: The Educational Experience of 'Problem' Pupils*. Stoke-on-Trent: Trentham Books.

Daly, K. (1994) *Gender, Crime and Punishment*. New Haven, CT: Yale University Press.

Daly, K. (1998) 'Women's Pathways to Felony Court: Feminist Theories of Lawbreaking and Problems of Representation', in K. Daly and L. Maher (eds.) *Criminology at the Crossroads: Feminist Readings in Crime and Justice*. New York: Oxford University Press.

Daly, K. (2008) 'Girls, Peer Violence, and Restorative Justice', *Australian & New Zealand Journal of Criminology*, 41(1): 109–37.

Datesman, S.K. and Scarpitti, F.R. (1975) 'Female Delinquency and Broken Homes: A Reassessment', *Criminology*, 13(1): 33–55.

Davies, A. (2008) *The Gangs of Manchester*. Preston: Milo Books.

Davis, C.P. (2007) 'At-Risk Girls and Delinquency: Career Pathways', *Crime & Delinquency*, 53(3): 408–35.

Department for Children, Schools and Families. (2008) *First-Time Entrants Aged 10–17 to the Criminal Justice System in England, 2000–01 to 2007–08*. London: Department for Children, Schools and Families.

Department for Education and Skills. (2007) *Permanent and Fixed Period Exclusions from Schools and Exclusion Appeals in England, 2005/06*. Statistical First Release, 21/2007. London: Department for Education and Skills.

Donzelot, J. (1979) *The Policing of Families*. London: Hutchinson.

Douglas, N. and Plugge, E. (2006) *Female Health Needs in Young Offender Institutions*. London: Youth Justice Board.

DTZ Pieda Consulting.(2005) *Measurement of the Extent of Youth Crime in Scotland*. Edinburgh: Scottish Executive.

Duncan, S., Edwards, R. and Alexander, C. (eds.) (2010) *Teenage Parenthood: What's the Problem?* London: Tufnell Press.

Dweck, C. (2000) *Self-Theories: Their Role in Motivation, Personality, and Development*. Philadelphia, PA: Taylor and Francis.

Dwyer, P. and Wyn, J. (2001) *Youth, Education and Risk: Facing the Future*. London: Routledge Falmer.

Earle, R. (2005) 'The Referral Order', in T. Bateman and J. Pitts (eds.) *The RHP Companion to Youth Justice*. Lyme Regis: Russell House Publishing.

Eaton, M. (1993) *Women after Prison*. Buckingham: Open University Press.

Edwards, R. (2009) 'Violent attacks by teenage girls treble in seven years', *The Telegraph*, 1st March.

Evans, R. and Puech, K. (2001) 'Reprimands and Warnings: Populist Punitiveness or Restorative Justice?', *Criminal Law Review*, October: 794–805.

Fagan, A. (2001) 'The Gender Cycle of Violence: Comparing the Effects of Child Abuse and Neglect on Criminal Offending for Males and Females', *Violence and Victims*, 16: 457–74.

Fagan, J. and Tyler, T. (2005) 'Legal Socialisation of Children and Adolescents', *Social Justice Research*, 18(3): 217–41.

Farrington, D. (1996) *Understanding and Preventing Youth Crime*. York: Joseph Rowntree Foundation.

Farrington, D. (2007) 'Childhood Risk Factors and Risk-Focused Prevention', in M. Maguire, R. Morgan and R. Reiner (eds.) *The Oxford Handbook of Criminology* (4th edition). Oxford: Oxford University Press.

Farrington, D. and Morris, A. (1983) 'Sex, Sentencing and Reconviction', *British Journal of Criminology*, 23(3): 229–58.

Farrington, D. and Painter, K. (2004) *Gender Differences in Offending: Implications for Risk-Focussed Prevention*. Home Office Online Report 09/04. London: Home Office.

Federal Bureau of Investigation. (2009) *Crime in the United States, 2007. Uniform Crime Reports*. Washington, DC: FBI, Department of Justice.

Feeley, M. and Simon, J. (1992) 'The New Penology: Notes on the Emerging Strategy of Corrections and Its Implications', *Criminology*, 30: 449–74.

Feilzer, M. and Hood, R. (2004) In consultation with Fitzgerald, M. and Roddam, A. *Differences or Discrimination? Minority Ethnic Young People in the Youth Justice System*. London: Youth Justice Board.

Feld, B. (2009) 'Girls in the Juvenile Justice System', in M. Zahn (ed.) *The Delinquent Girl*. Philadelphia, PA: Temple University Press.

Field, S. (2007) 'Practice Cultures and the "New" Youth Justice in (England and) Wales', *British Journal of Criminology*, 47(2): 311–30.

Finch, J. (1984) '"It's Great to have Someone to Talk to": The Ethics and Politics of Interviewing Women', in C. Bell and H. Roberts (eds.) *Social Researching: Politics, Problems, Practice*. London: Routledge and Kegan Paul.

Flood-Page, C., Campbell, S., Harrington, V. and Miller, J. (2000) *Youth Crime: Findings from the 1998/99 Youth Lifestyles Survey*. Home Office Research Study 209. London: HMSO.

Ford, R. (2009) 'Ladettes push girl violence to new high', *The Times*, 30th January.

Foucault, M. (1977) *Discipline and Punish: The Birth of the Prison*. London: Allen Lane.

Furlong, A. and Cartmel, F. (2007) *Young People and Social Change: New Perspectives* (2nd edition). Maidenhead: McGraw-Hill/Open University Press.

Gaarder, E., Rodriguez, N. and Zatz, M.S. (2004) 'Criers, Liars and Manipulators: Probation Officers' Views of Girls', *Justice Quarterly*, 21(3): 547–78.

Garland, D. (1997) '"Governmentality" and the Problem of Crime: Foucault, Criminology, Sociology', *Theoretical Criminology*, 1: 173–214.

Garland, D. (2001) *The Culture of Control: Crime and Social Order in Contemporary Society*. Oxford: Oxford University Press.

Gelsthorpe, L. (1989) *Sexism and the Female Offender*. Aldershot: Gower.

Gelsthorpe, L. (1990) 'Feminist Methodologies in Criminology: A New Approach or Old Wine in New Bottles?', in L. Gelsthorpe and A. Morris (eds.) *Feminist Perspectives in Criminology*. Buckingham: Open University Press.

Gelsthorpe, L. (2004) 'Female Offending: A Theoretical Overview', in G. McIvor (ed.) *Women Who Offend*. London: Jessica Kingsley.

Gelsthorpe, L. (2005a) 'Girls in the Youth Justice System', in T. Bateman and J. Pitts (eds.) *The RHP Companion to Youth Justice*. Lyme Regis: Russell House Publishing.

Gelsthorpe, L. (2005b) 'The Experiences of Female Minority Ethnic Offenders: The Other "Other"', in S. Lewis, P. Raynor, D. Smith and A. Wardak (eds.) *Race and Probation*. Cullompton: Willan.

Gelsthorpe, L. and Loucks, N. (1997) 'Magistrates' Explanations of Sentencing Decisions', in C. Hedderman and L. Gelsthorpe (eds.) *Understanding the Sentencing of Women*. London: Home Office.

Gelsthorpe, L. and Morris, A. (1994) 'Juvenile Justice 1945–1992', in M. Maguire, R. Morgan and R. Reiner (eds.) *The Oxford Handbook of Criminology*. Oxford: Clarendon Press.

Gelsthorpe, L. and Sharpe, G. (2006) 'Gender, Youth Crime and Justice', in B. Goldson and J. Muncie (eds.) *Youth Crime and Justice*. London: Sage.

Gelsthorpe, L., Sharpe, G. and Roberts, J. (2007) *Provision for Women Offenders in the Community*. London: The Fawcett Society.

Gelsthorpe, L. and Worrall, A. (2009) 'Looking for Trouble: A Recent History of Girls, Young Women and Youth Justice', *Youth Justice*, 9(3): 209–23.

Ghate, D. and Ramella, M. (2002) *Positive Parenting. The National Evaluation of the Youth Justice Board's Parenting Programme*. London: Youth Justice Board.

Gibbens, T.C.N. (1959) 'Supervision and Probation of Adolescent Girls', *British Journal of Delinquency*, 10: 84–103.

Giddens, A. (1990) *The Consequences of Modernity*. Oxford: Polity.

Giddens, A. (1991) *Modernity and Self-Identity. Self and Society in the Late Modern Age*. Oxford: Polity.

Gil-Robles, A. (2005) Report by Mr Alvaro Gil-Robles, Commissioner for Human Rights, on his visit to the United Kingdom, 4th–12th November 2004. Office of the Commissioner for Human Rights, 8 June, CommDH(2005)6. Strasbourg: Council of Europe.

Gilfus, M. (1992) 'From Victims to Survivors to Offenders: Women's Routes of Entry into Street Crime', *Women & Criminal Justice*, 4(1): 63–89.

Gill, R. (2003) 'From Sexual Objectification to Sexual Subjectification: The Resexualisation of Women's Bodies in the Media', *Feminist Media Studies*, 3(1): 100–6.

Gillborn, D. (1998) 'Racism, Selection, Poverty and Parents: New Labour, Old Problems?', *Journal of Education Policy*, 13(6): 717–35.

Giller, H. (1982) *Community Homes with Education on the Premises: A Study of the Policy and Practice of Residential Treatment for Juvenile Offenders*. Unpublished Ph.D. thesis, University of Cambridge.

Gilligan, G. (1989) 'Teaching Shakespeare's Sister: Notes from the Underground of Female Adolescence', in C. Gilligan, N. Lyons and T. Hanmer (eds.) *Making Connections: The Relational Worlds of Adolescent Girls at Emma Willard School.* Cambridge, MA: Harvard University Press.

Gilligan, C. (1991) 'Women's Psychological Development: Implications for Psychotherapy', in C. Gilligan, A. Roger and D. Tolman (eds.) *Women, Girls and Psychotherapy.* Binghamton, NY: The Haworth Press.

Giordano, P. (1978) 'Girls, Guys and Gangs: The Changing Social Context of Female Delinquency', *The Journal of Criminal Law and Criminology*, 69(1): 126–32.

Giordano, P. (2009) 'Peer Influences on Girls' Delinquency', in M. Zahn (ed.) *The Delinquent Girl.* Philadelphia, PA: Temple University Press.

Giordano, P., Cernkovich, S. and Rudolph, J. (2002) 'Gender, Crime and Desistance: Toward a Theory of Cognitive Transformation', *American Journal of Sociology*, 107(4): 990–1064.

Giordano, P., Deines, J. and Cernkovich, S. (2006) 'In and Out of Crime: A Life Course Perspective on Girls' Delinquency', in K. Heimer and C. Kruttschnitt (eds.) *Gender and Crime: Patterns in Victimization and Offending.* New York: New York University Press.

Girlguiding UK. (2007) *Girls Shout Out! A UK-wide Research Report by Girlguiding UK.* London: The Guide Association.

Glaser, B. and Strauss, A. (1967) *The Discovery of Grounded Theory: Strategies for Qualitative Research.* Chicago, IL: Aldine.

Glueck, S. and Glueck, E. (1934) *Five Hundred Delinquent Women.* New York: Knopf.

Godfrey, B. (2004) 'Rough Girls, 1880–1930: The "Recent" History of Violent Young Women', inC. Alder and A. Worrall (eds.)*Girls' Violence: Myths and Realities.* Albany, NY: State University of New York Press.

Goldson, B. (1997) '"Childhood": An Introduction to Historical and Theoretical Analyses', in P. Scraton (ed.) *'Childhood' in 'Crisis'?* London: UCL Press.

Goldson, B. and Jamieson, J. (2002) 'Youth Crime, the "Parenting Deficit" and State Intervention: A Contextual Critique', *Youth Justice*, 2(2): 82–98.

Goldson, B. and Muncie, J. (2006) 'Critical Anatomy: Towards a Principled Youth Justice', in B. Goldson and J. Muncie (eds.) *Youth Crime and Justice.* London: Sage.

Goodkind, S., Ng, I. and Sarri, R.C. (2006) 'The Impact of Sexual Abuse in the Lives of Young Women Involved or at Risk of Involvement with the Juvenile Justice System', *Violence Against Women*, 12(5): 456–77.

Graham, J. and Bowling, B. (1995) *Young People and Crime.* Home Office Research Study 145. London: HMSO.

Griffin, C. (1997) 'Troubled Teens: Managing Disorders of Transition and Consumption', *Feminist Review*, 55: 4–21.

Griffin, C. (2004) 'Good Girls, Bad Girls: Anglocentrism and Diversity in the Constitution of Contemporary Girlhood', in A. Harris (ed.) *All About the Girl: Culture, Power, and Identity.* New York: Routledge.

Griffin, C., Bengry-Howell, A., Hackley, C., Mistral, W. and Szmigin, I. (2009) '"Every Time I Do It I Absolutely Annihilate Myself": Loss of (Self-)Consciousness and Loss of Memory in Young People's Drinking Narratives', *Sociology*, 43(3): 457–76.

Griffiths, V. (1995) *Adolescent Girls and Their Friends: A Feminist Ethnography.* Gower: Avebury.

Hall, S., Winlow, S. and Ancrum, C. (2008) *Criminal Identities and Consumer Culture: Crime, Exclusion and the New Culture of Narcissism.* Cullompton: Willan.

Hammersley, M. and Atkinson, P. (1983) *Ethnography: Principles in Practice.* London: Tavistock.

Hammersley, R., Marsland, L. and Reid, M. (2003) *Substance Use by Young Offenders: The Impact of the Normalisation of Drug Use in the Early Years of the 21st Century.* Home Office Research Study 261. London: HMSO.

Hannah-Moffat, K. (2005) 'Criminogenic Needs and the Transformative Risk Subject: Hybridizations of Risk/Need in Penality', *Punishment & Society*, 7(1): 29–51.

Harding, S. (ed.) (1987a) *Feminism and Methodology*. Milton Keynes: Open University Press.

Harding, S. (1987b) 'Introduction: Is There a Feminist Method?', in S. Harding (ed.) *Feminism and Methodology*. Milton Keynes: Open University Press.

Harrington, R. (2001) 'Depression, Suicide and Deliberate Self-Harm in Adolescence', *British Medical Bulletin*, 57: 47–60.

Harris, A. (2004) *Future Girl: Young Women in the Twentieth Century*. London: Routledge.

Hart, D. (2010) *Children and Young People in 'Breach': A Scoping Report on Policy and Practice in the Enforcement of Criminal Justice and Anti-Social Behaviour Orders*. London: National Children's Bureau.

Hartless, J.M., Ditton, J., Nair, G. and Phillips, S. (1995) 'More Sinned Against than Sinning: A Study of Young Teenagers' Experience of Crime', *British Journal of Criminology*, 35(1): 114–33.

Hawton, K., Fagg, J., Simkin, S., Bale, E. and Bond, A. (2000) 'Deliberate Self-Harm in Adolescents in Oxford 1985–1995', *Journal of Adolescence* (23): 47–55.

Haynie, D.L. (2003) 'Contexts of Risk? Explaining the Link Between Girls' Pubertal Development and Their Delinquency Involvement', *Social Forces*, 82(1): 355–97.

Hedderman, C. (2004) 'The "Criminogenic" Needs of Women Offenders', in G. McIvor (ed.) *Women Who Offend*. London: Jessica Kingsley.

Hedderman, C. and Gelsthorpe, L. (eds.) (1997) *Understanding the Sentencing of Women*. London: HMSO.

Heidensohn, F. (1968) 'The Deviance of Women: A Critique and an Enquiry', *British Journal of Sociology*, 19: 160–75.

Heidensohn, F. (1996) *Women and Crime* (2nd edition). Basingstoke: Macmillan.

Heidensohn, F. (2000) *Sexual Politics and Social Control*. Buckingham: Open University Press.

Hennessy, P. (2008) 'Teenage girl crime rises by 25pc: Britain is in the grip of an unprecedented crime wave among teenage girls, government figures will confirm this week', *The Telegraph*, 10th May.

Her Majesty's Government. (2008) *Youth Crime Action Plan 2008*. London: Home Office.

Her Majesty's Prison Service and Youth Justice Board. (2003) *Child Protection and Safeguards Review*. London: Her Majesty's Prison Service/Youth Justice Board.

Hester, M. (2009) *Who Does What to Whom? Gender and Domestic Violence Perpetrators*. Bristol: University of Bristol in association with the Northern Rock Foundation.

Hey, V. (1997) *The Company She Keeps: An Ethnography of Girls' Friendships*. Buckingham: Open University Press.

Hibell, B., Andersson, B., Bjarnason, T., Ahlström, S., Balakireva, O., Kokkevi, A. and Morgan, M. (2004) *The ESPAD Report 2003: Alcohol and Other Drug Use Among Students in 35 European Countries*. Stockholm: The Swedish Council for Information on Alcohol and Other Drugs.

Hibell, B., Guttormsson, U., Ahlström, S., Balakireva, O., Bjarnason, T., Kokkevi, A. and Kraus, L. (2009) *The 2007 ESPAD Report: Substance Use Among Students in 35 European Countries*. Stockholm: The Swedish Council for Information on Alcohol and Other Drugs.

Hinds, L. (2007) 'Building Police–Youth Relationships: The Importance of Procedural Justice', *Youth Justice*, 7(3): 195–210.

Hoghughi, M. (1978) *Troubled and Troublesome: Coping with Severely Disordered Children*. London: Burnett.

Holdaway, S., Davidson, N., Dignan, J., Hammersley, R., Hine, J. and Marsh, P. (2001) *New Strategies to Address Youth Offending: The National Evaluation of the Pilot Youth Offending Teams*. RDS Occasional paper 69. London: HMSO.

Hollin, C. and Palmer, E. (2006a) 'Criminogenic Need and Women Offenders: A Critique of the Literature', *Legal and Criminological Psychology*, 11: 179–95.

Hollin, C. and Palmer, E. (2006b) 'Offending Behaviour Programmes: Controversies and Resolutions', in C. Hollin and E. Palmer (eds.) *Offending Behaviour Programmes: Development, Application, and Controversies*. Chichester: Wiley.

Holsinger, K. (2000) 'Feminist Perspectives on Female Offending: Examining Real Girls' Lives', *Women & Criminal Justice*, 12(1): 23–51.

Holt, A. (2008) 'Room for Resistance? Parenting Orders, Disciplinary Power and the Production of "The Bad Parent"', in P. Squires (ed.) *ASBO Nation: The Criminalisation of Nuisance*. Bristol: Policy Press.

Home Office. (1968) *Children in Trouble*. Cmnd 3601. London: HMSO.

Home Office. (1997) *No More Excuses: A New Approach to Tackling Youth Crime in England and Wales*. Cmnd 3809. London: HMSO.

Home Office. (2001) *Criminal Statistics, England and Wales 2000*. London: The Stationery Office.

Home Office. (2003) *Criminal Statistics, England and Wales 2002*. London: The Stationery Office.

Honigsbaum, M. (2006) 'British girls among most violent in world, WHO survey shows. Link to binge-drinking "ladette" culture feared', *The Guardian*, 24th January.

Hough, A. (2010) 'Judge: "Ladette binge-drinking culture" to blame for "plague" of alcohol fuelled violence', *The Telegraph*, 28th May.

Howard League. (1997) *Lost Inside: The Imprisonment of Teenage Girls*. London: The Howard League.

Howard League. (2004) *Advice, Understanding and Underwear: Working with Girls in Prison*. London: The Howard League.

Hudson, A. (1989) 'Troublesome Girls': Towards Alternative Definitions and Policies', in M. Cain (ed.) *Growing Up Good. Policing the Behaviour of Girls in Europe*. London: Sage.

Hudson, B. (1984) 'Adolescence and Femininity', in A. McRobbie and M. Nava (eds.) *Gender and Generation*. London: Macmillan.

Hudson, B. (1989) 'Justice or Welfare? A Comparison of Recent Developments in the English and French Juvenile Justice Systems', in M. Cain, (ed.) *Growing Up Good: Policing the Behaviour of Girls in Europe*. London: Sage.

Hudson, B. (2003) *Justice in the Risk Society*. London: Sage.

Hunt, F. (1991) *Gender and Policy in English Education: Schooling for Girls 1902–44*. London: Harvester/Wheatsheaf.

Independent Commission on Youth Crime and Antisocial Behaviour. (2010) *Time for a Fresh Start: The Report of the Independent Commission on Youth Crime and Antisocial Behaviour*. London: The Police Foundation.

Jackson, C. and Tinkler, P. (2007) '"Ladettes" and "Modern Girls": "Troublesome" Young Femininities', *Sociological Review*, 55(2): 251–72.

Jacobson, J., Bhardwa, B., Gyateng, T., Hunter, G. and Hough, M. (2010) *Punishing Disadvantage: A Profile of Children in Custody*. London: Prison Reform Trust.

Jamieson, J., McIvor, G. and Murray, C. (1999) *Understanding Offending Among Young People*. Edinburgh: The Stationery Office.

Joe, K. and Chesney-Lind, M. (1995) '"Just Every Mother's Angel": An Analysis of Gender and Ethnic Variations in Youth Gang Membership', *Gender & Society*, 9: 408–31.

Jolliffe, D. and Farrington, D. (2007) *A Rapid Evidence Assessment of Mentoring*. London: Home Office.

Katz, J. (1988) *Seductions of Crime: Moral and Sensual Attractions in Doing Evil*. New York: Basic Books.

Kaufman, J.G. and Widom, C.S. (1999) 'Childhood Victimization, Running Away, and Delinquency', *Journal of Research in Crime and Delinquency*, 36(4): 347–70.

Kempf-Leonard, K. and Peterson, E. (2000) 'Expanding Realms of the New Penology: The Advent of Actuarial Justice for Juveniles', *Punishment & Society*, 2(1): 66–97.

Kemshall, H. (2004) 'Risk, Dangerousness and Female Offenders', in G. McIvor (ed.) *Women Who Offend*. London: Jessica Kingsley.

Kemshall, H. (2008) 'Risks, Rights and Justice: Understanding and Responding to Youth Risk', *Youth Justice*, 8(1): 21–37.

Kersten, J. (1990) 'A Gender Specific Look at Patterns of Violence in Juvenile Institutions: or Are Girls Really "More Difficult to Handle"?', *International Journal of the Sociology of Law*, 18: 473–93.

Konopka, G. (1966) *The Adolescent Girl in Conflict*. Englewood Cliffs, NJ: Prentice Hall.

Lanctôt, N. and LeBlanc, M. (2002) 'Explaining Deviance by Adolescent Females', in M. Tonry (ed.) *Crime and Justice: A Review of Research*, vol. 29. Chicago, IL: University of Chicago Press.

Layder, D. (1998) *Sociological Practice: Linking Theory and Social Research*. London: Sage.

Lees, S. (1993) *Sugar and Spice: Sexuality and Adolescent Girls*. London: Penguin.

Lees, S. (2002) *Carnal Knowledge: Rape on Trial*. London: The Women's Press

Lemert, E. (1972) *Human Deviance, Social Problems and Social Control*. Englewood Cliffs, NJ: Prentice Hall.

Leonard, E. (1982) *Women, Crime and Society: A Critique of Criminology Theory*. New York: Longman.

Liddle, M. and Solanki, A.-R. (2002) *Persistent Young Offenders: Research on Individual Backgrounds and Life Experiences*. London: Nacro.

Lipsky, M. (1980) *Street-Level Bureaucracy: Dilemmas of the Individual in Public Service*. New York: Russell Sage Foundation.

Lloyd, G. (2005) '"EBD Girls" – A Critical View', in G. Lloyd (ed.) *Problem Girls: Understanding and Supporting Troubled and Troublesome Girls and Young Women*. Abingdon: Routledge Falmer.

Lombroso, C. and Ferrero, G. (1895) *The Female Offender*. London: Fisher Unwin.

Lyon, J., Dennison, C. and Wilson, A. (2000) *'Tell Them So They Listen': Messages from Young People in Custody*. Home Office Research Study 201. London: Home Office.

McAra, L. and McVie, S. (2005) 'The Usual Suspects? Street-Life, Young People and the Police', *Criminal Justice*, 5(1): 5–36.

McAra, L. and McVie, S. (2007) 'Youth Justice? The Impact of System Contact on Patterns of Desistance from Offending', *European Journal of Criminology*, 4(3): 315–45.

McCarry, M. (2005) 'Conducting Social Research with Young People: Ethical Considerations', in T. Skinner, M. Hester and E. Malos (eds.) *Researching Gender Violence: Feminist Methodology in Action*. Cullompton: Willan.

McIvor, G. (2007) *What Women Want: Female Offenders' Experiences of Supervision*. Paper presented at *Monash University international conference, 'What works with women offenders: Challenging stereotypes and achieving change'*. Prato, Italy, 12th September.

McIvor, G., Murray, C. and Jamieson, J. (2004) 'Desistance from Crime: Is it Different for Women and Girls?', in S. Maruna and R. Immarigeon (eds.) *After Crime and Punishment: Pathways to Offender Reintegration*. Cullompton: Willan.

McLaughlin, C. (1991) 'Working with Individual Pupils', in C. McLaughlin, C. Lodge and C. Watkins (eds.) *Gender and Pastoral Care: The Personal–Social Aspects of the Whole School*. Oxford: Basil Blackwell.

McLaughlin, C. (2005) 'Exploring the Psychosocial Landscape of "Problem" Girls: Embodiment, Relationship and Agency', in G. Lloyd (ed.) *Problem Girls: Understanding and Supporting Troubled and Troublesome Girls and Young Women*. Abingdon: Routledge Falmer.

McLaughlin, E., Muncie, J. and Hughes, G. (2001) 'The Permanent Revolution: New Labour, New Public Management and the Modernization of Criminal Justice', *Criminal Justice*, 1: 301–18.

McMahon, J. and Clay-Warner, J. (2002) 'Child Abuse and Future Criminality: The Role of Social Service Placement, Family Disorganization, and Gender', *Journal of Interpersonal Violence*, 17(9): 1002–19.

McMurran, M., Tyler, P., Hogue, T., Cooper, K., Dunseath, W. and McDaid, D. (1998) 'Measuring Motivation to Change in Offenders', *Psychology, Crime and Law*, 4: 43–50.

McNeill, F. (2006) 'Community Supervision: Context and Relationships Matter', in B. Goldson and J. Muncie (eds.) *Youth Crime and Justice*. London: Sage.

McRobbie, A. (2004) 'Note on Postfeminism and Popular Culture: Bridget Jones and the New Gender Regime', in A. Harris (ed.) *All About the Girl: Culture, Power, and Identity*. New York: Routledge.

McRobbie. A. (2009) *The Aftermath of Feminism: Gender, Culture and Social Change*. London: Sage.

McRobbie, A. and Garber, J. (2000) 'Girls and Subcultures', in A. McRobbie (ed.) *Feminism and Youth Culture* (2nd edition). Basingstoke: Macmillan.

Maguire, M. (2007) 'Crime Data and Statistics', in M. Maguire, R. Morgan and R. Reiner (eds.) *The Oxford Handbook of Criminology* (4th edition). Oxford: Oxford University Press.

Maguire, M. (2008) 'Researching "Street Criminals" in the Field: A Neglected Art?', in R. King and E. Wincup (eds.) *Doing Research on Crime and Justice* (2nd edition). Oxford: Oxford University Press.

Maher, L. (1997) *Sexed Work: Gender, Race and Resistance in a Brooklyn Drug Market*. Oxford: Oxford University Press.

Maruna, S. (2001) *Making Good: How Ex-Convicts Reform and Rebuild Their Lives*. Washington, D.C.: American Psychological Association.

Maruna, S. and Copes, H. (2005) 'What Have We Learned from Five Decades of Neutralization Research?', *Crime and Justice: A Review of Research*, 32: 221–320.

Matza, D. (1964) *Delinquency and Drift*. New York: Wiley.

Matza, D. (1969) *Becoming Deviant*. Englewood Cliffs, NJ: Prentice Hall.

Matza, D. and Sykes, G.M. (1961) 'Juvenile Delinquency and Subterranean Values', *American Sociological Review*, 26: 712–19.

Maurutto, P. and Hannah-Moffat, K. (2006) 'Assembling Risk and the Restructuring of Penal Control', *British Journal of Criminology*, 46(3): 438–54.

Maurutto, P. and Hannah-Moffat, K. (2007) 'Understanding Risk in the Context of the Youth Criminal Justice Act', *Canadian Journal of Criminology and Criminal Justice*, 49(4): 465–91.

Maxwell, G., Kingi, V., Robertson, J., Morris, A. and Cunningham, C. (2004) *Achieving Effective Outcomes in Youth Justice: Final Report*. Wellington, New Zealand: Ministry of Social Development.

May, D. (1977) 'Delinquent Girls Before the Courts', *Medical Science and Law*, 17(3): 203–12.

May, T., Gyateng, T. and Hough, M. (2010) *Differential Treatment in the Youth Justice System*. London: Equalities and Human Rights Commission.

Measham, F. (2002) '"Doing Gender" – "Doing Drugs": Conceptualising the Gendering of Drugs Cultures', *Contemporary Drug Problems*, 29(2): 335–73.

Measham, F. (2004) 'The Decline of Ecstasy, the Rise of "Binge" Drinking and the Persistence of Pleasure', *Probation Journal*, 51(4): 309–26.

Measham, F. and Østergaard, J. (2009) 'The Public Face of Binge Drinking: British and Danish Young Women, Recent Trends in Alcohol Consumption and the European Binge Drinking Debate', *Probation Journal*, 56(4): 415–34.

Miller, J. (2001) *One of the Guys: Girls, Gangs, and Gender*. New York: Oxford University Press.

Miller, J. (2008) *Getting Played: African American Girls, Urban Inequality, and Gendered Violence*. New York: New York University Press.

Miller, J. and Glassner, B. (2004) 'The "Inside" and the "Outside": Finding Realities in Interviews', in D. Silverman (ed.) *Qualitative Research: Theory, Method and Practice* (2nd edition). London: Sage.

Miller, J. and Mullins, C.W. (2006a) 'Stuck Up, Telling Lies, and Talking Too Much: The Gendered Context of Young Women's Violence', in K. Heimer and C. Kruttschnitt (eds.) *Gender and Crime: Patterns in Victimization and Offending*. New York: New York University Press.

Miller, J. and Mullins, C.W. (2006b) 'The Status of Feminist Theories in Criminology', in F. Cullen, J. Wright and K. Blevins (eds.) *Taking Stock: The Status of Criminological Theory*. New Brunswick, NJ: Transaction Publishers.

Miller, J. and White, N.A. (2004) 'Situational Effects of Gender Inequality on Girls' Participation in Violence', in C. Alder and A. Worrall (eds.) *Girls' Violence: Myths and Realities*. Albany, NY: State University of New York Press.

Mills, C.W. (1940) 'Situated Actions and Vocabularies of Motive', *American Sociological Review*, 5(6): 904–13.

Ministry of Justice. (2010a) *Statistics on Women and the Criminal Justice System*. London: Ministry of Justice.

Ministry of Justice. (2010b) *Re-offending of Juveniles: Results from the 2008 Cohort, England and Wales*. London: Ministry of Justice.

Ministry of Justice. (2010c) *Sentencing Statistics: England and Wales 2008*. Statistics Bulletin. London: Ministry of Justice.

Ministry of Justice. (2010d) *Criminal Statistics: England and Wales 2008*. London: Ministry of Justice.

Ministry of Justice. (2010e) *Criminal Statistics: England and Wales 2009*. London: Ministry of Justice.

Ministry of Justice. (2010f) *Youth Justice Annual Workload Data 2008/09, England and Wales*. London: Ministry of Justice.

Ministry of Justice. (2010g) *Breaking the Cycle: Effective Punishment, Rehabilitation and Sentencing of Offenders*. Norwich: The Stationery Office.

Ministry of Justice. (2011) *Youth Justice Statistics 2009/10, England and Wales*. London: Ministry of Justice.

Moffitt, T. (1993) '"Life-Course-Persistent" and "Adolescence-Limited" Antisocial Behavior: A Developmental Taxonomy', *Psychological Review*, 100: 674–701.

Moffitt, T.E., Caspi, A., Rutter, M. and Silva, P.A. (2001) *Sex Differences in Antisocial Behaviour*. Cambridge: Cambridge University Press.

Moir, J. (2008) 'The female of the species is now just as deadly as the male', *The Daily Mail*, 2nd August.

Morgan, R. (2006) *Youth Justice – Problems and Possibilities*. Presentation delivered at *'Doing Youth Justice'* conference, SOAS, London, 7th April.

Morgan, R. (2008) *Summary Justice: Fast – But Fair?* London: Centre for Crime and Justice Studies.

Morgan, R. (2009) 'Children and Young People: Criminalisation and Punishment', in M. Barry and F. McNeill (eds.) *Youth Offending and Youth Justice*. London: Jessica Kingsley.

Morgan, R. and Newburn, T. (2007) 'Youth Justice', in M. Maguire, R. Morgan and R. Reiner (eds.) *The Oxford Handbook of Criminology* (4th edition). Oxford: Oxford University Press.

Morris, A. (1987) *Women, Crime and Criminal Justice*. Oxford: Blackwell.

Morris, A. and Gelsthorpe, L. (1981) 'False Clues and Female Crime', in A. Morris and L. Gelsthorpe (eds.) *Women and Crime*. Papers presented to the *Cropwood Round-Table Conference*, December 1980. Cambridge: Cropwood Conference Series.

Morris, A., Wilkinson, C., Tisi, A., Woodrow, J. and Rockley, A. (1995) *Managing the Needs of Female Prisoners*. London: Home Office.

Morris, R. (1964) 'Female Delinquency and Relational Problems', *Social Forces*, 43(1): 82–9.

Muncie, J. (1999) 'Institutionalised Intolerance: Youth Justice and the 1998 Crime and Disorder Act', *Critical Social Policy*, 19(2): 147–75.

Muncie, J. (2006) 'Governing Young People: Coherence and Contradiction in Contemporary Youth Justice', *Critical Social Policy*, 26(4): 770–93.

Muncie, J. (2008) 'Managerialism', in B. Goldson (ed.) *Dictionary of Youth Justice*. Cullompton: Willan.

Muncie, J. and Goldson, B. (2006) 'England and Wales: The New Correctionalism', in J. Muncie and B. Goldson (eds.) *Comparative Youth Justice*. London: Sage.

Muncie, J. and Hughes, G. (2002) 'Modes of Youth Governance: Political Rationalities, Criminalization and Resistance', in J. Muncie, G. Hughes and E. McLaughlin (eds.) *Youth Justice: Critical Readings*. London: Sage/The Open University.

Nacro. (2010) *Some Facts About Children and Young People Who Offend – 2008*. Youth crime briefing. London: Nacro.

National Audit Office/Audit Commission. (2003) *Magistrates' Survey*. London: National Audit Office/Audit Commission.

Ness, C. (2010) *Why Girls Fight: Female Youth Violence in the Inner City*. New York: New York University Press.

Newburn, T., Crawford, A., Earle, R., Goldie, S., Hale, C., Hallam, A., Masters, G., Netten, A., Saunders, R., Sharpe, K. and Uglow, S. (2002) *The Introduction of Referral Orders into the Youth Justice System: Final Report*. Home Office Research Study 242. London: Home Office.

Newburn, T. and Shiner, M. with Young, T. (2005) *Dealing with Disaffection: Young People, Mentoring and Social Inclusion*. Cullompton: Willan.

Nye, F.I. (1958) *Family Relationships and Delinquent Behavior*. New York: Wiley.

Oakley, A. (2000) *Experiments in Knowing: Gender and Method in the Social Sciences*. Cambridge: Polity Press.

Office for National Statistics. (2009) *Social Trends no. 39*. Basingstoke: Palgrave Macmillan.

Ofsted/Her Majesty's Inspectorate of Prisons. (2004) *Girls in Prison. The Education and Training of Under-18s Serving Detention and Training Orders*. London: Her Majesty's Inspectorate of Prisons.

O'Mahony, P. (2009) 'The Risk Factors Prevention Paradigm and the Causes of Youth Crime: A Deceptively Useful Analysis?', *Youth Justice*, 9(2): 99–114.

O'Neill, T. (2001) *Children in Secure Accommodation: A Gendered Exploration of Locked Institutional Care for Children in Trouble*. London: Jessica Kingsley.

Orbuch, T. (1997) 'People's Accounts Count: The Sociology of Accounts', *Annual Review of Sociology*, 23: 455–78.

Osler, A. and Vincent, K. (2003) *Girls and Exclusion: Rethinking the Agenda*. London: Routledge Falmer.

Parker, H., Aldridge, J. and Measham, F. (1998) *Illegal Leisure: The Normalization of Adolescent Recreational Drug Use*. London: Routledge.

Parker, H., Turnbull, D. and Casburn, M. (1981) *Receiving Juvenile Justice: Adolescents and State Care and Control*. Oxford: Basil Blackwell.

Pavis, S., Cunningham-Burley, S. and Amos, A. (1997) 'Alcohol Consumption and Young People: Exploring Meaning and Social Context', *Heath Education Research*, 12: 311–22.

Paylor, I. (2010) 'The Scaled Approach to Youth Justice: A Risky Business', *Criminal Justice Matters*, 81: 30–1.

Payne, A., Gottfredson, D. and Kruttschnitt, C. (2009) 'Girls, Schooling, and Delinquency', in M. Zahn (ed.) *The Delinquent Girl*. Philadelphia, PA: Temple University Press.

Pearce, J. (2004) 'Coming Out to Play? Young Women and Violence on the Street', in C. Alder and A. Worrall (eds.) *Girls' Violence: Myths and Realities*. Albany, NY: State University of New York Press.

Pearson, G. (1983) *Hooligan: A History of Respectable Fears*. Basingstoke: Macmillan.

Petrie, C. (1986) *The Nowhere Girls*. Aldershot: Gower.

Phillips, C. (2003) 'Who's Who in the Pecking Order? Aggression and "Normal Violence" in the Lives of Girls and Boys', *British Journal of Criminology*, 43(4): 710–28.

Phoenix, A. (1991) *Young Mothers?* Cambridge: Polity Press.

Phoenix, J. (2006) *Doing Justice: Analyzing 'Risk' and 'Need' Assessments in Youth Justice Practice*. ESRC full research report, 14th October.

Phoenix, J. (2009) 'Beyond Risk Assessment: The Return of Repressive Welfarism?' in M. Barry and F. McNeill (eds.) *Youth Offending and Youth Justice*. London: Jessica Kingsley.

Pike, L. (1876) *A History of Crime in England*. London: Smith, Elder.

Plant, M.L. (2008) 'The Role of Alcohol in Women's Lives: A Review of Issues and Responses', *Journal of Substance Use*, 13(3): 155–91.

Plummer, K. (2001) *Documents of Life: An Invitation to Critical Humanism*. London: Sage.

Pollack, S. (2000) 'Reconceptualizing Womens Agency and Empowerment: Challenges to Self-Esteem Discourse and Women's Lawbreaking', *Women & Criminal Justice*, 12(1): 75–89.

Povey, D., Hand, T., Rishiraj, A.J. and Mulchandani, R. (2010) *Police Powers and Procedures, England and Wales 2008/09*. London: Home Office.

Priestley, P., Fears, D. and Fuller, R. (1977) *Justice for Juveniles. The 1969 Children and Young Persons Act: A Case for Reform*. London: Routledge and Kegan Paul.

Puffett, N. (2009) 'YOT manger struck off over young offenders topless photos', *Children and Young People Now*, 5th August.

Rafter, N. (2006) 'Gender, Genes and Crime: An Evolving Feminist Agenda', in F. Heidensohn (ed.) *Gender and Justice: New Concepts and Approaches*. Cullompton: Willan.

Rafter, N.H. and Gibson, M. (2004) 'Introduction', in C. Lombroso and G. Ferrero *Criminal Woman, the Prostitute, and the Normal Woman*. Translated and with a new introduction by Nicole Hahn Rafter and Mary Gibson. Durham, NC: Duke University Press.

Ramazanoglu, C. with Holland, J. (2002) *Feminist Methodology: Challenges and Choices*. London: Sage.

Ramesh, R. (2010) 'Talking tough on teenage pregnancy', *The Guardian*, 17th March.

Reinharz, H.Z., Giaconia, R.M., Pakiz, B., Silverman, A.B., Frost, A.K. and Lefkowitz, E.S. (1993) 'Psychosocial Risks for Major Depression in Late Adolescence – A Longitudinal Community Study', *Journal of the American Academy of Child and Adolescent Psychiatry*, 32(6): 1153–63.

Ribbens McCarthy, J. with Jessop, J. (2005) *Young People, Bereavement and Loss: Disruptive Transitions?* London: National Children's Bureau.

Ribbens McCarthy, J. (2006) *Young People's Experiences of Loss and Bereavement: Towards an Interdisciplinary Approach*. Buckingham: Open University Press.

Richardson, H. (1969) *Adolescent Girls in Approved Schools*. London: Routledge and Kegan Paul.

Roberts, J. (2002) 'Women-Centred: The West Mercia Community-Based Programme for Women Offenders', in P. Carlen (ed.) *Women and Punishment: The Struggle for Justice*. Cullompton: Willan.

Roberts, Y. (2007) 'Asbos for the unborn?', *The Guardian*, 17th May.

Robinson, G. (2005) 'What Works in Offender Management?', *Howard Journal*, 44(3): 307–18.

Robinson, G. and McNeill, F. (2004) 'Purposes Matter: Examining the "Ends" of Probation', in G. Mair (ed.) *What Matters in Probation*. Cullompton: Willan.

Roe, S. and Ashe, J. (2008) *Young People and Crime: Findings from the 2006 Offending, Crime and Justice Survey*. Home Office Statistical Bulletin 09/08. London: Home Office.

Rose, N. (1989) *Governing the Soul: The Shaping of the Private Self* (2nd edition). London: Free Association Books.

Rumgay, J. (1998) *Crime, Punishment and the Drinking Offender*. Basingstoke: Macmillan.

Rumgay, J. (2004a) *When Victims Become Offenders: In Search of Coherence in Policy and Practice*. London: The Fawcett Society.

Rumgay, J. (2004b) 'Scripts for Safer Survival: Pathways Out of Female Crime', *Howard Journal*, 43(4): 405–19.

Rumgay, J. (2007) *Ladies of Lost Causes: Rehabilitation, Women Offenders and the Voluntary Sector*. Cullompton: Willan.

Rutherford, A. (1986) *Growing Out of Crime: Society and Young People in Trouble*. Harmondsworth: Penguin.

Rutherford, A. (1998) 'Criminal Policy and the Eliminative Ideal', in C.J. Finer and M. Nellis (eds.) *Crime and Social Exclusion*. Oxford: Blackwell.

Rutter, M., Giller, H. and Hagell, A. (1998) *Antisocial Behaviour by Young People*. Cambridge: Cambridge University Press.

Schaffner, L. (2006) *Girls in Trouble with the Law*. Piscataway, NJ: Rutgers University Press.

Scott, J. (1990) *A Matter of Record*. Cambridge: Polity Press.

Scott, M.B. and Lyman, S.M. (1968) 'Accounts', *American Sociological Review*, 33(1): 46–62.

Seng, M. and Lurigio, A.J. (2005) 'Probation Officers' Views on Supervising Women Probationers', *Women & Criminal Justice*, 16(1/2): 65–85.

Shacklady Smith, L. (1978) 'Sexist Assumptions and Female Delinquency: An Empirical Investigation', in C. Smart and B. Smart (eds.) *Women, Sexuality and Social Control*. London: Routledge and Kegan Paul.

Shapiro, E. (1999) 'Trauma, Shame, and Group Psychotherapy: A Self Psychology Perspective', *Group*, 23(2): 51–65.

Sharp, C. and Budd, T. (2005) *Minority Ethnic Groups and Crime: Findings from the Offending, Crime and Justice Survey 2003*. Home Office Online Report 33/05. London: Home Office.

Sharpe, G. (2008) *Girls in the Youth Justice System*. Unpublished Ph.D. thesis, University of Cambridge.

Sharpe, G. (2009) 'The Trouble with Girls Today: Professional Perspectives on Young Women's Offending', *Youth Justice*, 9(3): 254–69.

Sharpe, G. (2011) 'Beyond Youth Justice: Working with Girls and Young Women Who Offend', in R. Sheehan, G. McIvor and C. Trotter (eds.) *Working with Women Offenders in the Community*. Cullompton: Willan.

Sharpe, G. and Gelsthorpe, L. (2009) 'Engendering the Agenda: Girls, Young Women and Youth Justice', *Youth Justice*, 9(3): 195–208.

Shaw, M. and Hannah-Moffat, K. (2000) 'Gender, Diversity and Risk Assessment in Canadian Corrections', *Probation Journal*, 47(3): 163–72.

Shore, H. (2002) 'Reforming the Juvenile: Gender, Justice and the Chid Criminal in Nineteenth-Century England', in J. Muncie, G. Hughes and E. McLaughlin (eds.) *Youth Justice: Critical Readings*. London: Sage.

Siegel, J.A. and Williams, L.M. (2003) 'The Relationship Between Child Sexual Abuse and Female Delinquency and Crime: A Prospective Study', *Journal of Research in Crime and Delinquency*, 40(1): 71–94.

Simester, A. and von Hirsch, A. (2006) 'Regulating Offensive Conduct Through Two-Step Prohibitions', in A. von Hirsch and A. Simester (eds.) *Incivilities: Regulating Offensive Behaviour*. Oxford: Hart.

Simon, J. (2007) *Governing Through Crime: How the War on Crime Transformed American Democracy and Created a Culture of Fear*. New York: Oxford University Press.

Simon, R. (1975) *Women and Crime*. Lexington, MA: Lexington Books.

Skeggs, B. (1997) *Formations of Class and Gender: Becoming Respectable*. London: Sage.

Skeggs, B. (2004) *Class, Self, Culture*. London: Routledge.

Slack, J. (2009) 'Scourge of the ladette thugs: Rising tide of violent crime committed by young women', *Daily Mail*, 30th January.

Smart, C. (1976) *Women, Crime and Criminology: A Feminist Critique*. London: Routledge and Kegan Paul.

Smith, C. and Thornberry, T.P. (1995) 'The Relationship Between Childhood Maltreatment and Adolescent Involvement in Delinquency', *Criminology*, 33(4): 451–81.

Smith, D. (2004) *The Links Between Victimization and Offending*. Edinburgh Study of Youth Transitions and Crime Research Digest No. 5. Edinburgh: Centre for Law and Society, University of Edinburgh.

Smith, D. (ed.) (2010) *A New Response to Youth Crime*. Cullompton: Willan.

Smith, D. and McAra, L. (2004) *Gender and Youth Offending*. Edinburgh Study of Youth Transitions and Crime Research Digest No. 2. Edinburgh: Centre for Law and Society, University of Edinburgh.

Smith, R. (2007) *Youth Justice: Ideas, Policy, Practice* (2nd edition). Cullompton: Willan.

Snyder, H. and Sickmund, M. (2006) *Juvenile Offenders and Victims: 2006 National Report*. Washington, D.C.: US Department of Justice, Office of Juvenile Justice and Delinquency Prevention.

Souhami, A. (2007) *Transforming Youth Justice: Occupational Identity and Cultural Change*. Cullompton: Willan.

Sprott, J.B. and Doob, A.N. (2009) *Justice for Girls? Stability and Change in the Youth Justice Systems of the United States and Canada*. Chicago, IL: University of Chicago Press.

Stanley, L. and Wise, S. (1993) *Breaking Out Again: Feminist Ontology and Epistemology*. London: Routledge.

Steffensmeier, D. (1978) 'Crime and the Contemporary Woman: An Analysis of Changing Levels of Female Property Crime, 1960–75', *Social Forces*, 57: 566–84.

Steffensmeier, D. and Allan, E. (1996) 'Gender and Crime: Toward a Gendered Theory of Female Offending', *Annual Review of Sociology*, 22: 459–87.

Steffensmeier, D. and Schwarz, J. (2009) 'Trends in Girls' Delinquency and the Gender Gap: Statistical Assessment of Diverse Sources', in M. Zahn (ed.) *The Delinquent Girl*. Philadelphia, PA: Temple University Press.

Steffensmeier, D., Schwartz, J., Zhong, H. and Ackerman, J. (2005) 'An Assessment of Recent Trends in Girls' Violence Using Diverse Longitudinal Sources: Is the Gender Gap Closing?', *Criminology*, 43(2): 355–406.

Stephenson, M. (2006) *Young People and Offending: Education, Youth Justice and Social Inclusion*. Cullompton: Willan.

Strauss, A. and Corbin, J. (1998) *Basics of Qualitative Research: Techniques and Procedures for Developing Grounded Theory* (2nd edition). London: Sage.

Sweeting, H., West, P. and Richards, M. (1998) 'Teenage Family Life, Lifestyles and Life Chances: Associations with Family Structure, Conflict with Parents and Joint Family Activity', *International Journal of Law, Policy and the Family*, 12(1): 15–46.

Sutherland, A. (2009) 'The "Scaled Approach" in Youth Justice: Fools Rush in', *Youth Justice*, 9(1): 44–60.

Sykes, G. and Matza, D. (1957) 'Techniques of Neutralization: A Theory of Delinquency', *American Sociological Review*, 22: 664–73.

Taylor, C. (2006) *Young People in Care and Criminal Behaviour*. London: Jessica Kingsley.

Taylor, S.E. (1989) *Positive Illusions: Creative Self-Deception and the Healthy Mind*. New York: Basic Books.

The Telegraph. (2008) 'Our view: Police must toughen stance on anti-social girls', *The Telegraph*, 15 May.

Thomas, W.I. (1907) *Sex and Society*. Chicago, IL: University of Chicago Press.

Thomas, W.I. (1923) *The Unadjusted Girl*. New York: Harper and Row.

Toor, S. (2009) 'British Asian Girls, Crime and Youth Justice' *Youth Justice*, 9(3): 239–54.

Trotter, C. (2007) 'Parole and Probation', in R. Sheehan, G. McIvor and C. Trotter (eds.) *What Works with Women Offenders*. Cullompton: Willan.

Trotter, C. (2011) 'Mentoring', in R. Sheehan, G. McIvor and C. Trotter (eds.) *Working with Women Offenders in the Community*. Abingdon: Willan.

Tye, D. (2009) *Children and Young People in Custody 2008–2009: An Analysis of the Experiences of 15–18-year-olds in Prison*. London: Her Majesty's Inspectorate of Prisons/Youth Justice Board.

Tyler, T. (1990) *Why People Obey the Law*. New Haven, CT: Yale University Press.

Uggen, C. and Kruttschnitt, C. (1998) 'Crime in the Breaking: Gender Differences in Desistance', *Law & Society Review*, 32(2): 339–66.

UNICEF. (2005) *Child Poverty in Rich Countries, 2005*. Innocenti Report Card No.6. Florence: UNICEF Innocenti Research Centre.

van Mastrigt, S. (2008) *Co-offending: Relationships with Age, Gender and Crime Type*. Unpublished Ph.D. thesis, University of Cambridge.

van Mastrigt, S. and Farrington, D. (2011) 'Prevalence and Characteristics of Co-Offending Recruiters', *Justice Quarterly*, 28(2): 325–59.

Veblen, T. (1994) *The Theory of the Leisure Class*. London: Dover Publications.

Walker, J., Thompson, C., Laing, K., Raybould, S., Coombes, M., Procter, S. and Wren, C. (2007) *Youth Inclusion and Support Panels: Preventing Crime and Anti-Social Behaviour*. London: Department for Children, Schools and Families.

Walkerdine, V., Lucey, H. and Melody, J. (2001) *Growing Up Girl: Psychosocial Explorations of Gender and Class*. Basingstoke: Palgrave.

Walter, N. (2010) *Living Dolls: The Return of Sexism*. London: Virago.

Ward, L. (2007) 'Unborn babies targeted in crackdown on criminality', *The Guardian*, 16th May.

Warr, M. (2002) *Companions in Crime: The Social Aspects of Criminal Conduct*. Cambridge: Cambridge University Press.

Webb, D. (1984) 'More on Gender and Justice: Girl Offenders on Supervision', *Sociology*, 18(3): 367–81.

Widom, C.S. (1989) 'Child Abuse, Neglect and Violent Criminal Behavior', *Criminology*, 27(2): 251–71.

Wiggins, M., Oakley, A., Sawtell, M., Austerberry, H., Clemens, F. and Elbourne, D. (2005) *Teenage Parenthood and Social Exclusion: A Multi-Method Study: Summary Report of Findings*. London: Social Science Research Unit Report, Institute of Education.

Wilkinson, C. and Morris, A. (2002) 'Victims or Villains? Challenging the Use of Custody for Girls Who Offend', *Prison Service Journal*, 132: 48–52.

Williams, J. (2008) *Real Bad Girls: The Origins and Nature of Offending by Girls and Young Women Involved with a County Youth Offending Team and Systemic Responses to Them*. Unpublished Ph.D. thesis, University of Bedfordshire.

Wilson, H. (1980) 'Parental Supervision: A Neglected Aspect of Delinquency', *British Journal of Criminology*, 20(3): 203–35.

Worrall, A. (1990) *Offending Women: Female Lawbreakers and the Criminal Justice System*. London: Routledge.

Worrall, A. (1999) 'Troubled or Troublesome? Justice for Girls and Young Women', in B. Goldson (ed.) *Youth Justice: Contemporary Policy and Practice*. Aldershot: Ashgate.

Worrall, A. (2000) 'Governing Bad Girls: Changing Constructions of Female Juvenile Delinquency', in J. Bridgeman and D. Monk (eds.) *Feminist Perspectives on Child Law*. London: Cavendish Publishing.

Worrall, A. (2001) 'Girls at Risk? Reflections on Changing Attitudes to Young Women's Offending', *Probation Journal*, 48(2): 86–92.

Worrall, A. (2002) 'Rendering Women Punishable: The Making of a Penal Crisis', in P. Carlen (ed.) *Women and Punishment: The Struggle for Justice*. Cullompton: Willan.

Worrall, A. (2004) 'Twisted Sisters, Ladettes, and the New Penology: The Social Construction of "Violent Girls"', in C. Alder and A. Worrall (eds.) *Girls' Violence: Myths and Realities*. Albany,NY: State University of New York Press.

Worsley, R. (2006) *Young People in Custody 2004–2006: An Analysis of Children's Experiences of Prison*. London: Her Majesty's Inspectorate of Prisons/Youth Justice Board.

Yorkshire Post. (2009) 'Social worker is struck off over teenagers' topless photo shoots', *Yorkshire Post*, 5th August.

Young, T. (2009) 'Girls and Gangs: 'Shemale' Gangsters in the UK?', *Youth Justice*, 9(3): 224–38.

Youth Justice Board. (2004a) *Youth Justice Annual Statistics 2002/03*. London: Youth Justice Board.

Youth Justice Board. (2004b) *Identification of Specific Community and Custodial Resources for Girls and Young Women in the Youth Justice System*. Unpublished report.

Youth Justice Board. (2006) *MORI Five-Year Report: An Analysis of Youth Survey Data*. London: Youth Justice Board.

Youth Justice Board. (2007) *Youth Justice Annual Statistics 2005/06*. London: Youth Justice Board.

Youth Justice Board. (2008) *To Develop and Improve Reparation, as Part of the Youth Crime Action Plan: Good Practice Guidance for Youth Offending Teams (YOTs)*. London: Youth Justice Board.

Youth Justice Board. (2009) *Youth Justice Annual Workload Data 2007/08*. London: Youth Justice Board.

Zedner, L. (1991) *Women, Crime, and Custody in Victorian England*. Oxford: Oxford University Press.

Zedner, L. (2007) 'Pre-Crime and Post-Criminology?', *Theoretical Criminology*, 11(2): 261–81.

Index

Note: page numbers in **bold** refer to illustrations.